Eating Disorders

SOURCEBOOK

FIFTH EDITION

Health Reference Series

Eating Disorders
SOURCEBOOK

FIFTH EDITION

Basic Consumer Health Information about Anorexia Nervosa, Bulimia Nervosa, Binge-Eating Disorder, and Other Eating Disorders and Related Concerns, Such as Compulsive Exercise, Female Athlete Triad, and Body Dysmorphic Disorder, Including Details about Risk Factors, Warning Signs, Adverse Health Effects, Methods of Prevention, Treatment Options, and the Recovery Process

Along with Suggestions for Maintaining a Healthy Weight, Improving Self-Esteem, and Promoting a Positive Body Image, a Glossary of Related Terms, and a Directory of Resources for More Information

OMNIGRAPHICS

615 Griswold, Ste. 901, Detroit, MI 48226

Bibliographic Note
Because this page cannot legibly accommodate all the copyright notices, the Bibliographic Note portion of the Preface constitutes an extension of the copyright notice.

* * *

OMNIGRAPHICS
Angela L. Williams, *Managing Editor*
* * *

Copyright © 2019 Omnigraphics

ISBN 978-0-7808-1681-7
E-ISBN 978-0-7808-1682-4

Library of Congress Cataloging-in-Publication Data

Names: Omnigraphics, Inc., issuing body.

Title: Eating disorders sourcebook : basic consumer health information about anorexia nervosa, bulimia nervosa, binge eating disorder, and other eating disorders and related concerns, such as compulsive exercise, female athlete triad, and body dysmorphic disorder, including details about risk factors, warning signs, adverse health effects, methods of prevention, treatment options, and the recovery process; along with suggestions for maintaining a healthy weight, improving self-esteem, and promoting a positive body image, a glossary of related terms, and a directory of resources for more information.

Description: Fifth edition. | Detroit, MI : Omnigraphics, Inc., [2019] | Series: Health reference series | Includes bibliographical references and index.

Identifiers: LCCN 2018053294 (print) | LCCN 2018053722 (ebook) | ISBN 9780780816824 (ebook) | ISBN 9780780816817 (hard cover : alk. paper)

Subjects: LCSH: Eating disorders. | Consumer education.

Classification: LCC RC552.E18 (ebook) | LCC RC552.E18 E287 2019 (print) | DDC 616.85/26--dc23

LC record available at https://lccn.loc.gov/2018053294

Table of Contents

Part II: Risk Factors for Eating Disorders

Part III: Causes of Eating Disorders

Part VI: Preventing Eating Disorders and Achieving a Healthy Weight

Part VII: Additional Help and Information

Preface

About This Book

According to the National Eating Disorders Association (NEDA), 20 million women and 10 million men in the United States suffer from a clinically significant eating disorder at some time in their life. Suicide, depression, and severe anxiety are common, and eating disorders can lead to major medical complications, including electrolyte imbalance, cognitive impairment, osteoporosis, infertility, or even death. Furthermore, although eating disorders can be successfully treated—even to complete remission—estimates suggest that only one in ten people with an eating disorder receives treatment.

Eating Disorders Sourcebook, Fifth Edition provides basic consumer health information about anorexia nervosa, bulimia nervosa, binge-eating disorder, and other eating disorders and related concerns, such as female athlete triad, the abuse of laxatives and diet pills, and rumination disorder. It explains the factors that put people at risk for developing eating disorders, and it discusses their adverse health affects and the methods used to prevent, diagnose, and treat them. Tips for determining a healthy weight and promoting self-esteem and a positive body image are also included, along with guidelines for safe weight loss and exercise, and a glossary of terms related to eating disorders, and a list of resources for further information.

How to Use This Book

This book is divided into parts and chapters. Parts focus on broad areas of interest. Chapters are devoted to single topics within a part.

Part One: What Are Eating Disorders? defines eating disorders and explains how they differ from disordered and normal eating patterns. It describes the most common types of eating disorders, as well as other related disorders that often accompany them, such as body dysmorphic disorder and compulsive exercising. The part also examines popular eating disorder myths.

Part Two: Risk Factors for Eating Disorders discusses the potential risk factors for eating disorders, and the specific populations most at risk for eating disorders. It also describes other problems that frequently co-occur with eating disorders such as autism, anxiety, PTSD, diabetes, and others.

Part Three: Causes of Eating Disorders explains what is known about the biological factors and genetic predispositions that may lead to the development of certain eating disorders. Environmental factors that can cause eating disorders are described, as well as the effect of the media in distorting body image and encouraging these disorders.

Part Four: Medical Complications of Eating Disorders describes provides information about the adverse—and sometimes fatal—physical health effects of eating disorders, including infertility, pregnancy complications, oral health problems, and osteoporosis.

Part Five: Recognizing and Treating Eating Disorders describes the physiological and behavioral warning signs of an eating disorder and provides suggestions for confronting a person with an eating disorder. It explains the treatment process, from determining the level of care needed to choosing a treatment facility. It also details the different treatment options available, including medications, psychotherapeutic approaches, and insurance coverage for such treatments. Issues related to the recovery process are also discussed.

Part Six: Preventing Eating Disorders and Achieving a Healthy Weight offers guidelines for the prevention of eating disorders, including tips for promoting self-esteem and a positive body image. It explains how people can determine a medically optimal weight for themselves and offers suggestions for safe weight gain, loss, and maintenance. Nutrition guidelines and suggestions for exercising safely are also included.

Part Seven: Additional Help and Information includes a glossary of terms related to eating disorders and a directory of resources for additional help and support.

Bibliographic Note

This volume contains documents and excerpts from publications issued by the following U.S. government agencies: Agency for Healthcare Research and Quality (AHRQ); Agricultural Research Service (ARS); Brookhaven National Laboratory (BNL); Centers for Disease Control and Prevention (CDC); Early Childhood Learning and Knowledge Center (ECLKC); Federal Occupational Health (FOH); Federal Trade Commission (FTC); Food and Nutrition Service (FNS); Genetic and Rare Diseases Information Center (GARD); Genetics Home Reference (GHR); Health Resources and Services Administration (HRSA); National Heart, Lung, and Blood Institute (NHLBI); National Institute of Diabetes and Digestive and Kidney Diseases (NIDDK); National Institute of Mental Health (NIMH); National Institute on Aging (NIA); National Institutes of Health (NIH); National Oceanic and Atmospheric Administration (NOAA); NIH Osteoporosis and Related Bone Diseases ~ National Resource Center (NIH ORBD~NRC); Office of Dietary Supplements (ODS); Office of Disease Prevention and Health Promotion (ODPHP); Office on Women's Health (OWH); Substance Abuse and Mental Health Services Administration (SAMHSA); U.S. Department of Agriculture (USDA); U.S. Department of Education (ED); U.S. Department of Health and Human Services (HHS); U.S. Department of Veterans Affairs (VA); U.S. Environmental Protection Agency (EPA); U.S. Food and Drug Administration (FDA); and U.S. Senate Committee on Health, Education, Labor, and Pensions.

It may also contain original material produced by Omnigraphics and reviewed by medical consultants.

About the Health Reference Series

The *Health Reference Series* is designed to provide basic medical information for patients, families, caregivers, and the general public. Each volume takes a particular topic and provides comprehensive coverage. This is especially important for people who may be dealing with a newly diagnosed disease or a chronic disorder in themselves or in a family member. People looking for preventive guidance, information about disease warning signs, medical statistics, and risk factors for health problems will also find answers to their questions in the *Health Reference Series*. The *Series*, however, is not intended to serve as a tool for diagnosing illness, in prescribing treatments, or as a substitute for the physician/patient relationship. All people concerned about medical symptoms or the possibility of disease are encouraged to seek professional care from an appropriate healthcare provider.

A Note about Spelling and Style

Health Reference Series editors use *Stedman's Medical Dictionary* as an authority for questions related to the spelling of medical terms and the *Chicago Manual of Style* for questions related to grammatical structures, punctuation, and other editorial concerns. Consistent adherence is not always possible, however, because the individual volumes within the *Series* include many documents from a wide variety of different producers, and the editor's primary goal is to present material from each source as accurately as is possible. This sometimes means that information in different chapters or sections may follow other guidelines and alternate spelling authorities. For example, occasionally a copyright holder may require that eponymous terms be shown in possessive forms (Crohn's disease vs. Crohn disease) or that British spelling norms be retained (leukaemia vs. leukemia).

Medical Review

Omnigraphics contracts with a team of qualified, senior medical professionals who serve as medical consultants for the *Health Reference Series*. As necessary, medical consultants review reprinted and originally written material for currency and accuracy. Citations including the phrase "Reviewed (month, year)" indicate material reviewed by this team. Medical consultation services are provided to the *Health Reference Series* editors by:

Dr. Vijayalakshmi, MBBS, DGO, MD
Dr. Senthil Selvan, MBBS, DCH, MD
Dr. K. Sivanandham, MBBS, DCH, MS (Research), PhD

Our Advisory Board

We would like to thank the following board members for providing initial guidance on the development of this series:

- Dr. Lynda Baker, Associate Professor of Library and Information Science, Wayne State University, Detroit, MI

- Nancy Bulgarelli, William Beaumont Hospital Library, Royal Oak, MI

- Karen Imarisio, Bloomfield Township Public Library, Bloomfield Township, MI

- Karen Morgan, Mardigian Library, University of Michigan-Dearborn, Dearborn, MI

- Rosemary Orlando, St. Clair Shores Public Library, St. Clair Shores, MI

Health Reference Series *Update Policy*

The inaugural book in the *Health Reference Series* was the first edition of *Cancer Sourcebook* published in 1989. Since then, the *Series* has been enthusiastically received by librarians and in the medical community. In order to maintain the standard of providing high-quality health information for the layperson the editorial staff at Omnigraphics felt it was necessary to implement a policy of updating volumes when warranted.

Medical researchers have been making tremendous strides, and it is the purpose of the *Health Reference Series* to stay current with the most recent advances. Each decision to update a volume is made on an individual basis. Some of the considerations include how much new information is available and the feedback we receive from people who use the books. If there is a topic you would like to see added to the update list, or an area of medical concern you feel has not been adequately addressed, please write to:

Managing Editor
Health Reference Series
Omnigraphics
615 Griswold, Ste. 901
Detroit, MI 48226

Part One

What Are Eating Disorders?

Chapter 1

Eating Disorders: An Overview

Chapter Contents

Section 1.1

Understanding Eating Disorders

This section includes text excerpted from "Eating Disorders," Substance Abuse and Mental Health Services Administration (SAMHSA), May 12, 2017.

Eating disorders are complex mental disorders. They are serious and can be life-threatening. Eating disorders are not just a phase, trend, or lifestyle choice. They can harm physical health, mood, social ties, and functioning in daily life.

Eating disorders involve problematic behaviors with an emotional basis. The person has excessive fear and anxiety about eating, body image, and weight gain. This leads them to do things that can have serious health effects. A person with an eating disorder needs specialized care. With early treatment, the person is more likely to recover.

Anorexia nervosa (AN), bulimia nervosa (BN), and binge-eating disorder (BED) are three common eating disorders. Many people may have serious problems related to eating and body image, but not one of these three disorders.

Signs and Symptoms
Anorexia Nervosa

Anorexia nervosa—also called anorexia, which means "not eating"— has three key features. The person eats less, is afraid of gaining weight or becoming fat, and has a distorted body image (seeing oneself as fat or overweight). The person may weigh less than what is normal for their age, sex, and health. But the person may not have low weight.

Young people with anorexia, and some adults, may not know or admit they fear gaining weight. They may weigh themselves often, look at themselves in the mirror, and monitor their size. Parents and friends may notice that the person starts to favor low-calorie foods, eats special diets, or is preoccupied with dieting and exercise. Anorexia has the highest death rate of any mental disorder. A person may die from starvation, metabolic collapse, or suicide.

Symptoms of anorexia include:

- Excessive exercise

- Severe or rigid dieting, or very restrictive eating

- Extreme thinness or constant pursuit of thinness

- Strong fear of gaining weight

- Distorted body image, low self-esteem tied to body weight and shape, and denial of the seriousness of low body weight

- Depression and anxiety

Anorexia can lead to health problems. These vary in severity and differ among people with anorexia. Health concerns include:

- Lethargy, sluggishness, or feeling tired all the time

- Iron deficiency (anemia)

- Low body temperature, so the person often feels cold

- Dry, yellowish skin

- Growth of fine hair all over the body

- Brittle hair and nails

- Skipping or no longer having monthly menstruation

- Infertility

- Muscle wasting and weakness

- Low blood pressure, with slow breathing and pulse

- Severe constipation and abdominal pain

- Thinning of the bones (osteopenia or osteoporosis)

- Damage to the heart, including slow heart rate and possible heart rhythm problems

- Brain damage or multi-organ failure

Also, a person with anorexia may have dehydration. They may have fainting, increased urination, or low back pain. They may lose interest in sex, have sleep problems, be sensitive to loud noise and bright lights, or have problems concentrating.

Bulimia Nervosa

Bulimia nervosa, also called bulimia, involves binge eating plus unhealthy behaviors to compensate for overeating. Binge eating means eating an unusually large amount of food, which most people would see as excessive, while feeling out of control. Compensation for binge eating may include forced vomiting; taking medications such as laxatives, diuretics, or diet pills; and heavy exercise, fasting, or other methods to make up for calorie intake.

People with bulimia often stay at a normal weight or are overweight. The person often goes to the bathroom right after eating meals. They are often ashamed of their eating problems. They may try to hide their actions from others. Bulimia can cause life-threatening problems.

Symptoms of bulimia include:

- Repeated binge eating (eating an unusually large amount of food, compared to what most people would eat), while feeling unable to stop eating and a loss of control

- Repeated unhealthy actions to prevent weight gain, such as forced vomiting (purging); abuse of laxatives, diuretics, or other medications; fasting; heavy exercise; or a combination of these

- Excessive worry about how their body looks and their weight (poor self-image, with an overemphasis on body shape or weight)

Bulimia may cause health concerns, including:

- Inflamed and sore throat

- Swollen salivary glands (in the neck and jaw area)

- Worn tooth enamel and sensitive, decaying teeth due to stomach acid

- Acid reflux disease and other gastrointestinal problems

- Intestinal distress and irritation from laxative abuse

- Severe dehydration from purging

- Electrolyte imbalance (low or high levels of sodium, calcium, potassium, and other minerals) that can lead to stroke, heart failure, or death

Also, a person with bulimia may have inflammation, swelling of hands and feet, rupture of the esophagus, gum disease, or irregular menstrual cycles. They may have fatigue, headaches, depression, anxiety, or problems concentrating.

Binge-Eating Disorder

Binge-eating disorder is the most common eating disorder in the United States. It does not mean occasional overeating. It involves eating large amounts of food (often quickly, and causing discomfort) and feeling unable to stop eating.

Binge-eating disorder is similar to bulimia in the amount of food eaten. But it does not involve regular purging, heavy exercise, or fasting. People with this disorder often feel embarrassed and ashamed. They tend to hide their eating from family and friends. Parents and friends may notice that the person is preoccupied with dieting and fitness. People with binge-eating disorder often are overweight, but some are not. They struggle with negative views of their body and weight, and may have depression, anxiety, and thoughts of suicide.

Symptoms of binge-eating disorder include:

- Repeated binge eating, feeling a lack of control over eating, and feeling distressed by it
- Eating alone due to embarrassment
- Eating large amounts when not physically hungry
- Eating more rapidly than normal
- Eating until uncomfortably full
- Feeling disgust, sadness, or guilt after binge eating

Binge-eating disorder may cause health concerns, including:

- Weight gain, obesity, or weight cycling
- Bloating
- Restricted food intake
- Dehydration
- Problems getting along with friends and family
- Stress
- Feeling underappreciated
- Feeling dissatisfied with life
- High blood pressure, high cholesterol, diabetes, and other medical conditions

Avoidant/Restrictive Food Intake Disorder

Some people have problems with eating and food but do not have an eating disorder. They may have avoidant/restrictive food intake disorder (ARFID). The symptoms typically start in infancy or childhood and may last into adulthood. Symptoms may include avoiding

7

certain colors or textures of food, eating very small portions, or having no appetite. The person may be afraid to eat after a frightening event that caused choking or vomiting.

Risk Factors

Eating disorders often start in adolescence or young adulthood, but can occur in childhood or later in adulthood. The symptoms are the same in males and females. About one percent of Americans have anorexia. About 90 to 95 percent of people with anorexia are female. About 25 percent of children with anorexia are boys. Bulimia affects one to two percent of adolescents and young adults. Of those with bulimia, 80 percent are female. Binge-eating disorder affects one to five percent of the general population. Rates of binge-eating disorder are similar in males and females.

Some men with eating disorders have muscle dysmorphia. This involves concern about becoming more muscular. No single risk factor is likely to cause an eating disorder. Research suggests that multiple factors lead to eating disorders.

Genetics

Heredity may play a role. Eating disorders are more likely in people who have one or more family members with an eating disorder. Researchers are studying genetic factors linked to eating disorders. No single genetic factor causes eating disorders.

Brain Function

Changes in brain functions related to eating and emotions may help explain why some people develop eating disorders. Imaging studies have linked eating disorders to brain activity patterns.

Social Factors

These include being teased or ridiculed often about one's weight, participating in a sport that requires low weight or a certain body image, or being surrounded by negative messages about food and body. Frequent dieting can increase the risk of eating disorders.

Trauma

Traumatic events and major life stressors, especially in childhood, such as sexual assault or other abuse, may be a risk factor for an eating disorder.

Psychological Factors

Having another mental disorder can make an eating disorder more likely. Also, personality traits such as being a perfectionist, feeling inadequate, having low self-esteem, and rigid thinking are linked to increased risk of an eating disorder.

Evidence-Based Treatments

People with eating disorders can recover with care that deals with behavioral, emotional, and physical symptoms. Treatment can help people stop harmful behaviors, stay at a healthy weight, and learn to accept their bodies. The treatment plan should consider each person's needs and choices. Treatments generally include one or more of these:

- Individual, group, or family psychotherapy (sometimes called "talk" therapy)
- Nutritional counseling
- Medications
- Functional rehabilitation to help resume their roles (school, work, relationships)

A person should consult a healthcare professional when choosing the right treatment and consider his or her own gender, race, ethnicity, language, and culture.

Psychotherapy

Psychotherapy can help people change their eating and deal with emotions related to the eating disorder. Psychotherapy involves working with a professional one-on-one or in a group. Several therapies are helpful for treating eating disorders. Some target symptoms directly. Others focus on changing a person's thoughts, environment, or problems that affect their actions and ability to change their actions.

Cognitive behavioral therapy (CBT) helps adults with bulimia and binge-eating disorder. The person learns skills to help stop binge eating or using compensatory behaviors to control weight. This therapy can reduce unhealthy eating and negative thoughts the person may have about their body.

The Maudsley approach is a family-based therapy. It helps people with anorexia or bulimia achieve a normal weight, address problem behaviors, and function better. Parents learn to manage their child's dieting, exercising, binging, and purging.

Medications

Psychotropic medications can help manage some symptoms of bulimia and binge-eating disorders. Antidepressants or mood stabilizers can help control some symptoms for people with bulimia and binge-eating disorders. These medications may also help with symptoms of anxiety or depression.

Medications should be used with care in children and adolescents. A psychiatrist or other prescriber must consider many factors in deciding if treatment should include medication.

Levels of Care

Several levels of specialty care may be best for people with eating disorders. The goal is to help the person get to a normal weight and normal eating. The best treatment option depends on the severity of the disorder and the person's past response to treatment. The best treatment may not be available in some areas.

- **Inpatient medical stabilization** may be needed to deal with serious physical problems such as dehydration or heart problems.

- **Inpatient psychiatric treatment** can provide intensive services for medical stabilization and psychological support.

- **Day treatment or partial hospitalization** can deal with medical conditions and psychological support. This can be done as a transition from inpatient to outpatient care. It can also be an alternative to inpatient care.

- **Outpatient care** may be best for people who are not severely malnourished and don't need medical stabilization.

Complementary Therapies and Activities

Complementary therapies and activities can help people improve their well-being, and are meant to be used along with evidence-based treatments. Approaches that may help people with eating disorders include:

- Cognitive remediation therapy (CRT) helps people improve their attention span, memory, problem-solving, organization, and planning.

- Self-monitoring therapies help people record their actions or thoughts. They can look for patterns and situations that tend to cause problems.

Section 1.2

Myths about Eating Disorders

This section includes text excerpted from
"Busting 5 Myths about Eating Disorder," U.S. Department of
Health and Human Services (HHS), March 1, 2018.

You may notice a friend or family member who has dropped a considerable amount of weight or is obsessive about needing to lose weight. They may be reclusive and continuously pushing food away, bingeing or exercising excessively. They may be suffering from an eating disorder. In the United States, an estimated 30 million people may have an eating disorder in their lifetime.

Myth 1: Only women and girls can get an eating disorder.

False: According to the National Eating Disorders Association (NEDA), ten million exit disclaimer icon men and boys in the United States will suffer an eating disorder. Eating disorders affect a diverse array of people of various ethnicities, ages, genders, body weight, and socioeconomic groups.

Myth 2: You can tell someone is suffering with an eating disorder by the way they look.

False—sometimes: Anorexia nervosa is an eating disorder in which a person unreasonably limits food intake and excessively exercises to prevent weight gain. Individuals who suffer from this disorder appear extremely thin. However, the other most common eating disorder, bulimia nervosa, uses bingeing and purging to control weight. These people may appear healthy, despite the internal damage being done to their bodies.

Myth 3: Only external influences, such as peer pressure or distorted physical images, can cause the onset of an eating disorder.

False: While it is difficult to pinpoint the cause of an eating disorder, research conducted by National Institutes of Health (NIH)-suggests that genetic, psychological, behavioral, biological, and social factors can heighten the risk.

Myth 4: Eating disorders are a choice.

False: According to National Institute of Mental Health's (NIMH), eating disorders are not lifestyle choices. People don't choose to have an eating disorder like they might choose to eat only vegetables or fish. Eating disorders are a biologically influenced medical illness.

Myth 5: Eating disorders are not really serious.

False: Some research has shown a direct correlation between eating disorders and suicide attempts. If untreated, eating disorders can cause an imbalance in electrolytes that can result in a stroke or heart attack, intestinal distress, brain damage, and multi-organ failure.

Chapter 2

Normal Eating, Disordered Eating, and Eating Disorders

Chapter Contents

13

Section 2.1

What Are Normal Eating, Disordered Eating, and Eating Disorders?

"What Are Normal Eating, Disordered Eating, and Eating Disorders?" © 2016 Omnigraphics. Reviewed December 2018.

To be diagnosed with an eating disorder, an individual must meet the clinical definitions listed in the American Psychological Association's *Diagnostic and Statistical Manual of Mental Disorders* (DSM) for anorexia nervosa, bulimia nervosa, binge-eating disorder, or eating disorder not otherwise specified (EDNOS). Although only a small fraction of the U.S. population meets the diagnostic criteria for one of these conditions, research suggests that an estimated 50 percent of Americans demonstrate unhealthy or disordered eating patterns.

Experts point to a cultural obsession with weight, body shape, and diet as a primary factor in the prevalence of disordered eating. In comparing themselves to the unattainable ideals of thinness and fitness that are promoted in the media, many Americans develop a negative body image and an unhealthy relationship with food. Countless people follow extremely restrictive diets, feel ashamed or guilty about eating, exercise obsessively, or resort to harmful practices like bingeing and purging in an effort to lose weight. Although these are signs of a disordered relationship with food, many people view such behavior as normal, common, or even healthy. As a result, they never seek help for the problem and put both their physical and emotional health at risk.

Normal Eating

Although there is no medical definition of "normal" eating, experts generally agree on the basic characteristics of a healthy relationship with food. People who exhibit normal eating patterns eat when they are hungry and stop eating when they feel satisfied and comfortably full. Although they usually make food selections with proper nutrition in mind, they do not deny themselves foods they enjoy. Rather than considering certain foods "bad" or "off limits," they allow themselves to eat everything in moderation without judgment. They enjoy eating and do not feel guilty, ashamed, or embarrassed about satisfying their appetites. They focus on health and well-being and do not let concerns about food or weight interfere with their lives.

Yet the American media and popular culture routinely promote ideas that contradict these healthy eating principles. People are applauded for restricting their food intake and encouraged to follow fad diets and extreme fitness regimens in an effort to change their body proportions. These cultural influences contribute to disordered eating and eating disorders.

Disordered Eating versus Eating Disorders

An eating disorder is a form of mental illness in which an individual uses food and eating as a means of coping with a complex range of emotional and psychological issues. Although a person with disordered eating may engage in some of the same behaviors as someone with an eating disorder—such as restricting food intake, binge eating, self-induced vomiting, or abusing diet pills or laxatives—they typically do so less often or to a lesser extent. While the symptoms may not be as extreme, however, disordered eating can still cause health problems, and it also increases the risk of developing an eating disorder or other types of psychiatric issues.

Disordered eating is characterized by an unhealthy or abnormal relationship with food. People with disordered eating are likely to think about food obsessively and worry about every bite they consume. Eating too much or eating "bad" foods makes them feel terribly guilty and ashamed. They may respond by punishing themselves, restricting food even more severely, or exercising excessively in order to burn off the calories. They are likely to count calories and deny themselves certain foods or entire food groups, even if they experience cravings. They tend to be rigid and inflexible about food, and they may feel anxious about eating in restaurants, trying new foods, or attending social events where food is served because they cannot control what they consume. They often evaluate their self-worth based on their body shape, weight, and success in controlling what they eat.

Preventing and Managing Disordered Eating

Although disordered eating is quite common, it is not considered normal or healthy and can be self-destructive. Disordered eating may turn into an eating disorder that requires medical treatment if it affects an individual's daily functioning. Worrying about food and eating may take up so much time and attention that it affects a person's concentration, ability to focus, and performance at school or on the job. Disordered eating may also cause a person to avoid socializing

15

because they worry about consuming forbidden foods or disrupting an exercise routine. Finally, disordered eating may require treatment if a person's relationship to food becomes a source of anxiety or a way to cope with the problems and stresses of everyday life.

A mental-health professional can help people distinguish between disordered eating and eating disorders and determine whether they need treatment. Therapy can help people understand the complex relationships between food and self-image and establish healthier eating and exercise patterns. Some other tips to help prevent or manage disordered eating include avoiding restrictive fad diets, incorporating all foods in moderation, focusing on health rather than weight, limiting use of the scale, maintaining a positive and nonjudgmental attitude toward one's body, and setting healthy limits on exercise.

References

1. Gottlieb, Carrie. "Disordered Eating or Eating Disorder: What's the Difference?" *Psychology Today*, February 23, 2014.

2. Klein, Sarah. "14 Habits of People with a Healthy Relationship to Food," Huffington Post, April 17, 2014.

3. Narins, Elizabeth. "25 Signs You Have a Terrible Relationship with Food," Cosmopolitan, May 4, 2015.

4. Tartakovsky, Margarita. "What Is Normal Eating?" PsychCentral, August 26, 2009.

Section 2.2

Emotional Eating

This section contains text excerpted from the following sources:
Text in this section begins with excerpts from "Connection between
Children's Emotions, Mental Skills, and Eating Habits," U.S.
Department of Agriculture (USDA), March 22, 2016; Text under the
heading "Interventions for Emotional Eating" is excerpted from "A
One-Day Act Workshop for Emotional Eating," ClinicalTrials.gov,
National Institutes of Health (NIH), November 16, 2018; Text under
the heading "Tips to Avoid Emotional Eating" is excerpted from
"Maintain Your Weight," Smokefree Women, U.S. Department of
Health and Human Services (HHS), September 6, 2018.

American children are gaining weight. Obesity now affects one in
six children and adolescents in the United States, according to the
Centers for Disease Control and Prevention (CDC). This is a major
concern because extra pounds can increase risk for developing serious
health problems in children, including diabetes, high blood pressure,
and high cholesterol.

While strategies to reduce childhood obesity include improving diet
and increasing exercise, U.S. Department of Agriculture (USDA) scientists are looking for ways to prevent behaviors in children that may
lead to obesity. Nutritionist Kevin Laugero, who works at the USDA
Agricultural Research Service's (ARS) Western Human Nutrition
Research Center in Davis, California, investigated the relationship
between obesity, unhealthy eating behaviors, and decreased mental
skills in 3- to 6-year-olds.

Laugero and his colleagues at the University of California-Davis
discovered, for the first time, a connection between young children's
eating behaviors and experiencing an emotional state. The team also
found that mental skills, referred to here as "cognitive control," are
significantly associated with overeating and emotions.

Cognitive control allows us to remember, plan, organize, make
decisions, manage time, maintain emotional and self-control, and curb
inappropriate behavior.

"At an early age, these skills are rapidly developing," Laugero says.
"If we're able to understand the relationship between eating behaviors
and cognitive control, we may be able to develop preventive methods
for young children to help control obesity."

Researchers conducted several experiments to examine the balance
between emotional state, snacking, and cognitive control in preschool

children. Cognitive control was measured through computerized and hands-on tasks, parent questionnaires, and standardized teacher reports.

"Our research suggests that, even at a young age, children with lower cognitive control skills may be more likely to engage in emotional-based overeating," Laugero says. "On the other hand, our results suggest that children with higher cognitive control skills may be less likely to overeat."

Laugero and his colleagues are considering further studies, using intervention strategies, to improve cognitive control during preschool years. They would then follow up with children to see whether intervention encourages healthier eating habits, including less emotional eating, later in life.

Interventions for Emotional Eating

Emotional eating is defined as increased food consumption in response to negative emotions, and has been linked to weight concerns, mental health concerns, and disordered eating behaviors. Effective interventions have been developed that address emotional eating, namely to improve weight loss. Such interventions are based in acceptance and commitment therapy (ACT), which encourages tolerance of internal cues, such as emotions, and external cues, such as food.

Emotional eating, however, is not exclusive to those who struggle with their weight. Many individuals maintain a normal weight despite engaging in emotional eating. These individuals still consume an excess of high calorie (for which they somehow eventually compensate), high fat, and high sugar foods as part of their emotional eating. Unhealthy dietary habits such as these have been shown to be associated with an increased risk of all-cause mortality, as well as health concerns including diabetes and cardiovascular disease (CVD). Individuals with normal weight are not eligible for ACT programs, despite the increased risk of health concerns associated with emotional eating.

Tips to Avoid Emotional Eating

Similar to how some people smoke in specific places or to cope with their emotions, some people use eating to handle situations. Emotional eating often includes the least healthy foods, and lots of them. If you're trying to maintain or lose weight, emotional eating can set you back in your progress. Try these tips:

- **Take away temptation.** Avoid keeping unhealthy comfort foods at home, and don't go to the grocery store when you're stressed or feeling down.

- **Learn your patterns.** Keep a food diary of what and when you eat, your level of hunger, and how you're feeling when you eat. This can help you gain a better understanding of how your emotions affect your eating.

- **Find other stress busters.** There are many ways to deal with your feelings. Try practicing meditation, deep breathing, listening to music, calling a friend, or going for a walk when you are stressed or down.

- **Don't be too hard on yourself if you slip.** Forgive yourself if you stress eat and start fresh the next day. Think of it as an experience to learn from and make a plan for how you can prevent it in the future.

Section 2.3

Disordered Eating and Eating Disorders: What's the Difference?

This section contains text excerpted from the following sources: Text beginning with the heading "What Is the Difference between Disordered Eating and an Eating Disorder?" is excerpted from "Women Veterans Healthcare," U.S. Department of Veterans Affairs (VA), March 28, 2017; Text under the heading "Exploring the Link between Trauma and Disordered Eating for Female Vets" is excerpted from "Exploring the Link between Trauma and Disordered Eating for Female Vets," U.S. Department of Veterans Affairs (VA), February 2, 2017.

What Is the Difference between Disordered Eating and an Eating Disorder?

Disordered eating is common and affects all types of people. It can be defined as periods of food avoidance, food restriction, or overeating. An eating disorder is a psychiatric illness that is more frequent, sustained, and severe than disordered eating. The main factors that differentiate disordered eating patterns from eating disorders are the severity and frequency of disordered eating behaviors.

Potential Signs and Risk Factors of Disordered Eating

Disordered eating is a serious health concern that can be difficult to detect. Disordered eating might include any of the following:

- Decreased self-esteem based on body shape or weight (being either overweight or underweight)

- Obsessive calorie counting

- Anxiety about eating only certain foods or food groups

- The inability to control eating habits

- A rigid approach to eating, such as having inflexible meal times

- A refusal to eat in restaurants or outside one's own home

- An excessive or rigid exercise routine

Being stressed about your body, measuring what you eat, and frequently weighing yourself could be signs of disordered eating. A person with disordered eating habits and behaviors may also be experiencing significant physical, emotional, and mental stress.

Disordered Eating Can Harm Your Body

Many who suffer with disordered eating patterns deny, minimize, or fail to fully recognize the impact these behaviors can have on their mental and physical well-being. Consequences can include a greater risk for obesity, bone loss, gastrointestinal disturbances, electrolyte and fluid imbalances, low heart rate and blood pressure, increased anxiety and depression, and social isolation.

Exploring the Link between Trauma and Disordered Eating for Female Vets

The terms "eating disorders" and "disordered eating" are often confused with one another, but they hold subtle differences. The former relates to serious conditions such as anorexia, an obsessive desire to lose weight by refusing to eat; bulimia, when excess overeating is often followed by self-induced vomiting, purging, or fasting; and binge eating, which includes overeating without purging or other compensatory behaviors.

Disordered eating, a wide range of abnormal eating behaviors, may be linked to eating disorders but doesn't meet the criteria for an eating disorder diagnosis. It's much less talked about but far more common.

Now, a new VA-funded study involving a small group of female veterans says military trauma that is related to such conditions as depression and posttraumatic stress disorder (PTSD) can trigger disordered eating.

The study, published online in January 2017 in *Women & Health*, found that trauma was associated with disordered eating, often in relation to negative feelings and emotions and thoughts of panic, fear, and anxiety. The research also says disordered eating generally provides short-term but not long-term relief from negative feelings or emotions related to trauma, as well as a way to avoid unwanted attention from potential and past perpetrators of trauma.

The researchers defined disordered eating as changing eating patterns in response to stress, using food to cope with stress, gaining or losing more weight than desired, or starting to become very interested in healthier eating in an excessive or otherwise unusual or harmful way.

Examples of disordered eating include eating unbalanced meals where one intentionally avoids "fatty" foods or carbohydrates; skipping meals to either fast or to eat other foods, such as ice cream, in excess; or using a laxative to help release food from the body.

Trapped in a 'Vicious Cycle'

"We found that women reported eating more and/or eating less in response to trauma," the researchers write. "We also found that the relationship between trauma exposure and disordered eating seemed to trap participants in a vicious cycle. For many women, the cycle began with a reminder of past trauma that triggered negative affect and maladaptive thoughts, which then led women to cope using disordered eating. This disordered eating led to short-term relief, but ultimately resulted in additional negative affect and maladaptive thoughts that perpetuated further disordered eating."

Study coauthor Dr. Jessica Breland, an investigator with the Center for Innovation to Implementation at the VA Palo Alto (California) healthcare system, says although much research exists on the link between trauma and disordered eating, "we wanted to interview women veterans to hear, in their own words, why that relationship might exist. We think understanding this issue from a veteran perspective will help clinicians better understand how to help the veterans they serve."

In the study, 20 female veterans recruited mostly from outpatient mental health clinics took part in focus groups and interviews at the San Francisco VA Healthcare System. Women with various eating behaviors, stress levels, and histories of military trauma exposure were included.

The women answered questions about changes in their eating habits that might be related to traumatic or stressful experiences. One question asked: "Some veterans . . . say they eat when they experience stress or think of things that are just hard to deal with. Has this ever happened to you?"

The participants reported high rates of trauma exposure and disordered eating. Each of the 20 women noted exposure to a potentially traumatic event in the military such as a personal injury, and 17 said they experienced military sexual trauma. The study suggested that many women experienced multiple traumas. Some described the types of trauma they experienced, while others spoke broadly about trauma without offering details. Sixty-five percent of the participants reported psychological symptoms, namely depression and/or PTSD.

The participants averaged 48 years old and 15 years of military experience. Most were of relatively low income, and 11 were women of color.

The researchers identified three themes that related to trauma exposure and disordered eating:

- Trauma can be linked to disordered eating, often in relation to negative feelings, emotions, or thoughts. One participant said: "We're overeating because we had trauma and we're angry." Another explained: "When I got out of the service I don't think I thought I deserved to be healthy. I had a pretty low self-opinion, and [disordered eating] was just one thing on the list."

- Most of the participants said they used disordered eating to control their emotions in response to experiencing negative feelings and emotions. One women said, "I ate to comfort myself," while another said, "When crisis comes up, I'll start eating."

- Some participants reported disordered eating as a way to change their shape and weight to avoid attention that may lead to more traumatic experiences. One participant said trauma "made us not want to eat because then we felt like, okay, maybe they won't bother us [if we] lose weight." The same woman noted that trauma gave some women an urge to overeat because "maybe when we gain weight, [the perpetrators] will leave us alone."

According to Breland, some women began their disordered eating patterns while in the military. Others said their problems started after they left the service.

Clinicians Must Be Aware of Treatment Options

In analyzing the answers, the researchers looked for signs of anorexia, bulimia, and other eating disorders. Fourteen women had possible eating disorders based on the SCOFF, a five-question screening tool designed to help determine whether an eating disorder may exist, rather than to make a diagnosis. (i.e., "Do you believe yourself to be fat when others say you are too thin?) Five participants reported purging, and 15 reported being worried about losing control over their eating.

The results of the study, Breland says, suggest disordered eating is both a major problem that stands alone and a marker of other issues that may need attention.

"For some women, disordered eating is related to other problems," she says. "For example, the stress of leaving structured military environments or the difficulty of coping with past trauma. We think it's important for clinicians to ask questions when veterans describe disordered eating so they can figure out which is the case."

She says the results of the study suggest that veterans may benefit from different kinds of treatment depending on the cause of their eating disorder.

"For example, they might benefit from cognitive behavioral therapy (CBT) for eating disorders," she says. "Or if PTSD is driving the eating disorder, psychological treatment for PTSD may help treat their eating problems. If the eating problems are mainly driven by depression, then therapy, medication, and/or physical activity could help. That said, a lot more research needs to be conducted before we'll know for sure."

What about male veterans and active-duty service members? Are they also at risk for trauma exposure and disordered eating, or is it mostly a problem for women?

"In this study, we focused on women veterans because they are at increased risk for problems with eating, compared to men veterans," Breland says. "But we think that studying the relationship between trauma and disordered eating among men is a really important next step."

Chapter 3

How Are Eating Disorders and Obesity Related?

Loss of Control Eating and Obesity

Individuals with binge-eating disorder (BED) feel that they lose control of themselves when eating. They eat large quantities of food and do not stop until they are uncomfortably full. Usually, they have more difficulty losing weight and keeping it off than do people with other serious weight problems. Most people with the disorder are obese and have a history of weight fluctuations. Binge-eating disorder is found in about two percent of the general population—more often in women than men. Recent research shows that binge-eating disorder occurs in about 30 percent of people participating in medically supervised weight control programs.

People with binge-eating disorder are usually overweight, so they are prone to the serious medical problems associated with obesity, such as high cholesterol, high blood pressure, and diabetes. Obese

This chapter contains text excerpted from the following sources: Text under the heading "Loss of Control Eating and Obesity" is excerpted from "Eating Disorders," National Oceanic and Atmospheric Administration (NOAA), U.S. Department of Commerce (DOC), November 28, 2001. Reviewed December 2018; Text beginning with the heading "Brain's Reward/Motivation Circuits Are Linked to Compulsive Overeating" is excerpted from "Binge Eaters' Dopamine Levels Spike at Sight, Smell of Food," Brookhaven National Laboratory (BNL), U.S. Department of Energy (DOE), February 28, 2011. Reviewed December 2018.

individuals also have a higher risk for gallbladder disease, heart disease, and some types of cancer. Research at the National Institute of Mental Health (NIMH) and elsewhere has shown that individuals with binge-eating disorder have high rates of co-occurring psychiatric depression.

Brain's Reward/Motivation Circuits Are Linked to Compulsive Overeating

A brain imaging study at the U.S. Department of Energy's (DOE) Brookhaven National Laboratory (BNL) reveals a subtle difference between ordinary obese subjects and those who compulsively overeat, or binge: In binge eaters but not ordinary obese subjects, the mere sight or smell of favorite foods triggers a spike in dopamine—a brain chemical linked to reward and motivation. The findings suggest that this dopamine spike may play a role in triggering compulsive overeating.

"These results identify dopamine neurotransmission, which primes the brain to seek reward, as being of relevance to the neurobiology of binge-eating disorder," said study lead author Gene-Jack Wang, a physician at BNL and the Mount Sinai School of Medicine. Previous studies conducted by Wang's team have identified a similar dopamine spike in drug-addicted individuals when they were shown images of people taking drugs, as well as other neurochemical similarities between drug addiction and obesity, including a role for dopamine in triggering desire for drugs and/or food.

"In earlier studies of normal-weight healthy people who had been food-deprived for 16 hours, we found that dopamine releases were significantly correlated with self-reports of hunger and desire for food. These results provided evidence of a conditioned-cue response to food," Wang said.

In a study, the researchers suspected that binge-eating obese subjects would show stronger conditioned responses to food stimuli when compared with nonbinging obese subjects.

"Understanding the neurobiological mechanisms underlying food stimulation might point us toward new ways to help individuals regulate their abnormal eating behaviors," Wang said.

The scientists used positron emission tomography (PET) to scan the subjects' brains after injecting a radiotracer designed to bind to dopamine receptors in the brain. Because the tracer competes with the brain's natural dopamine to bind to these receptors, the signal picked up by the PET scanner provides an inverse measure of the brain's dopamine levels: a strong signal from the bound tracer indicates low levels of natural brain dopamine; a low signal from the tracer indicates high levels of dopamine in the brain.

Results

Food stimulation significantly increased dopamine levels in the caudate and putamen regions of the brain in binge eaters but not in the nonbinge eaters. Subjects with the most severe binge-eating disorder, as assessed by psychological evaluations, had the highest dopamine levels in the caudate.

"So the key difference we found between binge eaters and nonbinge eating obese subjects was a fairly subtle elevation of dopamine levels in the caudate in the binge eaters in response to food stimulation," Wang said.

"This dopamine response is in a different part of the brain from what we've observed in studies of drug addiction, which found dopamine spikes in the brain's reward center in response to drug-associated cues. The caudate, in contrast, is believed to be involved in reinforcement of action potentially leading to reward, but not in processing of the reward per se. That means this response effectively primes the brain to seek the reward, which is also observed in drug-addicted subjects," Wang said.

Inasmuch as binge eating is not exclusively found in obese individuals, the scientists believe further studies are warranted to assess the neurobiological factors that may differentiate obese and nonobese binge eaters.

Chapter 4

Binge-Eating Disorder

What Is Binge-Eating Disorder?

Binge-eating is when you eat a large amount of food in a short amount of time and feel that you can't control what or how much you are eating. If you binge eat regularly—at least once a week for three months, you may have binge-eating disorder (BED).

If you have binge-eating disorder, you may be very upset by your binge eating. You also may feel ashamed and try to hide your problem. Even your close friends and family members may not know you binge eat.

How Is Binge-Eating Disorder Different from Bulimia Nervosa?

Unlike people with binge-eating disorder, people who have bulimia nervosa (BN) try to prevent weight gain after binge eating by vomiting, using laxatives or diuretics, fasting, or exercising too much.

How Common Is Binge-Eating Disorder?

Binge-eating disorder is the most common eating disorder in the United States. About 3.5 percent of adult women and two percent of adult men have binge-eating disorder. For men, binge-eating disorder is most common in midlife, between the ages of 45 to 59.

This chapter includes text excerpted from "Binge Eating Disorder," National Institute of Diabetes and Digestive and Kidney Diseases (NIDDK), June 2016.

For women, binge-eating disorder most commonly starts in early adulthood, between the ages of 18 and 29. About 1.6 percent of teenagers are affected. A much larger number of adults and children have episodes of binge eating or loss-of-control eating, but the episodes do not occur frequently enough to meet the criteria for binge-eating disorder.

Binge-eating disorder affects African Americans as often as whites. More research is needed on how often binge-eating disorder affects people in other racial and ethnic groups.

Who Is More Likely to Develop Binge-Eating Disorder?

Binge-eating disorder can occur in people of average body weight but is more common in people with obesity, particularly severe obesity. However, it is important to note that most people with obesity do not have binge-eating disorder.

Painful childhood experiences—such as family problems and critical comments about your shape, weight, or eating—also are associated with developing binge-eating disorder. Binge-eating disorder also runs in families, and there may be a genetic component as well.

What Other Health Problems Can You Have with Binge-Eating Disorder?

Binge-eating disorder may lead to weight gain and health problems related to obesity. Overweight and obesity are associated with many health problems, including type 2 diabetes, heart disease, and certain types of cancer. People with binge-eating disorder may also have mental health problems such as depression or anxiety. Some people with binge-eating disorder also have problems with their digestive system, or joint and muscle pain.

What Are the Symptoms of Binge-Eating Disorder?

If you have binge-eating disorder, you may:

- Eat a large amount of food in a short amount of time; for example, within two hours

- Feel you lack control over your eating; for example, you cannot stop eating or control what or how much you are eating

You also may:

- Eat more quickly than usual during binge episodes
- Eat until you feel uncomfortably full
- Eat large amounts of food even when you are not hungry
- Eat alone because you are embarrassed about the amount of food you eat
- Feel disgusted, depressed, or guilty after overeating

If you think that you or someone close to you may have binge eating disorder, share your concerns with a healthcare provider who can connect you to helpful sources of care.

What Causes Binge-Eating Disorder

No one knows for sure what causes binge-eating disorder. Like other eating disorders, binge-eating disorder may result from a mix of factors related to your genes, your thoughts and feelings, and social issues. Binge-eating disorder has been linked to depression and anxiety.

For some people, dieting in unhealthy ways—such as skipping meals, not eating enough food, or avoiding certain kinds of food—may contribute to binge eating.

How Do Doctors Diagnose Binge-Eating Disorder?

Most of us overeat from time to time, and some of us often feel we have eaten more than we should have. Eating a lot of food does not necessarily mean you have binge-eating disorder.

To determine if you have binge-eating disorder, you may want to talk with a specialist in eating disorders, such as a psychiatrist, psychologist, or other mental-health professional. She or he will eats with you about your symptoms and eating patterns. If a healthcare provider determines you have binge-eating disorder, she or he can work with you to find the best treatment options.

How Do Doctors Treat Binge-Eating Disorder?

Talk to your doctor if you think you have binge-eating disorder. Ask her or him to refer you to a mental-health professional in your area. A specialist, such as a psychiatrist, psychologist, or other mental-health professionals, may be able to help you choose the best treatment for you.

Treatment may include therapy to help you change your eating habits, as well as thoughts and feelings that may lead to binge eating and other psychological symptoms. Types of therapy that have been shown to help people with binge-eating disorder are called psychotherapies and include cognitive behavioral therapy (CBT), interpersonal psychotherapy, and dialectical behavior therapy (DBT). Your psychiatrist or other healthcare providers may also prescribe medication to help you with your binge eating, or to treat other medical or mental health problems.

Should You Try to Lose Weight If You Have Binge-Eating Disorder?

Losing weight may help prevent or reduce some of the health problems related to carrying excess weight. Binge-eating may make it hard to lose weight and keep it off. If you have binge-eating disorder and are overweight, a weight loss program that also offers treatment for eating disorders may help you lose weight. However, some people with binge-eating disorder do just as well in a behavioral treatment program designed only for weight loss as people who do not binge eat. Talk with your healthcare professional to help you decide whether you should try to manage your binge eating before entering a weight management program.

Chapter 5

Anorexia Nervosa

What Is Anorexia?

Anorexia nervosa (AN), often called anorexia, is a type of eating disorder. Eating disorders are mental health problems that cause extreme and dangerous eating behaviors. These extreme eating behaviors cause other serious health problems and sometimes death. Some eating disorders also involve extreme exercise.

Women with anorexia severely limit the amount of food they eat to prevent weight gain. People with anorexia usually have an intense fear of gaining weight and may think they are fat even when they are thin. Women with anorexia may also exercise too much so that they do not gain weight. Over time, eating so little food leads to serious health problems and sometimes death.

What Is the Difference between Anorexia and Other Eating Disorders?

Women with eating disorders, such as anorexia, bulimia, and binge-eating disorder (BED), have a mental health condition that affects how they eat, and sometimes how they exercise. These eating disorders threaten their health.

Unlike women with bulimia and binge-eating disorder, girls and women with anorexia do not eat enough to sustain basic bodily

This chapter includes text excerpted from "Binge Eating Disorder," National Institute of Diabetes and Digestive and Kidney Diseases (NIDDK), June 2016.

functions. Women with bulimia and binge-eating disorder usually binge, or eat too much while feeling out of control.

It is possible to have more than one eating disorder in your lifetime. Regardless of what type of eating disorder you may have, you can get better with treatment.

Who Is at Risk for Anorexia?

Anorexia is more common among girls and women than boys and men. Anorexia is also more common among girls and younger women than older women. On average, girls develop anorexia at 16 or 17. Teen girls between 13 and 19 and young women in their early 20s are most at risk. But eating disorders are happening more often in older women. In one recent study, 13 percent of American women over 50 had signs of an eating disorder.

What Are the Symptoms of Anorexia?

Anorexia causes physical and psychological changes. A girl or woman with anorexia often looks very thin and may not act like herself.

Some other symptoms of anorexia include:

- Sadness
- Moodiness
- Confused or slow thinking
- Poor memory or judgment
- Thin, brittle hair and nails
- Feeling cold all the time because of a drop in internal body temperature
- Feeling faint, dizzy, or weak
- Feeling tired or sluggish
- Irregular periods or never getting a period
- Dry, blotchy, or yellow skin
- Growth of fine hair all over the body (called lanugo)
- Severe constipation or bloating
- Weak muscles or swollen joints

Girls or women with anorexia may also exhibit behavior changes such as:

- Talking about weight or food all the time
- Not eating or eating very little
- Refusing to eat in front of others
- Not wanting to go out with friends
- Making herself throw up
- Taking laxatives or diet pills
- Exercising a lot

People with anorexia may also exhibit other health problems, including depression, anxiety, or substance abuse.

What Causes Anorexia

Researchers are not sure exactly what causes anorexia and other eating disorders. Researchers think that eating disorders might happen because of a combination of a person's biology and life events. This combination includes having specific genes, a person's biology, body image and self-esteem, social experiences, family health history, and sometimes other mental-health illnesses.

Researchers are also studying unusual activity in the brain, such as changing levels of serotonin or other chemicals, to see how it may affect eating.

How Does Anorexia Affect a Woman's Health?

With anorexia, your body doesn't get the energy that it needs from food, so it slows down and stops working normally. Over time, anorexia can affect your body in the following ways:

- Heart problems, including low blood pressure, a slower heart rate, irregular heartbeat, heart attack, and sudden death from heart problems
- Anemia (when your red blood cells do not carry enough oxygen to your body) and other blood problems
- Thinning of the bones (osteopenia or osteoporosis)
- Kidney stones or kidney failure

- Lack of periods, which can cause problems getting pregnant

- During pregnancy, a higher risk for miscarriage, cesarean delivery, or having a baby with low birth weight

Anorexia is a serious illness that can also lead to death. Studies have found that more women and girls die from anorexia than any other eating disorder or serious mental health problem such as depression. Many people with anorexia also have other mental health problems such as depression or anxiety.

Long-term studies of 20 years or more show that women who had an eating disorder in the past usually reach and maintain a healthy weight after treatment.

How Is Anorexia Diagnosed?

Your doctor or nurse will ask you questions about your symptoms and medical history. It may be difficult to talk to a doctor or nurse about secret eating or exercise behaviors. But doctors and nurses want to help you be healthy. Being honest about your eating and exercise behaviors with a doctor or nurse is a good way to ask for help.

Your doctor will do a physical exam and other tests, such as blood tests and a urine test, to rule out other health problems that may cause severe weight loss.

Your doctor may also do other tests, such as kidney function tests, bone density tests, or an electrocardiogram (ECG or EKG), to see if or how severe weight loss has affected your health.

How Is Anorexia Treated?

Your doctor may refer you to a team of doctors, nutritionists, and therapists who will work to help you get better. If you live with family members they may be invited to participate in some of your treatment. Treatment plans may include one or more of the following:

- **Nutrition therapy.** Doctors, nurses, and counselors will help you eat healthy to reach and maintain a healthy weight. Some girls or women may need to be hospitalized or participate in a residential treatment program (live temporarily at a medical facility) to make sure they eat enough to recover. Hospitalization may also be required to monitor any heart problems in people with anorexia. Reaching a healthy weight is a key part of the recovery process so that your body's biology, including thoughts and feelings in your brain, work correctly.

- **Psychotherapy.** Sometimes called "talk therapy," psychotherapy is counseling to help you change any harmful thoughts or behaviors. This therapy may focus on the importance of talking about your feelings and how they affect what you do. You may work one-on-one with a therapist or in a group with others who have anorexia. For girls with anorexia, counseling may involve the whole family.

- **Support groups** can be helpful for some people with anorexia when added to other treatment. In support groups, girls or women and sometimes their families meet and share their stories.

- **Medicine.** Studies suggest that medicines like antidepressants can help some girls and women with anorexia by improving the depression and anxiety symptoms that often go along with anorexia.

Most girls and women do get better with treatment and are able to eat and exercise in healthy ways again. Some may get better after the first treatment. Others get well but may relapse and need treatment again.

How Does Anorexia Affect Pregnancy?

Anorexia can cause problems getting pregnant and during pregnancy.

Extreme weight loss can cause missed menstrual periods because you may not ovulate, or release an egg from the ovary. When you do not weigh enough to ovulate, it is difficult to get pregnant. However, if you do not want to have children right now and you have sex, you should use birth control.

Anorexia can also cause problems during pregnancy. Anorexia raises your risk for:

- Miscarriage (pregnancy loss)

- Premature birth (also called preterm birth), or childbirth before 37 weeks of pregnancy

- Delivery by cesarean section (C-section)

- Having a low birth weight baby (less than five pounds, eight ounces at birth)

- Depression after the baby is born (postpartum depression)

If I Had an Eating Disorder in the Past, Can I Still Get Pregnant?

Yes. Women who have recovered from anorexia, are at a healthy weight, and have normal menstrual cycles have a better chance of getting pregnant and having a safe and healthy pregnancy.

If you had an eating disorder in the past, it may take you a little longer to get pregnant (about six months to a year) compared to women who never had an eating disorder. Tell your doctor if you had an eating disorder in the past and are trying to become pregnant.

If I Take Medicine to Treat Anorexia, Can I Breastfeed My Baby?

Maybe. Some medicines used to treat anorexia can pass through breast milk. Certain antidepressants can be used safely during breastfeeding.

Talk to your doctor to find out which medicine works best for you. You can also enter a medicine into the LactMed® database (toxnet. nlm.nih.gov/newtoxnet/lactmed.htm) to find out if the medicine passes through breast milk and about any possible side effects for your nursing baby.

Chapter 6

Bulimia Nervosa

What Is Bulimia?

Bulimia nervosa (BN), often called bulimia, is a type of eating disorder. Eating disorders are mental-health problems that cause extreme and dangerous eating behaviors. These extreme eating behaviors cause other serious health problems and sometimes death. Some eating disorders also involve extreme exercise.

Women with bulimia eat a lot of food in a short amount of time and feel a lack of control over eating during this time (called binging). People with bulimia then try to prevent weight gain by getting rid of the food (called purging). Purging may be done by:

- Making yourself throw up

- Taking laxatives. Laxatives can include pills or liquids that speed up the movement of food through your body and lead to bowel movements.

Women with bulimia may also try to prevent weight gain after binging by exercising a lot more than normal, eating very little or not at all (fasting), or taking pills to urinate often.

The self-esteem of women with bulimia is usually closely linked to their body image.

This chapter includes text excerpted from "Bulimia Nervosa," Office on Women's Health (OWH), U.S. Department of Health and Human Services (HHS), August 28, 2018.

What Is the Difference between Bulimia and Other Eating Disorders?

Women with eating disorders, such as bulimia, anorexia, and binge-eating disorder (BED), have a mental-health condition that affects how they eat, and sometimes how they exercise. These eating disorders threaten their health.

Unlike women with anorexia, women with bulimia often have a normal weight. Unlike women with binge-eating disorder, women with bulimia purge, or try to get rid of the food or weight after binging. Binging and purging are usually done in private. This can make it difficult to tell if a loved one has bulimia or another eating disorder.

It is possible to have more than one eating disorder in your lifetime. Regardless of what type of eating disorder you may have, you can get better with treatment.

Who Is at Risk for Bulimia?

Bulimia affects more women than men. It affects up to two percent of women and happens to women of all races and ethnicities.

Bulimia affects more girls and younger women than older women. On average, women develop bulimia at 18 or 19. Teen girls between 15 and 19 and young women in their early 20s are most at risk. But eating disorders are happening more often in older women. In one study, 13 percent of American women over 50 had signs of an eating disorder.

What Are the Symptoms of Bulimia?

Someone with bulimia may be thin, overweight, or have a normal weight. It can be difficult to tell based on a person's weight whether someone has bulimia. This is because binging and purging is most often done in private. However, family or friends may see empty food wrappers in unexpected places or vomit in the home.

Over time, some symptoms of bulimia may include:

- Swollen cheeks or jaw area

- Calluses or scrapes on the knuckles (if using fingers to induce vomiting)

- Teeth that look clear instead of white and are increasingly sensitive and decaying

- Broken blood vessels in the eyes

- Acid reflux, constipation, and other gastrointestinal problems
- Severe dehydration

Girls or women with bulimia may also have behavior changes such as:

- Often going to the bathroom right after eating (to throw up)
- Exercising a lot, even in bad weather or when hurt or tired
- Acting moody or sad, hating the way she looks, or feeling hopeless
- Having problems expressing anger
- Not wanting to go out with friends or do activities she once enjoyed

People with bulimia often have other mental-health problems, including depression, anxiety, or substance abuse.

What Causes Bulimia

Researchers are not sure exactly what causes bulimia and other eating disorders. Researchers think that eating disorders might happen because of a combination of a person's biology and life events. This combination includes having specific genes, a person's biology, body image and self-esteem, social experiences, family health history, and sometimes other mental-health illnesses.

Researchers are also studying unusual activity in the brain, such as changing levels of serotonin or other chemicals, to see how it may affect eating.

How Does Bulimia Affect a Woman's Health?

Purging through vomiting or taking laxatives can prevent your body from getting the important nutrients it needs from food. Over time, bulimia can affect your body in the following ways:

- Stomach damage from overeating
- Electrolyte imbalance (having levels of sodium, potassium, or other minerals that are too high or too low, which can lead to heart attack or heart failure)
- Ulcers and other damage to your throat from vomiting

41

- Irregular periods or not having periods, which can cause problems getting pregnant

- Tooth decay from vomiting

- Dehydration

- Problems having bowel movements or damage to the intestines from laxative abuse

Long-term studies of 20 years or more show that women who had an eating disorder in the past usually reach and maintain a healthy weight after treatment.

How Is Bulimia Diagnosed?

Your doctor or nurse will ask you questions about your symptoms and medical history. It may be difficult to talk to a doctor or nurse about secret eating, purging, or exercise behaviors. But doctors and nurses want to help you get better. Being honest about your eating behaviors with a doctor or nurse is a good way to ask for help.

Your doctor may do blood or urine tests to rule out other possible causes of your symptoms. Your doctor may also do other tests to see whether you have any other health problems caused by bulimia. These tests may include kidney function tests or an electrocardiogram (ECG or EKG) to see if or how repeated binging and purging has affected your health.

How Is Bulimia Treated?

Your doctor may refer you to a team of doctors, nutritionists, and therapists who will work to help you get better.

Treatment plans may include one or more of the following:

- **Nutrition therapy.** People who purge (make themselves throw up or take laxatives) regularly should be treated by a doctor. Purging can cause life-threatening electrolyte imbalances. Some people with bulimia may need to be hospitalized if they have serious heart or kidney problems.

- **Psychotherapy.** Sometimes called "talk therapy," psychotherapy is counseling to help you change harmful thoughts or behaviors. This type of therapy may focus on the importance of talking about your feelings and how they affect what you do. For example, you might talk about how stress triggers a binge. You may work one-on-one with a therapist or in a group with others who have bulimia.

- **Nutritional counseling.** A registered dietitian or counselor can help you eat in a healthier way than binging and purging.

- **Support groups** can be helpful for some people with bulimia when added to other treatment. In support groups, girls or women and sometimes their families meet and share their stories.

- **Medicine.** Fluoxetine (Prozac) is the only medicine approved by the U.S. Food and Drug Administration for treating bulimia, but only in adults. It may help reduce binging and purging and improve your thoughts about eating. Some antidepressants may help girls and women with bulimia who also have depression or anxiety.

Most girls and women do get better with treatment and are able to eat and exercise in healthy ways again. Some may get better after the first treatment. Others get well but may relapse and need treatment again.

How Does Bulimia Affect Pregnancy?

Bulimia can cause problems getting pregnant and during pregnancy. Repeated purging and binging can make your menstrual cycle irregular (your period comes some months but not others) or your period may stop for several months. Irregular or missing periods mean you may not ovulate, or release an egg from the ovary, every month. This can make it difficult to get pregnant. However, if you do not want to have children right now and you have sex, you should use birth control.

Bulimia can also cause problems during pregnancy. Bulimia raises your risk for:

- Miscarriage (pregnancy loss)

- Premature birth (also called preterm birth), or childbirth before 37 weeks of pregnancy

- Delivery by cesarean section (C-section)

- Having a low birth weight baby (less than five pounds, eight ounces at birth)

- Having a baby with a birth defect

- Depression after the baby is born (postpartum depression)

If I Had an Eating Disorder in the Past, Can I Still Get Pregnant?

Women who have recovered from bulimia and have normal menstrual cycles have a better chance of getting pregnant and having a safe and healthy pregnancy.

If you had an eating disorder in the past, it may take you a little longer to get pregnant (about six months to a year) compared to women who never had an eating disorder.

Tell your doctor if you had an eating disorder in the past and are trying to become pregnant.

If I Take Medicine to Treat Bulimia, Can I Breastfeed My Baby?

Maybe. Some medicines used to treat bulimia can pass through breast milk. Certain antidepressants can be used safely during breastfeeding.

Talk to your doctor to find out what medicine works best for you. You can also enter a medicine into the LactMed® database (toxnet. nlm.nih.gov/newtoxnet/lactmed.htm) to find out if the medicine passes through breast milk and any about possible side effects for your nursing baby.

Chapter 7

Diet Pill, Diuretic, Ipecac, and Laxative Abuse

While maintaining a healthy weight is a positive goal, sometimes people become so focused on losing weight that they resort to unproven and dangerous weight-loss methods that can lead to serious health problems. Those with eating disorders such as bulimia, for instance, may use various methods of purging—such as self-induced vomiting, consuming ipecac syrup, or abusing laxatives or diuretics—in an effort to rid their body of the calories they consume. Although the idea behind purging is to force food to leave the body before the calories have been absorbed, it is not an effective weight-loss strategy. The body absorbs nutrients very quickly, and mainly fluids are expelled through vomiting or the use of laxatives and diuretics. Purging is also extremely dangerous and can cause many serious, long-term, and potentially fatal health complications. Some of the common purging methods employed by people with eating disorders include:

Self-Induced Vomiting

Many people with eating disorders force themselves to vomit after eating in an effort to absorb fewer calories and lose weight. In people with bulimia, purging through self-induced vomiting often follows overeating or binge eating. The process of digestion begins as soon as food enters the mouth however, so vomiting does not prevent the absorption of all the calories consumed. In addition, forced vomiting is associated with a wide range of dangerous health issues, such as:

- Dental problems from teeth coming into contact with stomach acid, including stained teeth, sensitivity to temperature, and erosion of tooth enamel

- Hardened skin or scarring on the back of the hand, known as Russell's sign, from inserting the fingers into the back of the throat to induce vomiting

- Swelling, tearing, or other damage to the esophagus (the tube that transports food from the mouth to the stomach)

- Dehydration and loss of minerals and electrolytes

- Irregular heartbeat and heart failure

Ipecac Syrup

Ipecac syrup is a liquid medication that induces vomiting. It can be helpful in emergency medical situations when a person swallows something that is poisonous or toxic. Taking ipecac syrup immediately afterward may enable the person to expel the poison by vomiting before it is absorbed into the bloodstream. But some people with eating disorders abuse ipecac syrup by using it to purge after eating. When overused or abused, ipecac syrup can be extremely harmful or even deadly. In addition to the problems associated with repeated vomiting, ipecac abuse can cause muscle weakness, difficulty breathing, seizures, internal bleeding, chest pain, and heart complications.

Laxatives

Laxatives are medications that can help relieve constipation by loosening stool and triggering the large intestine to produce bowel movements. Although laxatives can be helpful when used as directed, they are also commonly abused by people with eating disorders such as bulimia. People who abuse laxatives take them after overeating in an effort to empty the food out of their digestive system before their body can absorb the calories. Laxatives do not help people lose weight, however, because most calories and fat are absorbed before food reaches the large intestine. Instead, laxatives mainly cause the body to lose water, minerals, and electrolytes. Any weight that is lost is typically regained as soon as the person drinks fluids. Misusing laxatives can cause a number of serious health problems, including:

- Severe dehydration, with symptoms including weakness, confusion, and accelerated heart rate

- Electrolyte imbalance and loss of important minerals such as magnesium, potassium, and sodium

- Nausea, stomach pain, bowel problems, stretching or infection of the intestines, and an increased risk of colon cancer

- Damage to kidneys and other organs

- Heart attack

Diuretic Abuse

Diuretics are medications that are used to eliminate water from the body. When used as directed, they can be helpful for people who have high blood pressure or a severe form of swelling called edema. People with eating disorders sometimes misuse diuretics in the belief that they promote weight loss. In reality, however, any weight loss that occurs in conjunction with diuretic misuse is due to a loss of water. Not only will the water weight return as soon as the person consumes fluids, but the long-term abuse of diuretics may actually cause weight gain as the body chronically retains water to offset the effects of the medication. The health risks associated with diuretic abuse include dehydration, electrolyte imbalance, low blood pressure, fainting, irregular heartbeat, kidney damage, and death.

Diet Pills

Diet pills or appetite suppressants are another form of medication that can be abused by people with eating disorders. Many of these substances stimulate the central nervous system and have the potential to be addictive. Since they are considered supplements rather than food or drugs, they are poorly regulated and may contain harmful ingredients. Excessive use of diet pills can cause nausea, headaches, anxiety, irritability, insomnia, dizziness, diarrhea, skin rashes, elevated blood pressure, and heart complications.

Resisting the Urge to Purge

To avoid the health hazards associated with misuse of ipecac syrup, laxatives, diuretics, diet pills, and other medications, people should seek support from an organization or treatment center that focuses on eating disorders. Specialized programs and professional assistance from doctors, therapists, and nutritionists can help people stop abusing these products and recover their physical and mental health. Additional strategies for resisting the urge to purge include throwing away any laxatives, diet pills, or related products in the home; staying well hydrated and avoiding caffeine and alcohol; eating a fiber-rich diet to promote intestinal health; and exercising—especially in the morning—to stimulate digestive function.

References

1. Bano, Musarrat. "Dangerous Methods of Weight Loss," May 27, 2014.

2. "Laxative Abuse: A Common Practice among Bulimics," Casa Palmera, September 19, 2012.

3. "Purging," Kelty Eating Disorders, n.d.

Chapter 8

Female Athlete Triad

Being active is great. In fact, girls should be active at least an hour each day. Sometimes, though, a girl will be very active (such as running every day or playing a competitive sport), but not eat enough to fuel her activity. This can lead to health problems.

Read about what can happen when girls don't eat enough to fuel their activity:

- A problem called "low energy availability"

- Period (menstrual) problems

- Bone problems

These three sometimes are called the female athlete triad. ("Triad" means a group of three). They sometimes also are called athletic performance and energy deficit. (This means you have a "deficit," or lack, of the energy your body needs to stay healthy.)

A Problem Called "Low Energy Availability"

Your body needs healthy food to fuel the things it does, such as fight infections, heal wounds, and grow. If you exercise, your body needs extra food for your workout. You can learn how much food to eat based on your activity level using the MyPlate Checklist Calculator (www. choosemyplate.gov/MyPlatePlan).

This chapter includes text excerpted from "Do You Exercise a Lot?" girlshealth. gov, Office on Women's Health (OWH), May 7, 2018.

"Energy availability" means the fuel from food that is not burned up by exercise and so is available for growing, healing, and more. If you exercise a lot and don't get enough nutrition, you may have low energy availability. That means your body won't be as healthy and strong as it should be.

Some female athletes diet to lose weight. They may do this to qualify for their sport or because they think losing weight will help them perform better. But eating enough healthy food is key to having the strength you need to succeed. Also, your body needs good nutrition to make hormones that help with things like healthy periods and strong bones.

Sometimes, girls may exercise too much and eat too little because they have an eating disorder. Eating disorders are serious and can even lead to death, but they are treatable.

Period (Menstrual) Problems

If you are very active, or if you just recently started getting your period (menstruating), you may skip a few periods. But if you work out really hard and do not eat enough, you may skip a lot of periods (or not get your period to begin with) because your body can't make enough of the hormone estrogen.

You may think you wouldn't mind missing your period, but not getting your period should be taken seriously. Not having your period can mean your body is not building enough bone, and the teenage years are the main time for building strong bones.

If you have been getting your period regularly and then miss three periods in a row, see your doctor. Not having your period could be a sign of a serious health problem or of being pregnant. Also see your doctor if you are 15 years old and still have not gotten your period.

Bone Problems

Being physically active helps build strong bones. But you can hurt your bones if you don't eat enough healthy food to fuel all your activity. That's because your body won't be able to make the hormones needed to build strong bones.

One sign that your bones are weak is getting stress fractures, which are tiny cracks in bones. Some places you could get these cracks are your feet, legs, ribs, and spine. Even if you don't have problems with your bones when you're young, not taking good care of them now can be a problem later in life. Your skeleton is almost completely formed by age 18, so it's important to build strong bones early in life. If you don't, then later on you could wind up with osteoporosis, which is a disease that makes it easier for bones to break.

Signs of Not Eating Enough and Eating Disorders

Sometimes, girls exercise a lot and do not eat enough because they want to lose weight. Sometimes, exercising just lowers a person's appetite. And sometimes limiting food can be a sign that a girl may be developing an eating disorder. Here are some signs that you or a friend may have a problem:

- Worrying about gaining weight if you don't exercise enough
- Trying harder to find time to exercise than to eat
- Chewing gum or drinking water to cope with hunger
- Often wanting to exercise rather than be with friends
- Exercising instead of doing homework or other responsibilities
- Getting very upset if you miss a workout, but not if you miss a meal
- Having people tell you they are worried you are losing too much weight

If you think you or a friend has a problem, talk to a parent, guardian, or trusted adult.

Sometimes girls exercise a lot because they feel pressure to look a certain way. Soccer star Brandi Chastain knows how bad that can feel. It took a while, she says, for her to realize that only she was in charge of how she felt about her body. "Body image is tough, but it is something we have to take charge of," Brandi says. "Because inside, only we know who we are."

Chapter 9

Orthorexia

Orthorexia is a form of disordered eating that is characterized by an extreme obsession with consuming only foods that are perceived to be healthy or pure. Although orthorexia is not listed as an eating disorder in the American Psychiatric Association's (APA) *Diagnostic and Statistical Manual of Mental Disorders* (DSM), the condition is widely recognized by healthcare professionals and shares many traits with eating disorders. Orthorexia was first described in 1997 by Dr. Steven Bratman, who coined the name from the Greek words meaning "correct diet."

As part of their fixation with eating only healthy foods, people with orthorexia carefully avoid foods that they consider to be unwholesome or harmful. They typically establish strict rules to determine which foods they will eat and which foods they will avoid. For instance, they may eliminate entire food groups, such as fats or carbohydrates, or they may refuse to eat any food that contains artificial ingredients or additives. For many people with orthorexia, the need to plan meals and restrict food choices prevents them from attending social events or eating at restaurants because they cannot control the menu. They may also feel superior to people who do not follow a strict diet and who consume foods they reject as unhealthy.

Orthorexia resembles anorexia and bulimia because all of these conditions involve an obsession with controlling food intake. People with these eating disorders often experience severe anxiety surrounding meal planning and food consumption, and they may evaluate their

"Orthorexia," © 2016 Omnigraphics. Reviewed December 2018.

self-worth based on their success in restricting their diet. Orthorexia differs from anorexia and bulimia, however, because people with orthorexia are primarily concerned with the quality of the food they consume, rather than the quantity. In addition, the main goal of their dietary limitations is typically to feel clean, pure, and healthy rather than to lose weight.

Signs of Orthorexia

Doctors, nutritionists, and public-health agencies all emphasize the benefits of eating healthy foods. In addition, the media promotes an endless array of fad diets that recommend limiting food choices or even eliminating food groups as a path to better health. As a result, it can be difficult to sort through all the contradictory dietary advice and determine the point at which an interest in healthy eating becomes disordered eating. Orthorexia occurs when people take healthy eating to such an extreme point that it actually compromises their health or well-being. Some of the common warning signs of orthorexia include the following:

- Strictly limiting food choices, including eliminating entire food groups, in an effort to achieve a "perfect" diet

- Spending extreme amounts of time and money planning meals and preparing "healthy" foods

- Experiencing severe anxiety regarding meal planning or food preparation

- Avoiding social events where food is served for fear of being unable to comply with a strict diet

- Feeling fulfilled or virtuous when self-imposed rules for eating "healthy" are followed successfully

- Feeling guilty or embarrassed when unable to adhere to strict dietary standards

- Viewing others negatively if they lack the self-control to avoid "unhealthy" foods

Treatment for Orthorexia

The behaviors associated with orthorexia extend beyond reasonable efforts to eat well and maintain a healthy lifestyle. As the condition progresses, such extreme dietary restrictions can take a toll on a person's physical, emotional, and mental health. In fact, some of the potential negative health effects are similar to those seen in people with anorexia or bulimia, such as malnutrition, loss of bone density, heart or kidney problems, social isolation, and emotional instability.

People with orthorexia may benefit from working with a team of eating disorder specialists, including physicians, psychiatrists, therapists, and nutritionists. Professional treatment can help people with orthorexia identify and address the underlying issues that may contribute to the condition and develop dietary practices that support overall health.

References

1. Ekern, Jacquelyn. "Orthorexia, Excessive Exercise, and Nutrition," Eating Disorder Hope, January 31, 2014.

2. Ekern, Jacquelyn, and Crystal Karges. "How to Recognize Orthorexia," Eating Disorder Hope, May 17, 2014.

Chapter 10

Pica and Rumination Disorder

Chapter Contents

Section 10.1

Pica

This section includes text excerpted from "Pica Behavior and Contaminated Soil," Centers for Disease Control and Prevention (CDC), September 15, 2017.

What's the Problem?

Pica behavior is the craving to eat nonfood items, such as dirt, paint chips, and clay. Some children, especially preschool children, exhibit pica behavior. Pica behavior is most common in 1- and 2-year-old children and usually diminishes with age. Elementary-age children seldom exhibit pica behavior. Soil ingestion is the consumption of soil resulting from various behaviors including, but not limited to, mouthing objects or dirty hands, eating dropped food, and intentionally consuming soil. All children (and even adults) ingest small amounts of soil daily from these behaviors. The distinguishing factor for soil-pica is the recurrent ingestion of unusually high amounts of soil either intentionally by eating dirt or unintentionally from excessive mouthing behavior or eating dropped food. While the typical child might ingest 1/8 teaspoon of soil daily (or about 100 to 200 milligrams), children with soil-pica behavior ingest about a teaspoon or more of soil daily (or about 1,000 to 5,000 mg or more per day).

Pica and specifically soil-pica is a public health issue that has gotten little attention because people do not realize that it can lead to significant exposure to chemicals. However, soil ingestion has already been shown to be a significant risk factor for increased blood lead levels (BLL) and for exposure to soil-transmitted parasites. Up to 20 percent of preschool children exhibit soil-pica behavior, which parents may not notice since their preschool children may play unattended in the safety of their backyards.

In addition, pica behavior has also been observed in adults, and in particular pregnant women. In many cases of adult pica, the practice has cultural significance or is the result of craving during pregnancy. In some cases, the craving is due to a nutritional deficiency, such as iron-deficiency anemia.

An example of an element that may be found in soil is arsenic. Inorganic arsenic doesn't degrade and binds to soil particles at the surface. Historically, repeated applications of arsenic-containing pesticides and herbicides may have increased arsenic levels in topsoil to very high concentrations and can be a potential problem for children with soil-pica behavior. Pesticides containing arsenic are no longer commercially available. However, in many cases, soils were treated decades ago and the arsenic remains at the surface and increases the risk of contact from children's play activities. If soil ingestion is suspected among children, it is important to know the amount of soil ingested, the frequency of ingestion, and the type of material ingested.

Who's at Risk?

Groups at risk of soil-pica behavior include children aged six years and younger as well as individuals of any age who are developmentally delayed. Soil-pica behavior is highest in 1- and 2-year-old children and declines as the children grow older.

Can It Be Prevented?

Parents and guardians must be responsible for closely monitoring young children and persons who have developmental delays to ensure that soil is not ingested. Additionally, proper handwashing techniques must be employed after being outside and before eating to ensure that contaminants and parasites in soil do not pose any further threats through hand-to-mouth contact.

Section 10.2

Rumination Disorder

This section includes text excerpted from " Rumination disorder," Genetic and Rare Diseases Information Center (GARD), National Center for Advancing Translational Sciences (NCATS), April 23, 2015. Reviewed December 2018.

Rumination disorder is the backward flow of recently eaten food from the stomach to the mouth. The food is then re-chewed and swallowed or spat out. A nonpurposeful contraction of stomach muscles is involved in rumination. It may be initially triggered by a viral illness, emotional distress, or physical injury. In many cases, no underlying trigger is identified. Behavioral therapy is the mainstay of treatment.

What Are the Symptoms of Rumination Disorder?

Signs and symptoms of rumination disorder include the backward flow of recently eaten food from the stomach to the mouth. This typically occurs immediately to 15 to 30 minutes after eating. Rumination often occurs without retching or gagging. Rumination may be preceded by a feeling of pressure, the need to belch, nausea, or discomfort. Some people with rumination disorder experience bloating, heartburn, diarrhea, constipation, abdominal pain, headaches, dizziness, or sleeping difficulties. Complications of severe disorder include weight loss, malnutrition, and electrolyte imbalance.

Rumination disorder may occur following a viral illness, emotional stress, or physical injury. It is theorized that while the initial stressor improves, an altered sensation in the abdomen persists. This ultimately results in the relaxation of the muscle at the bottom of the esophagus. To relieve this discomfort people with rumination disorder use abdominal wall muscles to expel and regurgitate foods. As a result of the relief of symptoms, the person repeats the same response when the discomfort returns. Overtime the person unconsciously adopts this learned behavior.

What Causes Rumination Disorder

Some cases of rumination disorder occur without a precipitating event or illness. Other people with the disorder describe also having ingestion, which may serve as a trigger. Studies have shown that some people with rumination disorder also have depression, anxiety, or an eating disorder. These conditions may likewise play a role in rumination disorder. Conditions like depression and anxiety are known to be more common in people with other functional gastrointestinal conditions as well, for example irritable bowel syndrome.

How Is Rumination Disorder Diagnosed?

Diagnosis can be made by a clinical evaluation of the person's signs and symptoms and history. The following diagnostic criteria is used to aid in diagnosis. These criteria must be met for the last three months, with symptoms beginning at least six months prior to diagnosis:

1. Repeated regurgitation and rechewing or expulsion of food that:

   a. Begins soon after eating

   b. Does not occur during sleep

   c. Does not respond to standard treatment for gastroesophageal reflux disease (GERD)

2. No retching

3. Symptoms are not explained by inflammatory, anatomic, metabolic, or neoplastic processes

These criteria help distinguish rumination syndrome from other disorders of the gastrointestinal (GI) tract, such as gastroparesis and achalasia where vomiting occurs hours after eating, gastroesophageal reflux where symptoms occur at night, and cyclic vomiting syndrome (CVS) where the symptoms are chronic/persistent.

Antroduodenal manometry can assist in making and confirming the diagnosis. Antroduodenal manometry involves putting a catheter through the nose into the stomach and small bowel to measure pressure changes.

How Is Rumination Disorder Treated?

The main treatment of rumination disorder is behavioral therapy. This may involve habitat reversal strategies, relaxation, diaphragmatic breathing, and biofeedback. These types of therapies can often be administered by a gastroenterologist. Other professionals, such as nurse practitioners, psychologists, massage therapists, and recreational therapists may also be involved in care. Ensuring adequate nutrition is essential and treatment will also involve managing other symptoms, such as anxiety, nausea and stomach discomfort (which may involve antidepressive agents or selective serotonin reuptake inhibitors (SSRIs)).

If behavioral therapy is unsuccessful, treatment with baclofen may be considered. There is limited data regarding optimal treatment of rumination disorder, but success with baclofen has been reported.

Chapter 11

Nocturnal Sleep-Related Eating Disorder

About 1 to 3 percent of the general population appears to be affected by sleep-related eating disorder (SRED). Both men and women can have this disorder, but it is more common among women. Sleep eating is also known to run in the family. The onset of this disease is typically between the ages 20 and 40. SRED can also be triggered by other sleep disorders or medical conditions.

What Is Nocturnal Sleep-Related Eating Disorder?

Sleep eating is a disorder in which the patient is hungry and eats at night. Patients diet during the day and are vulnerable to eating at night, but have no memory of doing so. In most cases, people with SRED have a history of alcoholism, drug abuse, and other sleep disorders. They often eat different types of food at odd hours, and may even eat inedible substances. They lose their appetite for food, which often results in anxiety, stress, or depression.

More than 50 percent of these individual's gain weight from consuming food during sleeping hours. They also feel drowsy and experience extreme emotions. Sometimes, low blood sugar (hypoglycemia) can also cause SRED. Dyssomnia is a conscious behavior, while parasomnia is an unconscious behavior. People with SRED usually:

- Become ill from inadequately cooked food or ingesting toxic substances

- Develop metabolic conditions (Type 2 diabetes or elevated cholesterol)

- Develop cavities or tooth decay from eating sugary foods

- Have unrefreshing sleep and feel sleepy or tired during the day

- Injure themselves preparing food (lacerations, burns)

- Gain weight

Sleep eating is an arousal disorder in which:

- The patient indulges in abnormal behavior during arousal from slow-wave sleep

- The patient indulges in repetitive and automatic motor activity

- The patient is unaware of the entire episode as it is occurring

- The patient finds it difficult to wake up despite vigorous attempts

Symptoms

People with sleep-related eating disorders often eat toxic substances and often in strange combinations. Continuous episodes of binge eating only occur when the patients are partially awake. The following conditions are seen in people with sleep-related eating disorder:

- Do something dangerous while getting or cooking food

- Continuous episodes of binge eating and drinking during the time when they sleep

- Have eating episodes that disturb their sleep and cause insomnia, resulting in unrefreshing sleep

- Decline in health from eating foods that are high in calories

- Have a loss of appetite in the morning

If something else is causing the problem, it may be one of the following reasons:

- A mental-health disorder

- A medical condition

- Another sleep disorder

- Substance abuse

- Medication use

Risk Factors

About 65 to 80 percent of SRED patients are females between the ages of 22 and 29. SRED can also occur from the use of certain medicines that are used to treat depression and other sleep problems. Sleep disorder is an ongoing problem and most people with SRED were sleepwalkers as children. Sleep-related disorders include the following:

- Restless legs syndrome

- Periodic limb movement disorder

- Obstructive sleep apnea

- Irregular sleep–wake rhythm

- Sleep-related dissociative disorders

SRED symptoms typically include the following:

- Dieting during the day

- Daytime eating disorders

- Ending the abuse of alcohol or drugs

- Use of certain medications

- Quitting smoking

SRED may result in:

- Encephalitis (brain swelling)

- Hepatitis (liver infection)

- Narcolepsy

- Stress

Diagnosis

It is important for patients to inform their doctor when this eating disorder begins. Keep your doctor informed about your complete medical history. Make sure to inform the doctor of any medication that you have been taking. Maintain a sleep diary to help the doctor understand your sleeping patterns. The doctor will do an overnight sleep study called a "polysomnogram." The polysomnogram will chart your brain waves, heartbeat, and breathing as you sleep. The unusual behaviors that occur during the night will be recorded on a video, which will help your doctor determine the patterns of your sleep eating disorder.

Treatment

Treatment for sleep-related disorders involves stress-management-classes, counseling, a clinical interview, and limited intake or avoidance of alcohol and caffeine. The physician may change some of your medicines to make it easier for you to treat SRED. Plenty of sleep is required on a daily basis. It is important to consult a sleep specialist to check for signs of sleep disorders.

Consulting a psychotherapist may help reduce stress and anxiety. The physician may recommend medicines such as benzodiazepine to treat your sleep-related disorder. Mirapex and Sinemet are effective dopaminergic agents for sleep eaters.

References

1. "Sleep-Related Eating Disorders," National Center for Biotechnology Information (NCBI), U.S. National Library of Medicine (NLM), November 2006.

2. "Sleep-Related Eating Disorders," The Cleveland Clinic Foundation, April 22, 2017.

3. "Sleep Eating Disorder—Overview and Facts," American Academy of Sleep Medicine (AASM), n.d.

Chapter 12

Other Specified and Unspecified Feeding and Eating Disorders

The *Diagnostic and Statistical Manual of Mental Disorders* (DSM) published by the American Psychiatric Association (APA) and regarded as an authoritative literature on the taxonomy and diagnosis of psychiatric disorders classifies "Other Specified Feeding and Eating Disorders (OSFED)" as a category of feeding and eating disorders that does not fall within the purview of other broad and easily identifiable categories of disorders including anorexia nervosa, bulimia nervosa, or binge-eating disorder. Earlier, the umbrella classification of "Eating Disorder Not Otherwise Specified (EDNOS)" was used to classify disorders that did not fit the strict criteria for typical eating disorders.

The presentation and diagnosis of EDNOS once posed numerous challenges to clinicians. First, a majority of the patients presenting with an eating disorder of this type were assigned a diagnosis in the residual category, which increased the risk of the condition being perceived as less severe than other threshold eating disorders.

Second, there was a distinct lack of specific information on the disease pathology conveyed in the diagnosis of EDNOS. And third, there was no specific treatment protocol for this residual category of eating disorders. Although health-insurance companies opine that patients diagnosed with EDNOS do not merit classification under mental disorders, and therefore, are not eligible for reimbursement of treatment costs by the insurance companies, the APA argues that certain eating disorders that may not exactly meet the diagnostic criteria of bulimia or anorexia nervosa are nonetheless comparable to them in clinical severity, and therefore, their classification under mental disorders is justifiable.

The DSM-5 Classification of Other Specified Feeding or Eating Disorder

In October 2016, the diagnostic category of EDNOS was revised in the DSM-5 and replaced by what is now termed "Other Specified Feeding or Eating Disorder," or "OSFED." This category is no longer as expansive as the residual category of EDNOS and also attempts to resolve some of the problems related to it. In addition, it removes some of the ambiguity surrounding the EDNOS category by outlining specific diagnostic protocols for its various subtypes, which include:

1. **Atypical anorexia nervosa:** This meets all criteria for anorexia nervosa, but despite significant weight loss, the patient's weight is well within the normal range.

2. **Atypical bulimia nervosa:** Patients in this subtype meet all criteria (binge eating and abnormal compensatory behavior) of bulimia nervosa, but exhibit significantly lower frequency and/or limited duration of the binge–purge cycle.

3. **Binge-eating disorder** that is low in frequency and/or of a limited duration.

4. **Purging disorder** aimed to control weight and not associated with binge eating.

5. **Night-eating syndrome** characterized by frequent episodes of eating after awakening from sleep (at least twice per week) and excess calorie intake (around 25 percent of the daily caloric requirement) following the evening meal.

Clinical Presentation and Diagnosis of Other Specified Feeding or Eating Disorder

Clinical studies show that atypical eating disorders are the most common type of EDs in adults and adolescents. Population surveys show that these subthreshold disorders represent around 75 percent and 80 percent of those with an eating disorder in adults and adolescents, respectively. However, there has been much less research on atypical EDs as compared to the broad classes of EDs. Also, it is now known that, over time, a person with atypical ED can be afflicted with various subtypes of the disorder, and may also, over the course of time, go on to develop a full-blown eating disorder that meets the threshold for anorexia or bulimia nervosa.

Individuals diagnosed with OSFED often experience the same level of clinical distress and metabolic impairment as those with full-threshold eating disorders. They have a distorted body image and experience an intense fear of weight gain. They present with extremely unhealthy eating patterns and may also engage in inappropriate compensatory behavior, such as self-induced vomiting or laxative abuse.

Further, a significant number of people diagnosed with specified or unspecified may also suffer from comorbid psychiatric illnesses, including depressive, bipolar, and anxiety disorders. Studies show that psychiatric comorbidity strongly influences disruptive brain patterns that predispose eating disorder behavior. Whether comorbid conditions drive disturbed thinking and behavior patterns in EDs or whether the ED itself is a result of the existing dysregulation of the brain arising from the mental illness, it is now known that comorbidity not only influences the manifestation of EDs by increasing its chronicity, but also negatively impacts treatment outcomes.

Treatment for Other Specified Feeding or Eating Disorder

As in the case of the more common eating disorders, early diagnosis and treatment are key to recovery and important for reducing morbidity and mortality rates associated with the disturbed eating pattern. Commonly used interventions for OSFED involve treating both physical and psychological health and usually include medication management, medical nutritional therapy, and psychotherapy. Treatment is tailored to meet individual requirements, and healthcare services are usually delivered by a team of professionals that includes a psychiatrist, psychologist, dietician, family therapist, and—sometimes—a social worker.

Medication Management

Pharmacotherapy often plays a role in the treatment and recovery processes. When used along with psychotherapy and nutritional guidance, medications can help patients with eating disorders stabilize their mental and physical conditions and control their symptoms. Prescription drugs may help people with bulimia suppress their urges to binge and purge, for instance, and may help people with anorexia manage their obsessive thinking about food and weight.

Psychiatric medications are useful in treating the underlying depression, anxiety, obsessive-compulsive disorder, and other mental-health conditions that often affect people with eating disorders.

Cognitive Behavioral Therapy

Cognitive behavioral therapy (CBT) is one of the most widely practiced forms of psychological intervention for treating eating disorders. Developed by psychotherapist Aaron Beck, M.D., in the 1960s, CBT combines two therapies—cognitive therapy (CT) and behavioral therapy—and is based on the theory that negative thoughts and negative behavior are interlinked. This kind of therapy focuses on helping individuals recognize the irrational thinking patterns associated with food and body image, then develop positive and healthy behavior patterns.

Medical Nutrition Therapy

Medical nutrition therapy (MNT) is an essential part of the treatment plan for eating disorders, and focuses on helping patients normalize their eating patterns. Creating a healthy-eating regimen includes maintaining a nutritious and balanced diet, promoting a harmonious and sustainable relationship with food devoid of negative or harmful rationale, and learning to trust the body's natural response to feelings of hunger or fullness. MNT can be implemented in all kinds of treatment settings, including inpatient, outpatient, and residential-care facilities. In all cases, a registered dietician formulates a structured meal plan on the basis of the patient's medical history, as well as his or her dietary and laboratory evaluations, and supervises the implementation of the dietary plan.

Family Therapy

In recent years, family therapy has emerged as an important component in the treatment of eating disorders, particularly for anorexia and bulimia. Family-based therapy was developed from the premise that involving family in and improving relationships between family members increases the likelihood of a positive treatment outcome. Therapists work at resolving conflicts within the family, educating relatives about the patient's condition and early signs of problems, and charting an action plan to manage the condition effectively.

Unspecified Feeding and Eating Disorder

The DSM-5 categorization of EDs has also introduced a new category of eating disorders, "Unspecified Feeding and Eating Disorders," or "UFED." Like OSFED, the thoughts and behavior patterns associated with this type of ED do not meet criteria for the broad categories of EDs; nor do they meet any of the five diagnostic categories of the OSFED subtypes. Sometimes, the clinician may choose this category when there is insufficient information to make a specific diagnosis. Regarded as a residual-eating disorder, UFED is nonetheless associated with significant physiological, psychological, and social disturbances that can adversely impact both physical and mental health if left undiagnosed and untreated. While it is true that more research to unravel the pathophysiology of this clinically heterogeneous group of eating disorder may further improve diagnostic guidelines and treatment interventions, what stands out now is the fact that UFED, like any other eating disorder, can have life-threatening consequences and must be treated on par with the broad categories of EDs.

Support Groups and Services

There are a number of self-help and support groups for people living with typical and atypical eating disorders, but they do not effectively replace therapeutic interventions provided by healthcare professions. These groups offer support and referral services for people living with eating disorders. They also offer information and coping strategies to help increase understanding of your or your loved one's eating disorder.

References

1. "Eating Disorder NOS (EDNOS): An Example of the Troublesome "Not Otherwise Specified" (NOS) Category in DSM-IV," National Center for Biotechnology Information (NCBI), June 18, 2004.

2. "EDNOS Is an Eating Disorder of Clinical Relevance, on a Par with Anorexia and Bulimia Nervosa" National Center for Biotechnology Information (NCBI), 2015.

3. "Diagnostic and Statistical Manual of Mental Disorders, Fifth Edition," The American Psychiatric Association (APA), n.d.

Chapter 13

Disorders Often Accompanying Eating Disorders

Chapter Contents

Section 13.1

Body Dysmorphic Disorder

This section includes text excerpted from "Body Dysmorphic Disorder," Office on Women's Health (OWH), U.S. Department of Health and Human Services (HHS), August 30, 2018.

We all sometimes worry about how we look, but body dysmorphic disorder (BDD) is a serious illness in which a person is overly worried about minor or imaginary physical flaws. These perceived flaws are usually not apparent to anyone else or are seen as minor. A person with BDD may feel so anxious about these physical flaws that she or he avoids social situations and relationships. The person may also try to fix perceived flaws with cosmetic surgery.

What Is Body Dysmorphic Disorder?

Body dysmorphic disorder (BDD) is a serious illness in which a person is overly worried about their appearance or about minor or imaginary physical flaws. Most of us worry about our appearance sometimes or are unhappy with some part of the way we look, but these worries don't usually affect our daily lives, such as whether we go to work or school. People with BDD check their appearance in a mirror constantly, try to cover up their perceived flaw, or worry about it for at least an hour a day, and that worry interferes with their life in some way.

Women with BDD may worry about any part of their body, such as acne or another skin problem, a scar, the size and shape of their nose, their breast size, or their body shape.

What Are the Symptoms of Body Dysmorphic Disorder?

The symptoms of BDD include:

- Being preoccupied with minor or imaginary physical flaws, which usually can't be seen by others
- Having a strong belief that you have a defect in your appearance that makes you ugly or deformed
- Having a lot of anxiety and stress about the perceived flaw and spending a lot of time focusing on it
- Frequently picking at skin

- Excessively checking your appearance in a mirror and grooming yourself

- Hiding the perceived imperfection

- Constantly comparing appearance with others to the point that it becomes your biggest focus or worry

- Constantly seeking reassurance from others about how you look and not believing them when they compliment your appearance

- Getting cosmetic surgery but not being happy with the outcome many times

Who Gets Body Dysmorphic Disorder

One in every 50 people may have BDD. The condition is more common in women and usually starts in the teen years. People with BDD often have other mental health conditions, especially eating disorders, depression, and anxiety.

What Causes Body Dysmorphic Disorder

Researchers aren't sure exactly what causes BDD, but certain factors probably play a role:

- **Brain differences.** Physical changes in the brain's shape or how it works may play a role in causing BDD.

- **Family history.** Some studies show that BDD is more common in people whose mother, father, or siblings also have BDD or obsessive-compulsive disorder (OCD).

- **Childhood experiences.** Situations or events that happened in your childhood may make you more likely to develop BDD. For example, people who are teased about their bodies, whose families focused on the child's worth only through physical appearance, or who were abused during childhood may be more likely to develop BDD.

Who Is at Risk for Body Dysmorphic Disorder?

Certain things seem to increase the risk of developing or triggering body dysmorphic disorder, including:

- A mother, father, or sibling with BDD or obsessive-compulsive disorder

- Negative life experiences, such as being teased, bullied, or abused

- Another mental-health condition, such as depression or an anxiety disorder

How Is Body Dysmorphic Disorder Treated?

Your doctor may treat BDD with therapy and medicines.

- **Cognitive behavioral therapy (CBT).** This type of therapy may involve putting yourself in social situations while forcing yourself not to check or cover up your "flaws." Your therapist may also ask you to change your behaviors or environment at home by removing mirrors, taking less time with your beauty routine, or not using makeup.

- **Medicines**. Certain antidepressants can help with obsessive and compulsive thoughts and behaviors.

Getting cosmetic surgery can make BDD worse. People with BDD are often not happy with the outcome of the surgery and continue to obsess over imaginary defects.

Section 13.2

Compulsive Exercise

"Compulsive Exercise," © 2017 Omnigraphics.
Reviewed December 2018.

What Is Compulsive Exercise?

Compulsive exercise (also known as anorexia athletica) is a type of addiction in which a person feels that they must work out frequently, often several times a day, and feels anxious and guilty if they don't work out enough. For those struggling with a compulsive exercise disorder, working out is not a choice. Exercise becomes an obligation, one that takes over the person's life to an extreme degree. Working out becomes the most important priority, often at the expense of other activities. A person with compulsive exercise disorder will strive to work out even with an injury or illness that would normally prevent physical exertion. For this reason, compulsive exercise often creates severe physical and psychological problems.

Research has shown that the majority of people with compulsive exercise disorder are female. Many people exercise compulsively in order to feel more in control of their lives, and they define their self-worth through athletic achievements. Some use exercise as a way to try to handle difficult emotions or depression, believing that physical exhaustion will eliminate negative feelings. Others develop compulsive exercise disorder through participation in competitive sports. External and internal pressure to succeed or excel in sports can drive an athlete to push workouts too far, too frequently. In these cases, exercise compulsion is driven by the belief that additional workouts will provide the edge needed to win.

What Are the Health Effects of Compulsive Exercise?

Compulsive exercise is dangerous and can result in serious physical and psychological harm.

Stress fractures can develop in weight-bearing areas of the body (such as feet and lower legs) as a result of repetitive, high-impact, weight-bearing activities such as running or jumping. Stress fractures produce pain during exercise and can develop into more serious bone breaks if not allowed to heal properly.

Damage to muscle and connective tissue is one common side effect of compulsive exercise. Fitness experts advocate for periods of rest between workouts to allow the body to heal from minor injuries and muscle strains. Long-term damage can result from insufficient rest time, including loss of muscle mass, particularly for those who also struggle with eating disorders. A malnourished body begins to break down muscle tissue for fuel when calories are not available to burn.

Low heart rate (bradycardia) is a condition that develops from metabolic disruptions due to over-exercising. The body's normal response to rapid weight loss is to slow the metabolism in an effort to burn as few calories as possible. Low heart rate typically results in low body temperature and decreased resting heart rate. Low heart rate can easily be mistaken as a positive result of exercise, but in cases of exercise compulsion, low heart rate can produce serious arrhythmias (irregular heart function) and even sudden death.

Osteoporosis results in bone loss which increases the risk of stress fractures. This is a particularly dangerous risk for those suffering from both compulsive exercise and eating disorders, due to malnutrition from a poor diet.

Amenorrhea is the loss of normal menstruation that often develops during rapid and severe weight loss. Amenorrhea can result in loss of bone density and other serious problems including reproductive issues.

Exercising to the point of exhaustion on a frequent basis overloads the body with adrenaline and cortisol hormones, which in turn compromise the body's natural immune system. This increases the likelihood of illness, fatigue, insomnia or other sleep-related problems, irritability, short attention span, and mood swings.

What Are the Signs of Compulsive Exercise?

Some of the warning signs of a compulsive exercise disorder include:

- Feeling guilty, anxious, or irritable about missing workouts
- Pushing yourself to exercise even when injured or ill
- Persistent exhaustion and fatigue
- Chronic insomnia or disrupted sleep
- Slower than normal heart rate
- Inability to rest or even to sit still
- Giving up social time with friends in order to work out
- Obsessive focus on the number of calories eaten and burned
- Constantly thinking about working out
- Working out even in bad weather
- Low body weight, being underweight for your height
- Feeling obligated to exercise
- Lack of enjoyment of physical activity
- Making up for eating by exercising more
- Lack of satisfaction from personal achievements, always feeling there is more to do

How Is Compulsive Exercise Treated?

Treatment and recovery from compulsive exercise disorder can take months to years, depending on the individual person and situation. Some common treatment approaches include psychotherapy and medication to help manage compulsive disorders. Cognitive behavioral therapy can help to identify and correct negative thoughts and attitudes. Therapy can also help provide healthy strategies to address negative emotions, stress, low self-esteem and negative body image. Family therapy can be useful when external pressures to excel may have inadvertently caused a compulsive exercise disorder. Family members may not be aware of overly high expectations and the resulting stress that is placed on a young person. This can be particularly critical for athletes who participate in sports that emphasize being thin, such as ice skating, gymnastics, and dancing. Participating in these sports can create an unhealthy focus on body weight.

References

1. "Compulsive Exercise," KidsHealth®. October 2013.

2. "Compulsive Exercise: Are You Overdoing It?" WebMD. February 26, 2016.

3. "Exercise Compulsion and Its Dangers," Eating Disorder Hope. October 5, 2012.

Part Two

Risk Factors for Eating Disorders

Chapter 14

Factors That Increase Risk for Eating Disorders

Eating disorders frequently appear during the teen years or young adulthood but may also develop during childhood or later in life. These disorders affect both genders, although rates among women are higher than among men. Like women who have eating disorders, men also have a distorted sense of body image. For example, men may have muscle dysmorphia, a type of disorder marked by an extreme concern with becoming more muscular.

Researchers are finding that eating disorders are caused by a complex interaction of genetic, biological, behavioral, psychological, and social factors.

One approach involves the study of human genes. Eating disorders run in families. Researchers are working to identify deoxyribonucleic acid (DNA) variations that are linked to the increased risk of developing eating disorders.

Brain imaging studies are also providing a better understanding of eating disorders. For example, researchers have found differences in patterns of brain activity in women with eating disorders in comparison with healthy women.

This chapter contains text excerpted from the following sources: Text in this chapter begins with excerpts from "Eating Disorders," National Institute of Mental Health (NIMH), February 2016; Text under the heading "Risk Factors" is excerpted from "Eating Disorders," Substance Abuse and Mental Health Services Administration (SAMHSA), May 12, 2017.

Risk Factors
Genetics

Heredity may play a role. Eating disorders are more likely in people who have one or more family members with an eating disorder. Researchers are studying genetic factors linked to eating disorders. No single genetic factor causes eating disorders.

Brain Function

Changes in brain functions related to eating and emotions may help explain why some people develop eating disorders. Imaging studies have linked eating disorders to brain activity patterns.

Social Factors

These include being teased or ridiculed often about one's weight, participating in a sport that requires low weight or a certain body image, or being surrounded by negative messages about food and body. Frequent dieting can increase the risk of eating disorders.

Trauma

Traumatic events and major life stressors, especially during childhood, such as sexual assault or another form of abuse, may be a risk factor for an eating disorder.

Psychological Factors

Having another mental disorder can make an eating disorder more likely. Also, personality traits such as being a perfectionist, feeling inadequate, having low self-esteem, and rigid thinking are linked to increased risk of an eating disorder.

Chapter 15

Eating Disorders in Youth and Young Adults

Chapter Contents

Section 15.1

Eating Disorders and Adolescents

This section includes text excerpted from "April 2018:
Eating Disorders in Adolescence," U.S. Department of
Health and Human Services (HHS), April 18, 2018.

It is common for adolescents to feel a little insecure about their appearance or body. However, adolescents who have eating disorders can become obsessed with their weight, how their body looks, and eating or not eating to the point that they can cause serious harm to their bodies. Eating disorders have many causes, including biological and psychological factors, but they are treatable. While treatment should include mental-health services, adults can help adolescents establish a positive body image, healthy eating behaviors, and other habits that will set them on a healthier path.

How Common Are Eating Disorders?

Almost three percent of adolescents ages 13 to 18 are diagnosed with an eating disorder. Generally, adolescent girls are at a higher risk for developing an eating disorder than are boys. Eighty percent of adolescents and young adults with bulimia are female and about one-quarter of children with anorexia are boys. Adolescents also have an increased risk of developing an eating disorder if they have a family history of eating disorders, other mental-health or substance-use disorders, or experienced negative childhood events such as parental death or abuse.

What Are the Most Common Eating Disorders?

The three most common eating disorders include anorexia, bulimia, and binge-eating disorder.

- **Anorexia:** People with anorexia limit how much they eat, which can cause weak bones, seizures, and heart issues. Women and girls die from anorexia more than any other mental health disorder.

- **Bulimia:** People who have bulimia eat a lot of food at one time and then try to get rid of the food or weight they may have gained by engaging in behaviors such as throwing up, taking laxatives, or exercising heavily. Over time, bulimia can damage the throat, teeth, stomach, and heart.

- **Binge-eating disorder:** People who eat a large amount of food in a short time but do not try to get rid of the food may have a binge-eating disorder (BED). This disorder can cause obesity, which is associated with health conditions such as Type 2 diabetes and heart disease.

Adolescents who seek treatment but do not meet the criteria for a specific eating disorder may be diagnosed with Other Specified Feeding and Eating Disorder (OSFED).

What Are the Signs of an Eating Disorder?

Though symptoms vary by eating disorder, common symptoms include:

- Excessive worry about weight gain
- A severe or rigid diet
- The desire to eat alone due to embarrassment
- Using the bathroom often after meals
- Repeated unhealthy actions to lose or gain weight
- Obsession with physical appearance and how others perceive their body
- Feelings of guilt and shame around eating habits
- Experiencing abnormal stress or discomfort about eating habits

How to Prevent Eating Disorders

Although more research is needed to better understand eating disorders and how to prevent them, there are strategies you can use to help children and adolescents develop healthy behaviors and relationships with food.

- **Encourage healthy eating habits.** Adolescents begin making their own eating choices as they become more independent. Have meals as a family to ensure they get the nutrition they need and have conversations about healthy eating to make nutrition a priority. Adolescents may eat at restaurants with friends more often, become interested in different diets for humanitarian reasons, or be concerned with eating enough protein to participate in sports. For these reasons and more, providing guidance on nutrition and healthy eating is essential for all adolescents.

- **Avoid unhealthy dieting around your adolescent**, and eat a balanced diet instead. Making healthy changes to improve your diet can be an important step, but extremely restrictive and unbalanced diets can be harmful. If you or your adolescent want to make dietary changes because of a health concern, consult your healthcare provider to ensure you are doing so safely.

- **Nurture a healthy body image** by discussing self-image and reassuring the teen that body shapes can vary. Also, talk with your adolescent about the messages they receive from media and avoid criticizing your own body.

- **Get help from your child's healthcare provider.** At well-child visits, providers may be able to identify early indicators of an eating disorder.

What Should I Do If I See the Signs?

It is important to recognize that eating disorders are real medical illnesses, and they are treatable. Here are steps you should take if an adolescent shows signs of an eating disorder.

- **Don't wait.** Approximately a quarter of teen boys and half of the teen girls have dieted; this includes more than one in three girls who are at a healthy weight. Extreme dieting could evolve into an eating disorder, so seek help if you are worried about a change in your adolescent's weight or relationship with food.

- **Talk to a professional.** If you're concerned that an adolescent may have an eating disorder, talk to a healthcare provider. Most adolescents with eating disorders receive treatment for mental-health issues but only a minority receive services specifically for eating disorders.

- **Identify treatment options.** Treatment varies based on the type of eating disorder that an adolescent may have and an individual's needs. It may include talk therapy, medicine, and nutrition counseling. In extreme cases, hospitalization may be needed to recover.

- **For immediate support, call a helpline.** If an adolescent (or anyone) needs immediate support, call the National Eating

Disorders Association (NEDA) Helpline at 800-931-2237. People who are uncomfortable speaking on the phone can text "NEDA" to 741741 to connect with a trained crisis counselor at Crisis Text Line.

Section 15.2

Eating Disorders: Information for Teens

This section includes text excerpted from "Take Charge of Your Health: A Guide for Teenagers," National Institute of Diabetes and Digestive and Kidney Diseases (NIDDK), December 2016.

As you get older, you're able to start making your own decisions about a lot of things that matter most to you. You may choose your own clothes, music, and friends. You also may be ready to make decisions about your body and health.

Making healthy decisions about what you eat and drink, how active you are, and how much sleep you get is a great place to start. Here you'll learn:

- How your body works—how your body uses the food and drinks you consume and how being active may help your body "burn" calories

- How to choose healthy foods and drinks

- How to get moving and stay active

- How getting enough sleep is important to staying healthy

- How to ease into healthy habits and keep them up

- How to plan healthy meals and physical activities that fit your lifestyle

How Does the Body Use Energy?

Your body needs energy to function and grow. Calories from food and drinks give you that energy. Think of food as energy to charge up your battery for the day. Throughout the day, you use energy from the battery to think and move, so you need to eat and drink to stay powered up. Balancing the energy you take in through food and beverages with the energy you use for growth, activity, and daily living is called "energy balance." Energy balance may help you stay a healthy weight.

How Many Calories Does Your Body Need?

Different people need different amounts of calories to be active or stay a healthy weight. The number of calories you need depends on whether you are male or female, your genes, how old you are, your height and weight, whether you are still growing, and how active you are, which may not be the same every day.

How Should You Manage or Control Your Weight?

Some teens try to lose weight by eating very little; cutting out whole groups of foods like foods with carbohydrates, or "carbs"; skipping meals; or fasting. These approaches to losing weight could be unhealthy because they may leave out important nutrients your body needs. In fact, unhealthy dieting could get in the way of trying to manage your weight because it may lead to a cycle of eating very little and then overeating because you get too hungry. Unhealthy dieting could also affect your mood and how you grow.

Smoking, making yourself vomit, or using diet pills or laxatives to lose weight may also lead to health problems. If you make yourself vomit, or use diet pills or laxatives to control your weight, you could have signs of a serious eating disorder and should talk with your healthcare professional or another trusted adult right away. If you smoke, which increases your risk of heart disease, cancer, and other health problems, quit smoking as soon as possible.

If you think you need to lose weight, talk with a healthcare professional first. A doctor or dietitian may be able to tell you if you need to lose weight and how to do so in a healthy way.

Healthy Eating

Healthy eating involves taking control of how much and what types of food you eat, as well as the beverages you drink. Try to replace foods high in sugar, salt, and unhealthy fats with fruits, vegetables, whole grains, low-fat protein foods, and fat-free or low-fat dairy foods.

Fruits and Vegetables

Make half of your plate fruits and vegetables. Dark green, red, and orange vegetables have high levels of the nutrients you need, like vitamin C, calcium, and fiber. Adding tomato and spinach—or any other available greens that you like—to your sandwich is an easy way to get more veggies in your meal.

Grains

Choose whole grains like whole-wheat bread, brown rice, oatmeal, and whole-grain cereal, instead of refined-grain cereals, white bread, and white rice.

Protein

Power up with low-fat or lean meats like turkey or chicken, and other protein-rich foods, such as seafood, egg whites, beans, nuts, and tofu.

Dairy

Build strong bones with fat-free or low-fat milk products. If you can't digest lactose—the sugar in milk that can cause stomach pain or gas—choose lactose-free milk or soy milk with added calcium. Fat-free or low-fat yogurt is also a good source of dairy food.

Fats

Fat is an important part of your diet. Fat helps your body grow and develop, and may even keep your skin and hair healthy. But fats have more calories per gram than protein or carbs, and some are not healthy.

Some fats, such as oils that come from plants and are liquid at room temperature, are better for you than other fats. Foods that contain healthy oils include avocados, olives, nuts, seeds, and seafood such as salmon and tuna fish.

Solid fats such as butter, stick margarine, and lard, are solid at room temperature. These fats often contain saturated and trans fats, which are not healthy for you. Other foods with saturated fats include fatty meats, and cheese and other dairy products made from whole milk. Take it easy on foods such as fried chicken, cheeseburgers, and fries, which often have a lot of saturated and trans fats. Options to consider include a turkey sandwich with mustard or a lean-meat, turkey, or veggie burger.

Your body needs a small amount of sodium, which is mostly found in salt. But getting too much sodium from your foods and drinks can raise your blood pressure, which is unhealthy for your heart and your body in general. Even though you're a teen, it's important to pay attention to your blood pressure and heart health now to prevent health problems as you get older.

Try to consume less than 2,300 mg, or no more than one teaspoon, of sodium a day. This amount includes the salt in already prepared food, as well as the salt you add when cooking or eating your food.

Processed foods, like those that are canned or packaged, often have more sodium than unprocessed foods, such as fresh fruits and vegetables. When you can, choose fresh or frozen fruits and veggies over processed foods. Try adding herbs and spices instead of salt to season your food if you make your own meals. Remember to rinse canned vegetables with water to remove extra salt. If you use packaged foods, check the amount of sodium listed on the Nutrition Facts label. Figure 15.1 below shows an updated food label, which the U.S. Food and Drug Administration (FDA) has approved for use on most packaged foods beginning in 2018.

Figure 15.1. *Side-by-Side Comparison of Original and New Nutrition Facts Label* (Source: U.S. Food and Drug Administration (FDA).)

Limit Added Sugars

Some foods, like fruit, are naturally sweet. Other foods, like ice cream and baked desserts, as well as some beverages, have added sugars to make them taste sweet. These sugars add calories but not vitamins or fiber. Try to consume less than ten percent of your daily calories from added sugars in food and beverages. Reach for an apple or banana instead of a candy bar.

Control Your Food Portions

A portion is how much food or beverage you choose to consume at one time, whether in a restaurant, from a package, at school or a friend's, or at home. Many people consume larger portions than they need, especially when away from home. Ready-to-eat meals—from a restaurant, grocery store, or at school—may give you larger portions than your body needs to stay charged up. The Weight-control Information Network (www.niddk.nih.gov/health-information/communication-programs/win) has tips to help you eat and drink a suitable amount of food and beverages for you, whether you are at home or somewhere else.

Don't Skip Meals

Skipping meals might seem like an easy way to lose weight, but it actually may lead to weight gain if you eat more later to make up for it. Even if you're really busy with school and activities, it's important to try not to skip meals. Follow these tips to keep your body charged up all day and to stay healthy:

- **Eat breakfast every day.** Breakfast helps your body get going. If you're short on time in the morning, grab something to go, like an apple or banana.

- **Pack your lunch on school days.** Packing your lunch may help you control your food and beverage portions and increases the chances that you will eat it because you made it.

- **Eat dinner with your family.** When you eat home-cooked meals with your family, you are more likely to consume healthy foods. Having meals together also gives you a chance to reconnect with each other and share news about your day.

- **Get involved in grocery shopping and meal planning at home.** Going food shopping and planning and preparing meals with family members or friends can be fun. Not only can you choose a favorite grocery store, and healthy foods and recipes, you also have a chance to help others in your family eat healthy too.

Other Tips

- Try to limit foods such as cookies, candy, frozen desserts, chips, and fries, which often have a lot of sugar, unhealthy fat, and salt.

- For a quick snack, try recharging with a pear, apple, or banana; a small bag of baby carrots; or hummus with sliced veggies.

- Don't add sugar to your food and drinks.

- Drink fat-free or low-fat milk and avoid sugary drinks. Soda, energy drinks, sweet tea, and some juices have added sugars, a source of extra calories. The *2015–2020 Dietary Guidelines* calls for getting less than ten percent of your daily calories from added sugars.

Get Moving

Physical activity should be part of your daily life, whether you play sports, take physical education (PE) classes in school, do chores, or get around by biking or walking. Regular physical activity can help you manage your weight, have stronger muscles and bones, and be more flexible.

Aerobic versus Lifestyle Activities

You should be physically active for at least 60 minutes a day. Most of the 60 minutes or more of activity a day should be either moderate or intense aerobic physical activity, and you should include intense physical activity at least three days a week. Examples of aerobic physical activity, or activity that makes you breathe harder and speeds up your heart rate, include jogging, biking, and dancing.

For a more moderate workout, try brisk walking, jogging, or biking on flat streets or paths. To pick up the intensity, turn your walk into a jog, or your jog into a run—or add hills to your walk, jog, or bike ride. You don't have to do your 60 minutes a day all at once to benefit from your activity.

Routine activities, such as cleaning your room or taking out the trash, may not get your heart rate up the way biking or jogging does. But they are also good ways to keep active on a regular basis.

Fitness apps that you can download onto your computer, smartphone, or other mobile device can help you keep track of how active you are each day.

Have Fun with Your Friends

Being active can be more fun with other people, like friends or family members. You may also find that you make friends when you get active by joining a sports team or dance club. Mix things up by choosing a different activity each day. Try kickball, flashlight tag, or other activities that get you moving, like walking around the mall. Involve your friends and challenge them to be healthy with you. Sign up for active events together, like charity walks, fun runs, or scavenger hunts.

Take It Outside

Maybe you or some of your friends spend a lot of time indoors watching TV, surfing the web, using social media, or playing video games. Try getting in some outdoor activity to burn calories instead. Here are other activities to try:

- Have a jump rope or hula hoop contest

- Play Frisbee

- Build an obstacle course or have a scavenger hunt

- Play volleyball or flag football

If you're stuck indoors or don't have a lot of time, try climbing up and down the stairs in your apartment or home. You can also find dance and other fitness and exercise videos online or on some TV channels. Some routines are only 15 or 20 minutes so you can squeeze them in between homework, going out, or other activities. You also can choose active sports games if you have a gaming system.

Get Enough Sleep

Sometimes it's hard to get enough sleep, especially if you have a job, help care for younger siblings, or are busy with other activities after school. Like healthy eating and getting enough physical activity, getting enough sleep is important for staying healthy.

You need enough sleep to do well in school, work and drive safely, and fight off infection. Not getting enough sleep may make you moody and irritable. While more research is needed, some studies have shown that not getting enough sleep may also contribute to weight gain.

If you're between 13 and 18 years old, you should get eight to ten hours of sleep each night. Find out what you can do to make sure you get enough sleep.

Take Your Time

Changing your habits can be hard. And developing new habits takes time. Use the tips below and the checklist under "Be a health champion" to stay motivated and meet your goals. You can do it!

- **Make changes slowly.** Don't expect to change your eating, drinking, or activity habits overnight. Changing too much too fast may hurt your chances of success.

- **Figure out what's holding you back.** Are there unhealthy snack foods at home that are too tempting? Are the foods and drinks you're choosing at your school cafeteria too high in fat and sugar? How can you change these habits?

- **Set a few realistic goals.** If you're a soda drinker, try replacing a couple of sodas with water. Once you are drinking less soda for a while, try cutting out all soda. Then set another goal, like getting more physical activity each day. Once you have reached one goal, add another.

- **Get a buddy at school or someone at home to support your new habits.** Ask a friend, brother or sister, parent, or guardian to help you make changes and stick with your new habits.

Planning Healthy Meals and Physical Activities Just for You

Being healthy sounds like it could be a lot of work, right? Well, it doesn't have to be. A free, online tool called the MyPlate Daily Checklist can help you create a daily food plan. All you have to do is type in whether you are male or female, your weight, height, and how much physical activity you get each day. The checklist will tell you how many daily calories you should take in and what amounts of fruit, vegetables, grains, protein, and dairy you should eat to stay within your calorie target.

Another tool, called the National Institutes of Health (NIH) Body Weight Planner lets you tailor your calorie and physical activity plans to reach your personal goals within a specific time period.

Breakfast: a banana, a slice of whole-grain bread with avocado or tomato, and fat-free or low-fat milk

Lunch: a turkey sandwich with dark leafy lettuce, tomato, and red peppers on whole-wheat bread

Dinner: two whole-grain taco shells with chicken or black beans, fat-free or low-fat cheese, and romaine lettuce

Snack: an apple, banana, or air-popped popcorn

Be a Health Champion

Spending much of your day away from home can sometimes make it hard to consume healthy foods and drinks. By becoming a "health champion," you can help yourself and family members, as well as your friends, get healthier by consuming healthier foods and drinks and becoming more active. Use this checklist to work healthy habits into your day, whether you're at home or on the go:

- Each night, pack a healthy lunch and snacks for the next day. Consume the lunch you packed. Try to avoid soda, chips, and candy from vending machines.

- Go to bed at a regular time every night to recharge your body and mind. Turn off your phone, TV, and other devices when you go to bed. Try to get between 8 and 10 hours of sleep each night.

- Eat a healthy breakfast.

- Walk or bike to school if you live nearby and can do so safely. Invite friends to join you.

- Between classes, stand up and walk around, even if your next subject is in the same room.

- Participate in gym classes instead of sitting on the sidelines.

- Get involved in choosing food and drinks at home. Help make dinner and share it with your family at the dinner table.

Section 15.3

Eating Disorders among College Students

Transitioning to college can be a challenging period in the lives of young people. College students experience a sudden increase in independence and responsibility as they leave their parents' home and establish their own routines for eating, sleeping, exercising, and studying. They also face the pressures of living among peers in a dormitory environment, making new friends, and competing academically. Although the flurry of changes can be exciting, students who have trouble adjusting may feel overwhelmed and anxious, which can impact their physical and mental health.

The stressful nature of the transition to college life is reflected in the high incidence of eating disorders among college students. Studies have shown that of the estimated 30 million Americans with eating disorders, 95 percent are between the ages of 12 and 25. In addition, over 90 percent of women on college campuses report having dieted in an effort to control their weight, while 25 percent of college-aged women have engaged in binging and purging as a weight-management technique. Some studies suggest that upwards of 20 percent of college students develop eating disorders. Although the majority of people with eating disorders are female, research indicates that the prevalence rates are increasing among college-aged males as well.

Diagnosing College Student Eating Disorders

Early diagnosis and treatment of eating disorders is key to preventing the development of serious medical conditions and improving the chances of recovery. Some of the warning signs and behaviors that increase the risk of developing eating disorders include:

- Symptoms of depression and anxiety relating to the adjustment to college life and the pressures of academia

- Changes in appearance, such as significant weight gain or loss

- Social withdrawal or pronounced changes in emotional state

- Associating with roommates, teammates, or sorority/fraternity members who have eating disorders, which may create peer pressure and establish norms of disordered eating

- Adopting unhealthy, extreme measures of weight management, such as skipping meals, exercising obsessively, taking diet pills, trying fad diets, substituting caffeine or tobacco for food, or purging after meals by inducing vomiting or abusing laxatives or diuretics

- Demonstrating bingeing behavior, such as not eating all day and then overeating at night or drinking excessively at parties, which is common on college campuses

Eating disorders can be tricky to diagnose because college students often try to hide them. They may not believe their behavior is dangerous, or they may come to view extreme dieting, bingeing, or purging as normal because they see others engaging in it. Some individuals do not seek treatment for eating disorders because they feel shame or embarrassment, they are not aware of the treatment resources available, or they worry that treatment will not be covered by health insurance.

Educating college students and their families about eating disorders is an important way to help them determine whether they may be at risk. Many people recover from eating disorders when they are treated at an early stage. Left untreated, however, eating disorders can cause serious health problems and even death. Some tips for helping a college student who appears to have an eating disorder include:

- Discussing concerns and mentioning specific observations of behavior

- Offering to provide help and support

- Contacting the family doctor and obtaining a referral to a nutritionist, therapist, or eating-disorder treatment center

- Setting realistic goals for recovery and being prepared for the possibility that it may be too dangerous for the student to return to school

References

1. "Eating Disorders among College Students," Walden Center, 2015.

2. Kramer, Jennie J. "Might Your College Student Have an Eating Disorder? How to Tell, What to Do," Huffington Post, December 12, 2014.

3. Wolf, Nancy L. "A Guide to Choosing a College for Teens with Eating Disorders," Noodle, May 21, 2015.

Chapter 16

How Eating Disorders Affect Males

Eating disorders primarily affect girls and women, but boys and men also are vulnerable. Boys with eating disorders show the same types of emotional, physical, and behavioral signs and symptoms as girls, but for a variety of reasons, boys are less likely to be diagnosed with what is often considered a stereotypically "female" disorder. Males account for an estimated 5 to 15 percent of patients with anorexia or bulimia and an estimated 35 percent of those with binge-eating disorder (BED).

Like females who have eating disorders, males with the illness have a distorted sense of body image and often have muscle dysmorphia, a type of disorder characterized by an extreme concern with becoming more muscular. Some boys with the disorder want to lose weight, while others want to gain weight or "bulk up." Boys who think they are too small are at a greater risk for using steroids or other dangerous drugs to increase muscle mass.

This chapter contains text excerpted from the following sources: Text in this chapter begins with excerpts from "Males and Eating Disorders," MedlinePlus, National Institutes of Health (NIH), 2008. Reviewed December 2018; Text beginning with the heading "Eating Disorders among Men" is excerpted from "Eating Disorders among Men," Substance Abuse and Mental Health Services Administration (SAMHSA), April 19, 2016.

Eating Disorders among Men

"Body dysmorphic disorder is a chronic mental illness, wherein the afflicted individual is concerned with body image, manifested as excessive concern about and preoccupation with a perceived defect of their physical appearance. An individual with BDD has perpetual negative thoughts about their appearance."—Hunt, T.J., Thienhaus, O., and Ellwood, authors of The Mirror Lies: Body Dysmorphic Disorder, *American Family Physician*.

"Men have anorexia. Men have bulimia. Both are just as life threatening for men as they are for women. There are specific challenges in identifying and treating men for eating disorders, but the biggest challenge is getting men to admit they have a problem because they do not recognize the behavior or understand how much damage it can do," said Leigh Cohn. Cohn is a writer and publisher of several books about eating disorders.

Eating disorders in men are multidimensional, the result of genetic factors, peer pressure, family issues, cultural messages, and possible trauma such as the death or serious illness of the father, according to Cohn.

"The incidence is higher in gay males, but we are seeing eating disorders cross the cultural line into the straight population," Cohn said.

The drivers for men's eating disorders are similar to those for women: an unrealistic ideal in body type, coupled with the notion that looking right will bring success in unrelated areas such as getting a good job and finding the right partner. This is tied to the cultural notion that men need to be in control, an impulse displaced onto the bodies of those with eating disorders. Some sports such as wrestling, boxing, and horse racing foster behaviors of eating disorders due to strict weight restrictions.

The National Institute of Mental Health reports on eating disorders such as anorexia, bulimia, and binge eating among men.

Brian Cuban discussed his own eating disorder, which was coupled with drug and alcohol use that pushed him to a very dangerous bottom.

"I probably became anorexic and bulimic when I was a freshman at Penn State. When I was young, I was heavy and my mother used fat-shaming behaviors. I was the victim of a weight-related assault in junior high school when I was stripped of my pants on a public street and forced to walk home in my underwear. No one helped. I was brought very low by substance abuse but was able to recover with help from my family. However, I still could not admit to the eating disorders. In fact, I first admitted my behavior on a blog before I was able to talk about it with my psychiatrist and my family. I really thought I was the only man out there with this. Then I Googled it and found some message boards: I was not the only one! Writing the blog was my coming out."

"People should remember that words do damage," Cuban continued. "It was when I understood how my mother was raised that I was able to forgive her and understand my body issue, my body dysmorphia." The use of social media and connecting with other men impacted by eating disorders virtually has begun to embolden advocates seeking more nuanced treatment options to overcome discrimination associated with these disorders.

Cohn notes that treating males with eating disorders may require a unique approach.

"One of the biggest challenges is getting men to show up. Men are unaware they are engaging in odd behaviors such as excessive exercise without enough nutrition. There is also comorbidity with alcohol abuse, getting calories from alcohol. But once a male enters treatment, they can be the better patients because they want to fix things. 'Explain it to me, and I will work on it' is how they approach it. Once they get past the stigma, they can get better," Cohn said.

"Eventually there won't be a stigma for male eating disorders, same as for females now. There are excellent information resources out there, including the National Eating Disorders Association. Things are slow to change."

Chapter 17

Eating Disorders in Athletes

Athletes are well known for their self-esteem, physical fitness, and teamwork. They tend to be highly disciplined and competitive individuals who go to great lengths to excel in their sports and achieve their goals. Athletes, however, have to face a lot of physical and psychological pressure during sports competition, and pressure caused by cultural ideals about body types. These stressors may lead to anxiety and depression among athletes, and eventually lead to some sort of eating disorder.

Risk Factors of Eating Disorders in Athletes

The major reason for athletes developing eating disorders is the extreme stress placed on their bodies. A few factors that are detrimental in stressing the mind and body of an athlete follow:

- Families and coaches who give more importance to performance and victory than to the health of the athletes

- An overvalued idea that reducing body weight will improve the performance

- Being an elite athlete

"Eating Disorders in Athletes," © 2019 Omnigraphics. Reviewed December 2018.

- Training for a sport since childhood
- Excessive practice
- Obsessive exercise
- Performance anxiety
- Chronic dieting
- Self-starvation
- Low self-esteem
- Peer pressure
- Social and cultural pressure to be thin
- Other traumatic life experiences

Eating disorders can occur in all kinds of sports. But athletes in certain sports that focus more on appearance, body weight, and endurance are considered to have a greater risk of developing eating disorders. Such sports include:

- Gymnastics
- Skating/figure skating
- Diving
- Swimming
- Running
- Horse racing
- Wrestling
- Weight lifting
- Ballet/dance

Some studies indicate a higher rate of eating disorders among athletes involved in individual sports (such as gymnastics, running, swimming, etc.) than those involved in team sports (such as soccer, basketball, hockey, etc.).

Symptoms of Eating Disorders in Athletes

Some of the common and most noticeable symptoms of eating disorders among athletes are:

- Decreased energy level, speed, and performance
- Lack of coordination

- Loss of endurance

- Experiencing light-headedness and dizziness during practice

- Prolonged recovery time after workouts

- Increased fatigue

- Frequent trips to the bathroom, especially after meals

- Repeated complaints about gastrointestinal problems such as nausea and vomiting

- Excessive drinking of water/soda

- Excessive use of laxatives

- Frequent muscle strains and fractures

- Increased sensitivity to cold

- Isolation from teammates

- Lack of interaction with coaches and teammates

- Impatience

- Seeking perfection

Consequences of Eating Disorders in Athletes

Although disordered eating behaviors may improve the performance of some athletes in the initial stage, it will pose a serious threat to their physical, mental, and emotional health over time. Some of the major medical consequences of eating disorders in athletes are:

- Dehydration

- Swollen joints

- Muscle cramps and pain

- Osteoporosis

- Anemia

- Decrease in blood pressure

- Irregular heartbeat

- Heart failure

- Electrolyte imbalance leading to sudden death

Female Athlete Triad

Female athlete triad is a distinct condition caused by eating disorders among female athletes. As the term "triad" suggests, it is a combination of three interrelated health conditions:

- Lack of energy

- Amenorrhea—irregular menstrual cycles

- Osteoporosis—bone weakness

Each condition may be a simple medical concern, but together they may pose life-threatening risks.

Preventing Eating Disorders in Athletes—Tips for Coaches

Coaches are one of the most influential and inspiring persons in the life of athletes. They motivate athletes to live up to their potentials both on and off the field. Coaches are also in the first position to notice the signs of eating disorders in an athlete. Hence, it is their responsibility to approach athletes with eating disorders in the right way and to help rid them of the problem. Here are few tips for how coaches handle athletes with eating disorders.

- Educate yourself about the various signs and symptoms of eating disorders.

- People with eating disorders often try to hide their problems, so take the warning signs seriously. Act immediately, as soon as you identify one or more warning signs.

- Provide athletes with proper education about nutrition, diet, and healthy body weight. You may also employ the assistance of local nutritionists to guide the athletes.

- Do not place too much emphasis on the body weight of athletes.

- Do not force the athletes to reduce their body weight in order to enhance their performance. While reducing weight may improve the performance, it cannot be true in the cases of all the athletes.

- Avoid making derogatory comments about the bodies of the athletes. Also, do not allow fellow athletes to do this.

- Teach the athletes about the ill effects and the health risks of low weight.

- When you suspect that an athlete has an eating disorder, set up a private meeting to discuss her or his issues.

- Discuss your concerns with the parents or caregivers of the athlete you suspect to be suffering from an eating disorder.

- Make sure that the athletes play their sport and lead their life with a positive self-image and self-esteem.

References

1. "Eating Disorders and Athletes," National Eating Disorders Association (NEDA), August 5, 2005.

2. Quinn, Elizabeth. "Eating Disorders in Athletes," Verywell Fit, February 16, 2018.

3. "Resources for Athletic Directors, Coaches, and Trainers," Eating Disorders Center for Treatment and Research, July 7, 2016.

4. "Tips for Coaches: Preventing Eating Disorders in Athletes," National Eating Disorders Association (NEDA), February 1, 2001.

5. "10 Things Coaches and Trainers Can Do to Help Prevent Eating Disorders in Their Athletes," The Renfrew Center Foundation, June 30, 2017.

Chapter 18

Eating Disorders among Gays, Lesbians, and Bisexuals

Eating disorders are serious psychological problems that may affect anyone irrespective of age, race, gender, or sexual orientation. Members of the lesbian, gay, bisexual, and transgender (LGBT) community are no exception from being affected by eating disorders. In fact, LGBT people are more vulnerable to such disorders when compared to others. It is estimated that over half of LGBT teens suffer from eating disorders. LGBT-identified people experience distinctive stressors and are prone to rejections and harassments. These stressors can contribute to the increased anxiety, depression, low self-esteem, body dissatisfaction, etc. that may put LGBT people at a greater risk of developing eating disorders.

Potential Factors That Trigger Eating Disorders in Lesbian, Gay, Bisexual, and Transgender People

Eating disorders are not actually about food, but rather about control. People who do not have control over their emotions, feelings, relationships, and other aspects of life often end up with disordered eating behaviors. They see food as a way to suppress their emotions. This scenario leaves LGBT people at special risk of developing eating disorders. Several risks and challenges impose immense psychological pressure on LGBT people and can trigger eating disorders. Here is a list of such challenges faced by the LGBT community:

- Gender dysphoria

- Confusion and shame regarding one's gender identity

- Discrimination or fear of discrimination due to sexual orientation and gender identity

- Rejections by family, friends, and loved ones

- Being a victim of bullying and violence at schools and workplaces

- Posttraumatic stress disorder (PTSD) caused by violent acts committed against them

- Negative self-perceptions Low self-esteem and confidence

- Poor interpersonal relationships Isolation Lack of support

- Body dissatisfaction Inability to attain the body image ideals within their sociocultural context. (This is especially prevalent among transgender people.) Socioeconomic oppression

Treatment for Eating Disorders in Lesbian, Gay, Bisexual, and Transgender People

Treating eating disorders in LGBT community involves the same methodologies—psychotherapy approaches, nutritional counseling, and so on—used to treat members of other populations. However, the primary concern within this group is to focus on the specific internal struggles that affect LGBT people in order to help them learn or relearn how to accept their appearance, body image, gender identity, and sexual orientation. It is also important to raise social awareness of how to best treat members of the LGBT community. Some of the common barriers that impede the treatment of LGBT people are:

- Lack of support from friends and family

- Lack of culturally competent treatment facilities that can address the complexity of gender-identity issues

LGBTQ+ community centers, LGBTQ+ healthcare resource centers, and so on, are some of the places where members of the LGBT community can find safe access to healthcare support and treatment. Every LGBT person deserves the right to be treated with respect and compassion. Hence, treatment staff should be trained and informed on how to maintain a safe environment for members of the LGBT community.

The Support Groups

If, as an LGBT person, you find it difficult to get support from others for your treatment or recovery, then you may want to join LGBT community groups. If you cannot find such a group in your area, then create one through social media or another public forum. Sharing personal stories, struggles, and experiences in a support-group setting is very useful for someone seeking help. These groups help to connect people, create awareness, and allow members of the community to support each other during a time of crisis.

References

1. "Eating Disorders in LBBTQ+ Populations," National Eating Disorders Association (NEDA), February 24, 2018.

2. "Eating Disorders in the LGBT Community," Center For Discovery Eating Disorder Program, August 11, 2017.

3. Slager, Emily. "Eating Disorder Recovery Tips for the LGBT Community," Walden, September 10, 2018.

4. "Over Half of All LGBT Teens Have an Eating Disorder," Gay Star Health, March 1, 2018.

Chapter 19

Problems Frequently Co-Occurring with Eating Disorders

Chapter Contents

Section 19.1

What Are Co-Occurring Disorders?

"What Are Co-Occurring Disorders?"
© 2016 Omnigraphics. Reviewed December 2018.

Individuals suffering from eating disorders often tend to experience other emotional or behavioral issues as well. These can include depression, anxiety disorder, and substance abuse. An accompanying condition is called a "co-occurring disorder," and the two illnesses together are termed a "dual diagnosis."

The co-occurring illness can sometimes be the actual cause of the eating disorder, so it is crucial to treat not just the eating disorder itself, but also to understand and address the factors that led to its development.

Unfortunately, serious coexisting conditions, such as depression, are often ignored, and an individual may get treated only for the eating disorder itself. Although a person might keep this disorder under control for a short time, unless the co-occurring illnesses are also addressed, she or he might soon revert back to poor eating habits once treatment stops. Hence, a comprehensive treatment strategy that focuses on both illnesses is vital to a successful outcome.

Reference

Ekern, Jacquelyn. "Dual Diagnosis and Co-Occurring Disorders," Eating Disorder Hope, April 25, 2012.

Section 19.2

Eating Disorders and Obsessive-Compulsive Disorder

"Eating Disorders and Obsessive-Compulsive Disorder," © 2016
Omnigraphics. Reviewed December 2018.

A type of anxiety disorder, obsessive-compulsive disorder (OCD) is characterized by uncontrollable thoughts and repetitive behaviors. The individual often feels anxious, and therefore, engages in ritualistic or repetitive behaviors to reduce the feeling of uneasiness. OCD often co-occurs with other illnesses, including eating disorders and substance abuse.

- Numerous indications of OCD, some more complex than others, may be observed in the behavior of an individual with an eating disorder. Examples include:

- Obsessive thoughts (about food, weight, and body image)

- An obsession with healthy eating and fear of food-borne impurities or diseases (called orthorexia)

- Rituals such as cutting food into tiny pieces or picking food items based on color or shape

- Hoarding large quantities of food

- Spitting out food immediately after chewing

- Excessive or compulsive exercise

These types of abnormal behaviors and thought patterns can take a significant toll on the quality of life (QOL), as they can be time-consuming and may create feelings of anxiety and discomfort, especially when in the company of others. Moreover, this situation can lead to a host of other problems, such as depression, irritability, and social isolation.

Because a strong relationship between eating disorders and OCD has been established, a comprehensive treatment plan that addresses both forms of illness is crucial. In addition to medication and therapy to treat eating disorders, various forms of psychotherapy may also be employed to bring about a change in the co-occurring unwanted behaviors and thought patterns.

Reference

Ekern, Jacquelyn. "Dual Diagnosis and Co-Occurring Disorders," Eating Disorder Hope, April 25, 2012.

Section 19.3

Eating Disorders and Autism Spectrum Disorder

Autism spectrum disorder (ASD) is a type of developmental disorder that is characterized by difficulties in interacting or communicating with others, repetitive or constrained behavior, abnormal sensory responses, and occasional delays in cognition. The term "spectrum" refers to a wide range of symptoms, skills, and levels of impairment. Thus, each individual suffering from ASD is affected differently and requires a unique approach to care and support.

Individuals on the autism spectrum can be extremely particular about what they eat. They may, for example, have an aversion to the physical properties of some food, such as texture, appearance, smell, and even the sound it makes when chewed. Another common symptom of those on the autism spectrum is pica, or the tendency to consume nonfood items, such as paper, dirt, or soap. Some individuals might also experience such problems as difficulty in chewing and swallowing, or gastrointestinal issues. Such eating difficulties, combined with other behaviors associated with the spectrum, can often result in poor body weight and other characteristics of eating disorders.

A number of shared behavioral patterns and personality traits have been identified among individuals suffering from both anorexia and ASD. A study in 2013 established that girls with ASD and those with anorexia had lower empathy and a stronger tendency to systemize (construct and follow rules or patterns) than other people. Keen interest in details, strict behavior patterns, and an inclination to focus on self were some of the common features identified among the two groups.

Since the majority of people diagnosed with eating disorders are females—and since both ASD and anorexia are characterized by symptoms like low body weight, poor or disordered eating habits, and preoccupation with systems—some girls and young women with ASD are incorrectly diagnosed or neglected because the signs of anorexia are the ones most obvious to medical professionals.

Reference

"Eating Disorders and Other Health Problems," Eating Disorders Victoria, June 19, 2015.

Section 19.4

Eating Disorders and Diabetes

In individuals suffering from type 1 diabetes, the pancreas is unable to produce insulin, which therefore, must be administered daily. A healthy eating plan that balances the periodic insulin injections, physical activity, and food intake is crucial for an individual with this condition. The presence of an eating disorder can cause inadequate glucose control and an increase in the chances of developing secondary complications in the eyes, nerves, and kidneys. In addition to the long-term complications from extreme weight-loss, high blood-glucose levels induced by omitted or reduced insulin doses can cause diabetic ketoacidosis (DKA), an acidic blood condition that may lead to coma.

Eating disorders that involve episodes of purging or restricting food intake can cause severe low blood sugar (hypoglycemia), which can make it difficult to determine the proper insulin dose for the individual. And those that involve "insulin-purging"—intentionally decreasing insulin dosage as a means of inducing weight loss—may result in a dangerously high blood sugar level (hyperglycemia).

Indications of an eating disorder in a diabetic individual include constant changes in weight, frequent changes in food intake, extreme fear of low blood-glucose level (hypoglycemia), anxiety about injecting or injecting in private, and other signs of unusual eating behavior that may not be directly related to diabetes.

Although many diabetic individuals may be prone to developing eating disorders, the risks are higher for adolescents and young women, as the physical and hormonal changes occurring in the body can have an impact on blood sugar levels. It is important for a diabetic individual to seek professional help if even some of these symptoms are present.

Reference

"Eating Disorders and Other Health Problems," Eating Disorders Victoria, June 19, 2015.

Section 19.5

Eating Disorders and Self-Injury

"Eating Disorders and Self-Injury,"
© 2016 Omnigraphics. Reviewed December 2018.

Common forms of self-injury include cutting skin, scratching, beating, or burning body parts; interfering with the healing of wounds; and the intake of poisonous substances. Self-injury can be caused by a combination of psychological, genetic, and social factors, along with a possible history of substance abuse and other destructive behavior. Rarely does an individual engage in self-harm with the intention of committing suicide, but these habits, if left unchecked, can increase the risk of death.

The reasons for self-injury can include establishing a sense of control, relieving negative emotions (such as anger, shame, distress, guilt, or loneliness), and attempting to escape traumatic memories. The consequences and complications of such behaviors may include depression, poor self-esteem, relationship difficulties, infections, hospitalization, or even death.

Self-injury is compulsive behavior that can also manifest as a co-occurring disorder. Signs of self-injury, such as fresh wounds, multiple scars, frequent withdrawal from friends and family, and covering wounds with long sleeves or pants, could be an indication of the presence of another illness.

The likelihood of engaging in self-injury is high for individuals with eating disorders. Similarly, certain behaviors associated with eating disorders—such as induced vomiting, excessive or compulsive exercise, and excessive consumption of laxatives—can be the cause self-harm. And self-injury could, alternatively, act as a means of expressing dissatisfaction with one's body, punishing oneself for not sticking to a routine, or even finding solace from a strict nutritional regimen.

During the diagnosis and treatment of eating disorders, identifying the signs of self-harm, as well as analyzing its causes, are essential for a successful outcome. Medication, along with various forms of psychotherapy, such as family intervention, group therapy, and cognitive behavioral therapy (CBT), will aid in faster recovery from both eating disorders and self-injurious behavior.

Reference

Ekern, Jacquelyn. "Dual Diagnosis and Co-Occurring Disorders," Eating Disorder Hope, April 25, 2012.

Section 19.6

Eating Disorders and Trichotillomania

"Eating Disorders and Trichotillomania,"
© 2016 Omnigraphics. Reviewed December 2018.

Trichotillomania—sometimes called "hair-pulling disorder"—is characterized by a compulsive urge to pull one's own hair from the scalp, eyebrows, eyelashes, limbs, or pubic area. This impulse-control disorder is self-induced and is sometimes classified under obsessive-compulsive disorder (OCD) or self-injury. Research suggests that the hair-pulling behavior could be a way of relieving stress and anxiety. Some outward signs of trichotillomania, in addition to hair loss, include playing with, chewing, or eating pulled-out hair.

Current thinking suggests that trichotillomania is most likely caused by multiple factors—genetic, biological, and environmental—and could result in low self-esteem and social withdrawal. Complications include infections, permanent hair loss, and gastrointestinal blockage caused by the ingestion of hair, along with other disorders, such as anxiety, depression, and eating disorders.

Both eating disorders and trichotillomania are often attempts by an individual to cope with negative internal emotions or issues. Obsessive-compulsive behavior is a common trait in both disorders, and the individual suffering from an eating disorder might sense momentary relief when hair is pulled.

Treatment for trichotillomania primarily includes psychotherapy, along with medication and—in some cases—surgery to remove intestinal blockage. A comprehensive treatment method that focuses on resolving underlying issues is usually employed to help the individual heal from both disorders.

Reference

Ekern, Jacquelyn. "Dual Diagnosis and Co-Occurring Disorders," Eating Disorder Hope, April 25, 2012.

Section 19.7

Eating Disorders and Posttraumatic Stress Disorder

"Eating Disorders and Posttraumatic Stress Disorder," © 2016 Omnigraphics. Reviewed December 2018.

Posttraumatic stress disorder (PTSD) develops as a result of exposure to a terrifying or life-threatening event, such as abuse (physical, emotional, or sexual), the sudden death of a loved one, war, major accidents, or natural disasters. The symptoms of PTSD can fall into the following categories:

- **Re-experiencing the traumatic incident.** The individual could have "flashback" episodes, recurring nightmares, and/or reminders or distressing thoughts about the traumatic event, all of which can affect daily life.

- **Avoidance.** The individual may exhibit emotional detachment and avoid people, places, or situations that remind her or him about the event.

- **Stimulation.** These are called "arousal symptoms" and may include getting alarmed easily, trouble with focusing or sleeping, and sudden emotional outbursts.

- **Negative perceptions and emotions.** These symptoms may include the inability to remember certain parts of the traumatic incident, pessimistic thoughts about people or the world in general, lack of interest in formerly enjoyable activities, and momentary feelings of guilt or blame.

If left untreated, PTSD can have serious adverse effects on the individual. It can take a toll on the person's role in society, interpersonal relationships, the way she or he functions on a daily basis, the ability to learn, and also social and emotional development.

To help cope with the effects of PTSD, individuals frequently develop other disorders, such as drug or alcohol abuse, or an eating disorder. Eating disorders, in particular, have been observed in individuals with a history of trauma, who often perceive this as a way to distract themselves from, or attain a sense of control over, the distressing emotions associated with PTSD. It thus becomes essential to seek help from experienced professionals to treat both conditions simultaneously. A comprehensive treatment strategy may include a combination of medication, nutritional support, and therapy to help resolve the underlying causes of the disorders.

Reference

Ekern, Jacquelyn. "Dual Diagnosis and Co-Occurring Disorders," Eating Disorder Hope, April 25, 2012.

Section 19.8

Eating Disorders, Anxiety, and Depression

"Eating Disorders, Anxiety, and Depression,"
© 2016 Omnigraphics. Reviewed December 2018.

Psychological conditions like depression and anxiety have been found to co-occur frequently in individuals suffering from eating disorders.

Depression

Depression is a mood disorder that comprises acute feelings of distress, helplessness, anxiety, and/or guilt. It is one of the most common mental-health problems, and it can seriously affect the overall well-being and productivity of the individual. Symptoms may include:

- Increased frustration

- Insomnia

- Reckless behavior

- Loss of interest in activities that were previously enjoyed

- Irritability

- Feelings of insignificance or self-hatred

- Tendency to abuse alcohol or drugs

- Frequent feelings of fatigue or pain

- Low energy level

- Fluctuations in eating habits and body weight

- Social withdrawal

- Poor concentration

- Delusions

- Suicidal thoughts

Depression can be caused by a number of factors, including hormonal imbalance, traumatic experiences, a previous history of substance abuse, and side-effects of certain medication. It can either co-occur with, or lead to the development of other mental illnesses, such as anxiety, phobias, panic disorders, and eating disorders.

It is not clear whether eating disorders take root in an individual due to existing depression, or whether eating disorders cause depression. Since no two eating disorders are the same, and each is a complex condition on its own, both arguments are considered valid in different cases. For instance, feelings of worthlessness and moodiness are often identified as a sign of an eating disorder—which, on the other hand, may also be symptoms of depression. Likewise, a depressed person can indulge in emotional eating, which can subsequently lead to an eating disorder.

Anxiety

It is quite normal for people to feel anxious in stressful situations, but when an individual experiences an extreme and unreasonable level of anxiety, it is characterized as a disorder. Anxiety disorder is generally identified as a combination of psychological states, such as nervousness, fear, worry, and mistrust, that extends over a long period of time and considerably affects daily activities. Anxiety may be caused by a combination of environmental, social, psychological, genetic, and physiological factors. Some examples include:

- Hormonal imbalance

- Substance abuse, or withdrawal from an illicit drug

- History of mental illness in the family

- Traumatic episodes

- Current physical ailment

Types of anxiety disorders include generalized anxiety disorder (GAD), obsessive-compulsive disorder (OCD), phobias, social anxiety disorder (SAD), panic disorder, and posttraumatic stress disorder (PTSD). Each has its own unique symptoms, which are further categorized as physical, behavioral, emotional, and cognitive. These symptoms include sweating, irregular heartbeat, difficulty breathing, headache, irregular sleeping patterns, nervous habits, irritability, restlessness, obsessive and unwanted thoughts, and irrational fear.

Like depression, anxiety disorder can co-occur with eating disorders. And similarly, an individual suffering from an anxiety disorder can develop an eating disorder as a means of coping with anxiety.

In most cases, anxiety precedes the onset of an eating disorder, such as when an individual briefly soothes symptoms of anxiety by trying to gain a sense of control over other aspects of life, such as food, exercise, and weight. This, in the long run, can lead to the development of eating disorders.

Because of the complex nature of eating disorders that co-occur with depression or anxiety, there is the need for a comprehensive treatment plan that analyzes the factors underlying these conditions. Since a number of similar factors can lead to the development of each of these illnesses, successful treatment requires an inclusive strategy that addresses the root cause of all the conditions and helps the individual learn to manage the co-occurring disorder separately and not associate it with food. In addition to medication and nutritional support, the treatment plan may also include various forms of therapy, such as group therapy, cognitive behavioral therapy, and music and art therapy.

Reference

"Eating Disorders and Other Health Problems," Eating Disorders Victoria, June 19, 2015.

Section 19.9

Eating Disorders and Alcohol and Substance Abuse

"Eating Disorders and Alcohol and Substance Abuse,"
© 2016 Omnigraphics. Reviewed December 2018.

The uncontrolled use and abuse of alcohol and drugs can lead to dependence or addiction, which may have severe mental and physical consequences. Alcohol and substance addiction are caused by various biological, social, psychological, environmental, and physiological factors and can co-exist with other medical conditions, as well.

A three-year study by the National Center on Addiction and Substance Abuse (CASA) at Columbia University in 2003 showed a strong link between substance abuse and eating disorders—anorexia nervosa and bulimia nervosa, in particular—and identified shared risk factors and characteristics. The exhaustive report states that about 50 percent of those with eating disorders were likely to abuse alcohol and illicit drugs, and up to 35 percent of people with alcohol or drug dependency also had eating disorders.

Other studies have also confirmed that eating disorders and addiction frequently co-occur, noting that characteristics common to both conditions often include intense obsession with the substance (food, alcohol, or drugs), compulsive behavior, a tendency to keep the disorder a secret, social withdrawal, strong cravings, and risk for suicide. Both eating and substance-abuse disorders are more likely to occur in times of stress and depression, low self-esteem, anxiety, when unhealthy dieting behavior or substance abuse is present in the family, and when physical or sexual abuse has occurred in the past.

Both types of disorders are life-threatening, recurrent, and can have the same impact on the functioning of the brain. Some other severe psychiatric conditions associated with eating disorders, as well as substance and alcohol abuse, include obsessive-compulsive disorder and mood disorders.

Eating disorders and alcohol or substance abuse are similar in terms of their addictive nature, and issues related to both conditions tend to coincide. Hence, there is the need for comprehensive treatment that can effectively address the requirements of both disorders simultaneously. Dual-diagnosis treatment and 12-step programs are commonly used in many treatment centers to facilitate eating-disorder and substance-abuse rehabilitation.

References

1. "Eating Disorders and Other Health Problems," Eating Disorders Victoria, June 19, 2015.

2. Ekern, Jacquelyn. "Dual Diagnosis and Co-Occurring Disorders," Eating Disorder Hope, April 25, 2012.

Part Three

Causes of Eating Disorders

Chapter 20

Identifying and Understanding the Causes of Eating Disorders

Chapter Contents

Section 20.1

What Causes Eating Disorders

This section contains text excerpted from the following
sources: Text in this section begins with excerpts from "Eating
Disorders Myths Busted—Myth #4: Eating Disorders are a Choice,"
National Institute of Mental Health (NIMH), February 25, 2014.
Reviewed December 2018; Text under the heading "Causes of Eating
Disorders" is excerpted from "Eating Disorders," National Institute
of Mental Health (NIMH), February 2016; Text under the heading
"Other Risk Factors" is excerpted from "Eating Disorders,"
Substance Abuse and Mental Health Services
Administration (SAMHSA), May 12, 2017.

One of the common myths about eating disorders—and families of
patients have suffered from this myth—is that families are to blame.
This is not true at all. But what we know in eating disorders is that
families are often our best allies in treatment. Another huge myth is
that eating disorders are a choice. This is perhaps the most damaging
myth that patients have had to deal with. People make an association
between the cultural thin ideal and what they imagine to be anorexia
nervosa. If you ask patients if something like People magazine or models was what put them on the path to develop anorexia nervosa, the
vast majority of them say no. There might have been a role in the very
beginning that made them think "I'm going to go on that first diet." But
the minute they go on that first diet, their anomalous biology kicks in
and anorexia nervosa just sends them down a path that they have no
control over. So eating disorders are illnesses not choices.

Causes of Eating Disorders

Eating disorders frequently appear during the teen years or young
adulthood but may also develop during childhood or later in life. These
disorders affect both genders, although rates among women are higher
than among men. Like women who have eating disorders, men also
have a distorted sense of body image. For example, men may have
muscle dysmorphia, a type of disorder marked by an extreme concern
with becoming more muscular.

Researchers are finding that eating disorders are caused by a complex interaction of genetic, biological, behavioral, psychological, and
social factors. Researchers are using the latest technology and science
to better understand eating disorders. One approach involves the study
of human genes. Eating disorders run in families. Researchers are

working to identify deoxyribonucleic acid (DNA) variations that are linked to the increased risk of developing eating disorders.

Changes in brain functions related to eating and emotions may help explain why some people develop eating disorders. Brain imaging studies are also providing a better understanding of eating disorders. For example, researchers have found differences in patterns of brain activity in women with eating disorders in comparison with healthy women. This kind of research can help guide the development of new means of diagnosis and treatment of eating disorders.

Other Risk Factors
Social Factors

These include being teased or ridiculed often about one's weight, participating in a sport that requires low weight or a certain body image, or being surrounded by negative messages about food and body. Frequent dieting can increase the risk of eating disorders.

Trauma

Traumatic events and major life stressors, especially during childhood, such as sexual assault or other abuse, may be a risk factor for an eating disorder.

Psychological Factors

Having another mental disorder can make an eating disorder more likely. Also, personality traits such as being a perfectionist, feeling inadequate, having low self-esteem, and rigid thinking are linked to increased risk of an eating disorder.

Section 20.2

Genetics and Anorexia

This section includes text excerpted from "Coming Together to
Calm the Hunger: Group Therapy Program for Adults Diagnosed
with Anorexia Nervosa," Education Resources Information
Center (ERIC), U.S. Department of Education (ED),
March 4, 2012. Reviewed December 2018.

The presence of eating disorders tends to be influenced by hereditary within families, with female relatives most often diagnosed. This
hereditary component may suggest that there is a genetic component
as well as environmental elements to the disorder onset. In terms of
the latter, the environmental factors that could be causes of an eating
disorder include the social pressure to be thin, high social class, high
social anxiety, elevated weight or obesity, high impulsivity, individual differences in biological response to starvation, and individual
differences in the reward value of starvation or eating. It is important to recognize that a genetic component may play a role in people
struggling with disordered eating, particularly since the diagnosis of
anorexia nervosa (AN) is currently based solely on signs and symptoms
as opposed to objective measures.

The criteria of AN remains the subject of considerable debate, in
large part because it fails to result in clearly defined subgroups or to
account for changing symptomatology over the course of the illness.
Many individuals who suffer from disordered eating do not meet the
criteria for AN and bulimia nervosa (BN), so they are placed in a residual group known as eating disorder not otherwise specified.

Striegel-Moore and Bulik (Authors of Risk Factors for Eating
Disorders, *American Psychologist*) stated that risk factor studies
that include both the genetic and environmental factors present an
untapped source of information of potential value for revising the
classification system. Understanding the genetic components of AN
is valuable for treatment. Treatment is best accomplished when the
causes of a disorder are known as this aids in the search for effective
interventions. It is interesting to note that some individuals with a
family history of AN do not develop AN, whereas others will develop
disordered eating; Striegel-Moore and Bulik asserted that this is a
gene plus an environmental interaction whereby varying genotypes
would render individuals differentially sensitive to environmental
events.

The authors provided an excellent example of this where an individual with Genotype A might experiment with her first extreme diet, find the experience aversive and uncomfortable, and reject the behavior on the basis of it not being at all reinforcing. In contrast, an individual with Genotype B might experience that first episode of severe caloric restriction to be highly reinforcing by reducing her innate dysphoria and anxiety, providing her with a sense of control over her own body weight and resulting in her receiving positive social attention for weight loss attempts.

Identification of risk factors is important for determining high-risk groups for targeted interventions, designing prevention program content, and informing public policy.

Section 20.3

Mediating Factors for Anorexia

This section includes text excerpted from "Coming Together to Calm the Hunger: Group Therapy Program for Adults Diagnosed with Anorexia Nervosa," Education Resources Information Center (ERIC), U.S. Department of Education (ED), March 4, 2012. Reviewed December 2018.

Various empirical and survey-based studies examined possible mediating factors that promote the onset and maintenance of anorexia nervosa (AN). The topic of mediating factors is worthy of exploring as it might aid counselors helping those with AN if an anorexic client has a history of childhood sexual abuse, obsessive-compulsive disorder (OCD), depression, borderline personality disorder (BPD), or posttraumatic stress disorder (PTSD). It is also necessary to present the mediating factors, as they may help guide treatment options and intervention techniques. For example, in the group program manual associated with this project, topics such as posttraumatic stress disorder and abuse can be addressed. The following sections explore the mediating factors in further detail. Specifically, the next section will address the prevalence of childhood sexual abuse in AN clients.

Childhood Sexual Abuse

Clinicians have long argued that childhood sexual abuse is a risk factor for the development of AN. The issue is whether a meaningful relationship exists between the two phenomena, or whether it is merely an illusory one because of the prevalence of both in a female population. Some studies have failed to identify a link between childhood sexual abuse and eating disorders. Cachelin et al. and Fullerton, Wonderlich, and Gosnell asserted that from the data it is clear that childhood sexual abuse is neither necessary nor sufficient for the development of AN; however, in a number of cases it may be an important etiological factor. Cachelin et al.'s study found that not all of the AN participants reported childhood sexual abuse and that some of the control participants did. What seemed to differentiate the two groups was the amount of abuse. The women with AN reported more separate instances and longer duration of sexual abuse than did healthy controls and were more likely to have been revictimized. Cachelin et al.'s study supported Wonderlich et al.'s research by finding that the individuals who had experienced both childhood sexual abuse and sexual assault in adulthood showed the highest rates of AN behavior and associated impulsivity, which also support the concept that early trauma may sensitize an individual's reaction to later adversity or traumatic experience. The results of these studies indicated a need for clinicians to be aware that repeated or prolonged abuse may increase the risk for developing AN. Therefore, screening questions that ask about abuse should be included during intake sessions.

Varner stated that pathological eating and other self-destructive behaviors may be a maladaptive mechanism for avoiding or dealing with the overwhelming depression and anxiety that accompany memories of abuse. The group program developed for this project, *Coming Together to Calm the Hunger: Group Therapy Program for Adults Diagnosed with Anorexia Nervosa* provides a venue for the recognition and exploration of overwhelming emotions that member's may feel. The following section reviews the mediating factor of OCD that may be present in individuals with AN.

Obsessive-Compulsive Disorder

Obsessive-compulsive disorder (OCD) involves a combination of dysfunctional thoughts and behaviors. Furthermore, Steinglass and Walsh asserted the obsessions of OCD are "persistent thoughts, impulses, or images that are intrusive or unwanted such that the client has some degree of insight that their worries are unrealistic." Individuals diagnosed with AN have persistent and intrusive thoughts about food and repetitive concerns about gaining weight. An individual with AN may avoid meals with friends or family in an attempt to reduce their anxiety; Steinglass and Walsh asserted this type of behavior is associated with an obsession characteristic of the disorder.

Compulsions, also part of OCD, are repetitive, purposeful actions that are usually intended to reduce anxiety raised by the obsessions. Compulsions and obsessions can also be identified within individuals diagnosed with AN. For example, an AN client might disclose how she is frequently spending her time considering how she is going to structure her day around food avoidance.

Halmi et al., Halmi, Tozzi, et al., Sallet, and Wu identified that OCD is comorbid with AN, however, there appears to be distinct differences in the desire for change. Steinglass and Wals asserted the motivation for change is often a critical component of treatment of AN, in a way that is qualitatively different from OCD. In OCD clients, there may be high degree of motivation to change. However, those with AN may have difficulty identifying their behaviors and thoughts as being maladaptive and thus do not see a need to change. Furthermore, it appears that clients with AN are unable to see the physical dangers associated with their dietary restrictions.

Depression

Depression has been found to coexist with AN at a relatively high rate such as 50 percent. Features that are common to both eating disorders and depression (i.e., weight change, social withdrawal, decreased self-esteem, sleep disturbance, and concentration problems) can make differential diagnosis of depression difficult. Depressive symptoms that do not meet full criteria for an affective disorder, such as low mood, sleep changes, and experiencing less pleasure in one's life, are also common in AN clients. Individuals suffering from depression are reported to have higher than expected rates of a history of trauma or victimization, and more often than not the trauma occurred during childhood or adolescence.

The implications for clinicians is that it would be advisable to assess and treat depressive disorders among those who present with eating or weight problems as this may also facilitate recovery from AN. Post-traumatic stress disorder is another mediating factor in the development of AN and is identified next.

Posttraumatic Stress Disorder

Posttraumatic stress disorder (PTSD) is currently conceptualized as a complex anxiety disorder with an oscillation between reexperiencing the trauma in memories and dreams, on one hand, and generalized avoidance of stimuli reminiscent of the event on the other. According to Levitt, trauma-related symptoms are generally diagnosed under either acute stress disorder or posttraumatic stress disorder.

Acute stress disorder and posttraumatic stress disorder are quite similar in symptomatology; however, acute stress disorder is only used for diagnosis during the first month after a traumatic event and acute stress disorder tends to have a great emphasis on dissociative symptoms. While a person with posttraumatic stress disorder may present with dissociative features, it is not a requirement for the diagnosis. Levitt stated that the individual who experiences a traumatic event may, soon after the experience, develop and present with a variety of symptoms including anxiety, depression, and dissociative symptoms along with other trauma-related symptoms.

Despite their apparent distance in presentation and clinical picture between PTSD and AN, there are similarities. According to Mantero and Crippa, both posttraumatic stress disorder and AN disorders contain ruminations, and these ruminations tend to be called obsessive by AN individuals and intrusive in posttraumatic stress disorder individuals. When compared with typical obsessions, both the intrusive thoughts of individuals with posttraumatic stress disorder and the obsessive thoughts of anorexics have a stronger link with objective external reality. Mantero and Crippa asserted that in both AN and posttraumatic stress disorder the resulting aggravated symptoms may worsen self-esteem and depressive states and the interruption of this vicious circle is vital to improvement.

Borderline Personality Disorder

Highly variable rates of comorbidity, ranging from 21 percent to 57 percent have been reported for the presence of any personality disorder in patients with a range of eating disorder diagnoses. Sansone and Sansone asserted that childhood trauma is a potential etiological factor in the development of both AN and borderline personality disorder. The relationship between childhood abuse and eating disorders may be mediated by personality dysfunction. Sansone and Sansone further postulated, "At the outset of life's journey, one's endowment with low adaptive genetics and exposure to an unstable family environment highlighted by abuse appears to establish the risk for personality disorder." In turn, this consolidated personality disorder may enhance the risk for AN. However, not all traumatized individuals develop personality disorders, and not all individuals with personality disorders develop AN. Sansone and Sansone suggested further research is needed to explore the various protective and augmenting factors for this pathway.

Section 20.4

Impaired Brain Activity Underlies Impulsive Behaviors in Bulimia

This section includes text excerpted from "Impaired Brain Activity Underlies Impulsive Behaviors in Women with Bulimia," National Institute of Mental Health (NIMH), January 12, 2009. Reviewed December 2018.

Women with bulimia nervosa (BN), when compared with healthy women, showed different patterns of brain activity while doing a task that required self-regulation. This abnormality may underlie binge eating and other impulsive behaviors that occur with the eating disorder.

Background

In the first study of its kind, Rachel Marsh, Ph.D., Columbia University, and colleagues assessed self-regulatory brain processes in women with BN without using disorder-specific cues, such as pictures of food.

In this study, 20 women with BN and 20 healthy controls viewed a series of arrows presented on a computer screen. Their task was to identify the direction in which the arrows were pointing while the researchers observed their brain activity using functional magnetic resonance imaging (fMRI).

People generally complete such tasks easily when the direction of the arrow matches the side of the screen it is on—an arrow on the left side pointing to the left—but respond more slowly and with more errors when the two do not match. In such cases, healthy adults activate self-regulatory processes in the brain to prevent automatic responses and to focus greater attention on resolving the conflicting information.

Results of the Study

Women with BN tended to be more impulsive during the task, responding faster and making more mistakes when presented with conflicting information, compared with healthy controls.

Patterns in brain activity also differed between the two groups. Even when they answered correctly to conflicting information, women with BN generally did not show as much activity in brain areas involved in self-regulation as healthy controls did. Women with the most severe cases of the disorder showed the least amount of self-regulatory brain activity and made the most errors on the task.

Significance

Altered patterns of brain activity may underlie impaired self-regulation and impulse control problems in women with BN. These findings increase the understanding of causes of binge eating and other impulsive behaviors associated with BN and may help researchers to develop better targeted treatments.

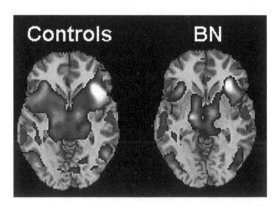

Figure 20.1. *Functional Magnetic Resonance Imaging (fMRI) Data*

fMRI data showing self-regulatory brain activity in healthy controls (left) and women with BN (right). Dark grey areas show increases in activity while answering correctly when given conflicting information. Light grey areas show increases in activity while answering correctly when given matching information. In both cases, women with BN showed less activity than healthy controls.

These differences in brain activity patterns may account for problems with impulse control and similar behaviors related to BN.

What's Next?

The researchers are currently conducting further studies on brain functioning in teens with BN, which would offer a closer look at the beginnings of the illness. They also recommend studying people in remission from an eating disorder. Comparison studies with impulsive people who have healthy weight and eating habits could also provide more information about which patterns of brain activity are most directly related to eating disorders.

Section 20.5

Congenital Leptin Deficiency and Obesity

This section includes text excerpted from "Congenital Leptin Deficiency," Genetics Home Reference (GHR), National Institutes of Health (NIH), December 11, 2018.

What Is Congenital Leptin Deficiency?

Congenital leptin deficiency is a condition that causes severe obesity beginning in the first few months of life. Affected individuals are of normal weight at birth, but they are constantly hungry and quickly gain weight. Without treatment, the extreme hunger continues and leads to chronic excessive eating (hyperphagia) and obesity. Beginning in early childhood, affected individuals develop abnormal eating behaviors such as fighting with other children over food, hoarding food, and eating in secret.

People with congenital leptin deficiency also have hypogonadotropic hypogonadism, which is a condition caused by reduced production of hormones that direct sexual development. Without treatment, affected individuals experience delayed puberty or do not go through puberty, and may be unable to conceive children (infertile).

How Common Is Congenital Leptin Deficiency?

Congenital leptin deficiency is a rare disorder. Only a few dozen cases have been reported in the medical literature.

What Genes Are Related to Congenital Leptin Deficiency?

Congenital leptin deficiency is caused by mutations in the *LEP* gene. This gene provides instructions for making a hormone called leptin, which is involved in the regulation of body weight. Normally, the body's fat cells release leptin in proportion to their size. As fat accumulates in cells, more leptin is produced. This rise in leptin indicates that fat stores are increasing.

Leptin attaches (binds) to and activates a protein called the leptin receptor, fitting into the receptor like a key into a lock. The leptin receptor protein is found on the surface of cells in many organs and tissues of the body including a part of the brain called the hypothalamus. The hypothalamus controls hunger and thirst as well as other functions such as sleep, moods, and body temperature. It also regulates the release of many hormones that have functions throughout the body. In the hypothalamus, the binding of leptin to its receptor triggers a series of chemical signals that affect hunger and help produce a feeling of fullness (satiety).

LEP gene mutations that cause congenital leptin deficiency lead to an absence of leptin. As a result, the signaling that triggers feelings of satiety does not occur, leading to the excessive hunger and weight gain associated with this disorder. Because hypogonadotropic hypogonadism occurs in congenital leptin deficiency, researchers suggest that leptin signaling is also involved in regulating the hormones that control sexual development. However, the specifics of this involvement and how it may be altered in congenital leptin deficiency are unknown.

Congenital leptin deficiency is a rare cause of obesity. Researchers are studying the factors involved in more common forms of obesity.

How Do People Inherit Congenital Leptin Deficiency?

This condition is inherited in an autosomal recessive pattern, which means both copies of the gene in each cell have mutations. The parents of an individual with an autosomal recessive condition each carry one copy of the mutated gene, but they typically do not show signs and symptoms of the condition.

What Other Names Do People Use for Congenital Leptin Deficiency?

- LEPD
- Leptin deficiency
- Obesity due to congenital leptin deficiency
- Obesity, morbid, due to leptin deficiency
- Obesity, morbid, nonsyndromic 1
- Obesity, severe, due to leptin deficiency

Chapter 21

Body Image and Eating Disorders

What Is Body Image?

Body image is how you think and feel about your body. It includes whether you think you look good to other people.

Body image is affected by a lot of things, including messages you get from your friends, family, and the world around you. Images we see in the media definitely affect our body image even though a lot of media images are changed or aren't realistic.

Why Does Body Image Matter?

Your body image can affect how you feel about yourself overall. For example, if you are unhappy with your looks, your self-esteem may start to go down. Sometimes, having body image issues or low self-esteem may lead to depression, eating disorders, or obesity.

This chapter contains text excerpted from the following sources: Text beginning with the heading "What Is Body Image?" is excerpts from "Having Body Image Issues," girlshealth.gov, Office on Women's Health (OWH), January 7, 2015. Reviewed December 2018; Text under the heading "Body Image and Mental Health" is excerpted from "Body Image and Mental Health," Office on Women's Health (OWH), U.S. Department of Health and Human Services (HHS), May 17, 2018.

How Can I Deal with Body Image Issues?

Everyone has something they would like to change about their bodies. But you'll be happier if you focus on the things you like about your body—and your whole self. Need some help? Check out some tips:

- **List your great traits.** If you start to criticize your body, tell yourself to stop. Instead, think about what you like about yourself, both inside and out.

- **Know your power.** Hey, your body is not just a place to hang your clothes! It can do some truly amazing things. Focus on how strong and healthy your body can be.

- **Treat your body well.** Eat right, sleep tight, and get moving. You'll look and feel your best—and you'll be pretty proud of yourself too.

- **Give your body a treat.** Take a nice bubble bath, do some stretching, or just curl up on a comfy couch. Do something soothing.

- **Mind your media.** Try not to let models and actresses affect how you think you should look. They get lots of help from makeup artists, personal trainers, and photo fixers. And advertisers often use a focus on thinness to get people to buy stuff. Don't let them mess with your mind!

- **Let yourself shine.** A lot of how we look comes from how we carry ourselves. Feeling proud, walking tall, and smiling big can boost your beauty—and your mood.

- **Find fab friends.** Your best bet is to hang out with people who accept you for you! And work with your friends to support each other.

If you can't seem to accept how you look, talk to an adult you trust. You can get help feeling better about your body.

Stressing about Body Changes

During puberty and your teen years, your body changes a lot. All those changes can be hard to handle. They might make you worry about what other people think of how you look and about whether your body is normal. If you have these kinds of concerns, you are not alone.

Here are some common thoughts about changing bodies.

- Why am I taller than most of the boys my age?
- Why haven't I grown?
- Am I too skinny?
- Am I too fat?
- Will others like me now that I am changing?
- Are my breasts too small?
- Are my breasts too large?
- Why do I have acne?
- Do my clothes look right on my body?
- Are my hips getting bigger?

If you are stressed about your body, you may feel better if you understand why you are changing so fast—or not changing as fast as your friends.

During puberty, you get taller and see other changes in your body, such as wider hips and thighs. Your body will also start to have more fat compared to muscle than before. Each young woman changes at her own pace, and all of these changes are normal.

What Are Serious Body Image Problems?

If how your body looks bothers you a lot and you can't stop thinking about it, you could have body dysmorphic disorder, or BDD.

People with BDD think they look ugly even if they have a small flaw or none at all. They may spend many hours a day looking at flaws and trying to hide them. They also may ask friends to reassure them about their looks or want to have a lot of cosmetic surgery. If you or a friend may have BDD, talk to an adult you trust, such as a parent or guardian, school counselor, teacher, doctor, or nurse. BDD is an illness, and you can get help.

Body Image and Mental Health

Body image is how you think and feel about your body. Women with a positive body image are more likely to have good mental health. But many women in the United States have negative body images, which can put them at higher risk of depression, eating disorders, or other mental- and physical-health problems. You can take steps to develop a healthier body image and get treatment for mental-health conditions.

Chapter 22

Environmental Factors in Eating Disorder Development

Researchers cannot pinpoint a single cause for eating disorders. Instead, they view eating disorders as complex illnesses that can have a variety of contributing causes, including genetic, biological, psychological, social, and environmental factors. Some of the environmental factors that may increase the likelihood of an individual developing an eating disorder include sociocultural pressures to attain a certain standard of thinness, media messages about diet and weight loss, exposure to traumatic events, stressful or chaotic family dynamics, and mothers who frequently express dissatisfaction with their own bodies or criticize their daughters' body shape or weight.

Sociocultural Ideals

American media and popular culture promote an image of the ideal or "perfect" body that is unattainable for most people. Fashion models, actors, and celebrities featured onscreen or in magazines tend to fall within a narrow set of norms that include only those who are extremely thin or extremely muscular, and editing technologies such

"Environmental Factors in Eating Disorder Development," © 2016 Omnigraphics. Reviewed December 2018.

as Photoshop and airbrushing are often employed to remove any blemishes, wrinkles, or love handles. When people internalize these unrealistic standards of beauty, it may contribute to the development of a negative body image, an obsession with weight and appearance, and eating disorders. Although many people who are exposed to sociocultural ideals of thinness do not develop eating disorders, studies have shown that some individuals are highly vulnerable to such environmental messages about weight and beauty.

Dieting

In response to societal pressures to attain a certain ideal body shape, many people resort to restrictive dieting or other extreme weight loss measures. Americans spend an estimated $60 billion each year on fad diets and dangerous weight loss products, despite the fact that 95 percent of people on diets fail to achieve permanent weight loss. In addition to their ineffectiveness, restrictive diets are also a common precipitating factor in the development of eating disorders. Dieting increases people's preoccupation with food and weight and generates feelings of guilt and shame surrounding eating. For some people, these feelings contribute to the development of eating disorders.

Traumatic Experiences

Studies have suggested that up to 50 percent of people with eating disorders have experienced a traumatic event, such as physical or sexual abuse. Such events often create feelings of guilt and shame and contribute to a negative body image. Some victims of trauma develop eating disorders as they restrict food in an attempt to regain control over their bodies or cope with the intense emotions generated by the event.

Family Dynamics

Stressful or chaotic family situations are another environmental factor that has been linked with an increase in the likelihood of eating disorders. While many people with eating disorders come from difficult family environments, however, there is no evidence to support the idea that certain family situations or parenting styles directly cause eating disorders. Instead, family dynamics are only one factor that may potentially contribute to the illness. In addition, research has found that the relationship may be reciprocal—the stress surrounding a member's struggle with an eating disorder may cause negative family dynamics to develop.

On the other hand, family support systems can also help young people ignore sociocultural pressures and establish a positive body image, which may help protect them from developing eating disorders. Finally, family involvement is a vital component in the treatment and recovery process.

The Mother–Daughter Relationship

Of all the family relationships, the one between mothers and daughters has been most extensively studied with respect to its impact on the development of eating disorders. Research has suggested a correlation between a mother's body image and eating behaviors and the likelihood of her daughter developing an eating disorder. Some of this the correlation may be explained by genetic predisposition, which is estimated to account for between 50 and 80 percent of eating disorder risk, yet many experts believe that behavior modeling also plays a role.

Studies have identified the following behaviors by mothers as factors that may increase the risk of daughters developing low self-esteem, negative body image, preoccupation with weight and appearance, and eating disorders:

- Mothers who have a negative body image or frequently express dissatisfaction with their own weight, shape, or size

- Mothers who have disordered eating habits and attitudes, such as restrictive dieting or binge eating

- Mothers who criticize or ridicule their daughters' food choices or eating habits

- Mothers who make negative comments about their daughters' weight and appearance

- Mothers who insist upon a relationship with their daughters that lacks boundaries and does not promote individual autonomy

It is important to note that eating disorders never have a single cause. Even if mothers engage in one or more of the above behaviors, they should not be blamed for having a daughter with an eating disorder. But being aware of the risks associated with the mother–daughter relationship can help people adjust their behavior and build healthier family dynamics. Mothers who focus on health and inner beauty rather than weight and appearance can help counteract other environmental factors and protect their daughters against disordered eating behaviors.

References

1. Fielder-Jenks, Chelsea. "Mothers, Daughters, and Eating Disorders," Eating Disorder Hope, 2016.

2. Jones, Megan. "Factors that May Contribute to Eating Disorders," National Eating Disorders Association, n.d.

Chapter 23

Bullying and the Link to Eating Disorders

What Is an Eating Disorder?

Eating disorders are complex mental disorders that cause a person to have excessive fear and anxiety about eating, body image, and weight gain that lead to unhealthy behaviors.

Three of the most commonly diagnosed eating disorders:

1. **Binge-eating disorder (BED):** A person with binge-eating disorder will eat too much and feel like they do not have control over how much they eat. What to look for: Eating in secret, eating a lot of food quickly, sadness, feeling guilty about eating.

This chapter contains text excerpted from the following sources: Text beginning with the heading "What Is an Eating Disorder?" is excerpted from "February 26-March 4, 2018 Is National Eating Disorders Awareness Week," StopBullying.gov, U.S. Department of Health and Human Services (HHS), February 28, 2018; Text beginning with the heading "Weight-Based Bullying and Binge-Eating Disorder" is excerpted from "Bullying and Binge Eating Disorder," StopBullying.gov, U.S. Department of Health and Human Services (HHS), May 12, 2015. Reviewed December 2018; Text under the heading "Research Brief: Childhood Bullying Linked to Adult Psychiatric Disorders" is excerpted from "Research Brief: Childhood Bullying Linked to Adult Psychiatric Disorders," StopBullying.gov, U.S. Department of Health and Human Services (HHS), June 3, 2013. Reviewed December 2018.

2. **Bulimia nervosa (BN):** A person with bulimia will overeat and then throw up on purpose or do something else to make up for what they ate so that they do not gain weight from eating too much. What to look for: Hidden food wrappers, vomit, always going to the bathroom after eating, overexercising, and moodiness.

3. **Anorexia nervosa (AN):** A person with anorexia often fears that they weigh too much, despite their weight being low. This fear drives them to try to lose weight or avoid weight gain by limiting the foods that they eat. What to look for: Weight loss, talking about food and eating all the time, not eating, withdrawing or other change in mood.

Eating disorders can lead to serious health problems, like heart failure and death, without help from a trained healthcare team. Anyone can get an eating disorder at any age, but eating disorders are more common in females and most start during the teen years. Recovering from an eating disorder can take a long time, but it is possible to fully recover. People who were teased about their weight as teens sometimes worry about their weight and engage in disordered eating behaviors into adulthood.

How Can I Support a Young Person I Know Who Is Being Bullied about Their Weight?

Supporting the young person who is being bullied is critical. Listen to the young person and let her/him know that it is not their fault and that they deserve to feel good about their body. Be aware that they may have a hard time talking about weight-based teasing, but knowing she or he has an adult who cares can make all the difference in preventing an eating disorder from further developing. Here are some more tips:

- Encourage youth to eat healthy and to be active.

- Set a good example—Avoid teasing youth about their weight and talking negatively about other people's bodies, including your own. Focus conversations on positive personality traits that emphasize the strengths and talents of youth.

- Help youth find activities that they like and that let them make friends with their peers.

- Ask children and adolescents who show signs and symptoms of an eating disorder about how they feel, and create a safe space for them to talk about their emotions and social relationships.

- Talk to your child's physician or other health providers if you notice signs and symptoms of an eating disorder.

- Join the conversation online during Eating Disorders Awareness Week and share resources on body image and eating disorders with your social media contacts and people you care about.

Weight-Based Bullying and Binge-Eating Disorder

Binge-eating disorder (BED) is a complex psychiatric disorder with countless risk factors, signs and symptoms, and potential accompanying physical and psychological complications (called comorbidities)—and that bullying can be a contributing factor.

Bullying has very serious consequences. Studies show bullying of any kind, but particularly weight-based bullying, leads to increased occurrence of low self-esteem, poor body image, social isolation, eating disorders, and poor academic performance.

Kids and teens who are overweight can be victims of many forms of bullying, including physical force, name-calling, derogatory comments, being ignored or excluded, or being made fun of.

Research conducted by Dr. Rebecca Puhl, Deputy Director of the Yale Rudd Center on Food Policy and Obesity found:

- Weight-based teasing predicted binge eating at five years of followup among both men and women, even after controlling for age, race/ethnicity, and socioeconomic status.

- Peer victimization can be directly predicted by weight.

- 64 percent of students enrolled in weight-loss programs reported experiencing weight-based victimization.

- One-third of girls and one-fourth of boys report weight-based teasing from peers, but prevalence rates increase to approximately 60 percent among the heaviest students.

- 84 percent of students observed students perceived as overweight being called names or getting teased during physical activities.

Bullying Is Trauma and Can Lead to Binge-Eating Disorder

Bullying because of body size can have a major negative impact on this vulnerable population. We know BED has the highest rate of trauma of all eating disorders. That is, individuals who have binge-eating disorder have experienced trauma at some point during their lives. Types of trauma include emotional, physical, and sexual abuse, a divorce or death, and, yes, bullying.

Trauma doesn't have to be catastrophic to have lasting catastrophic effects on a person's psychological, social, and physical health.

People living in larger bodies experience trauma every day by being assaulted by negative attitudes and messages about weight from all angles: in the media; at home, school, and work; even in doctors' offices. This increases stress and leads to internalized weight stigma, which further entrenches disordered eating patterns.

What Can We Do about It?

There are several things you can do to help stop weight-based bullying and all other types of bullying.

- Learn what bullying is and what it is not.

- Learn to recognize warning signs that your child is involved in bullying.

- Talk to your child about bullying and what to do if it happens.

- National Weight Stigma Awareness Week. Learn how you can get involved.

Research Brief: Childhood Bullying Linked to Adult Psychiatric Disorders

Duke University professors published research that shows the degree to which bullying can affect someone's mental health.

Authors Copeland, Wolke, Angold, and Costello discovered that victims of childhood bullying have a higher risk of developing mental health problems later in life. The study followed more than 1,000 youth, starting at the ages of 9, 11, and 13. The youth were interviewed each year until they turned 16. Follow-up interviews were then conducted into adulthood.

Results of the study showed bullying elevated the rate of mental health problems. Some of the key findings were:

- Youth who were victims of bullying had a higher chance of having agoraphobia, anxiety, and panic disorders

- Youth who bullied were at risk for antisocial personality disorder

- Youth who bullied who were also victims of bullying were at a higher risk for adult depression and panic disorder. For this group, there was an increased risk for agoraphobia in females and suicidality in males.

The link between bullying and mental illness is very real. This research brief only scratches the surface of this issue, and is not a synthesis of all mental health and bullying research. Bullying can have many different effects. Bullying is a serious problem for all involved and can have a lasting impact on someone's entire life—but it doesn't have to. You can help youth heal from the harmful effects of bullying.

A nationwide effort to "bring mental illness out of the shadows" has resulted in the launch of a new national dialogue on mental health.

Chapter 24

The Media and Eating Disorders

Chapter Contents

Section 24.1

Media Influence and Eating Disorders

This section contains text excerpted from the following
sources: Text in this section begins with excerpts from "A Change
of Attitude: Body Image," Federal Occupational Health (FOH), U.S.
Department of Health and Human Services (HHS), 2012. Reviewed
December 2018; Text under the heading "Media Exposure and the
"Perfect" Body" is excerpted from "If Those Dolls Were Real People,"
Centers for Disease Control and Prevention (CDC),
March 23, 2006. Reviewed December 2018.

In the scenery of spring there is nothing superior nothing infe-
rior; flowering branches are by nature different, some short some
long. — Zen proverb

We sometimes forget that variety is part of nature. When we think
of the characteristics of something as simple as a flower, we quickly
realize that they come in many colors, sizes, and shapes. We're glad
for this diversity in nature, but when it comes to our own bodies, we
often think we should fit the standard model (pun intended).

We have a mental disconnect, at times, and wonder why we don't
look like what is presented to us in advertisements. We forget that
everyone is different and that the people we tend to see in advertisements aren't necessarily meant to represent reality. Instead, the goal
of advertising is to inspire us to buy some product or service.

Media Exposure and the "Perfect" Body

According to research, a typical child in the United States watches
more than 19 hours of television a week. The average American child
also plays computer or video games for seven hours each week. The
American Academy of Pediatrics (AAP) estimates that kids see 40,000
television commercials each year, and they also are exposed to ads on
the Internet, in magazines, on billboards, in newspapers, on the radio,
and all around them.

Media conveys powerful messages — about what is "cool" to wear,
what music to listen to, which TV shows to watch. It also sends powerful messages about how people are supposed to look.

The problem is that many of the images children see in the media
bear little relationship to real life. According to the nonprofit organization Just Think, the average fashion model is much taller than the

average woman—but weighs about 23 percent (one-fifth) less. According to the National Eating Disorders Association (NEDA), while the average woman is 5'4" tall and weighs 140 pounds, the average model is 5'11" and weighs 117 pounds. In addition, media techniques ranging from airbrushing to the use of "body doubles" create photographs that are visually arresting, but simply no reflection of reality.

Unrealistic body image portrayed in the media, and even by forms of entertainment such as toys, may affect both mental and physical health. Seeing thin female and muscular male models can affect kids' thoughts about their own bodies, and may cause confusion, anxiety, insecurity, anger, or depression, especially for those who already have concerns about their body or place great importance on their appearance. Some kids may risk their physical health through unhealthy dieting or excessive physical activity. Some may begin smoking to control their appetite or develop eating disorders. Some may engage in unhealthy weight training, or use anabolic steroids or dietary supplements, for muscle growth.

Just as children need to learn how to be critical of the things they read, they also need to know how to do the same with pictures, video, and sound. MediaSharpSM, a media literacy education guide from the Centers for Disease Control and Prevention (CDC), outlines seven key questions that are critical to understanding media messages.

Who Is Communicating and Why?

Every message is communicated for a reason—to entertain, inform, and/or persuade. However, the basic motive behind most media programs is to profit through the sale of advertising space and sponsorships.

Who Owns, Profits from, and Pays for Media Messages?

Media messages are owned. They are designed to yield results, provide profits, and pay for themselves. Both news and entertainment programming try to increase listenership or viewership to attract advertising dollars. Movies also seek to increase box-office receipts. Understanding the profit motive is key to analyzing media messages.

How Are Media Messages Communicated?

Every message is communicated through sound, video, text, and/or photography. Messages are enhanced through camera angles, special effects, editing, and/or music. Analyzing how these features are used in any given message is critical to understanding how it attempts to persuade, entertain, or inform.

Who Receives Media Messages and What Sense Is Made of Them?

Messages are filtered through the "interpretive screens" of our beliefs, values, attitudes, and behaviors. Identifying the target audience for a given message and knowing its "filters" and the way in which it interprets media messages help make you media sharp!

What Are the Intended or Underlying Purposes and Whose Point of View Is behind the Message?

Behind every message is a purpose and point of view. The advertiser's purpose is more direct than the program producer's, though both may seek to entertain us. Understanding their purposes and knowing WHOSE point of view is being expressed and WHY is critical to being media sharp.

What Is Not Being Said and Why?

Because messages are limited in both time and purpose, rarely are all the details provided. Identifying the issues, topics, and perspectives that are NOT included can often reveal a great deal about the purposes of media messages. In fact, this may be the most significant question that can uncover answers to other questions.

Is There Consistency Both within and across Media?

Do the political slant, tone, local/national/international perspective, and depth of coverage change across media or messages? Because media messages tell only part of the story and different media have unique production features, it helps to evaluate multiple messages on the same issue. This allows you to identify multiple points of view, some of which may be missing in any single message or medium. This is typically referred to as the "multi-source rule."

Section 24.2

The Internet and Eating Disorders (Pro-Eating Disorders Websites)

The Internet can be a valuable source of information and support for people who are working to recover from eating disorders. It can help them feel less isolated by enabling them to connect with others who share their experiences and understand their feelings. Yet the Internet also contains thousands of dangerous websites that advocate extreme weight-loss methods and encourage disordered eating behaviors. Known as pro-anorexia (pro-ana), pro-bulimia (pro-mia), and pro-eating disorder (pro-ED) websites, these online communities can be harmful or even deadly for people who are vulnerable to their messages. Rather than promoting treatment and recovery, these sites spread strategies and ideas that may trigger or exacerbate an eating disorder.

The Dangers of Pro-Eating Disorders Websites

Some pro-ED websites seem fairly innocuous on the surface. They may seem to promote clean eating, fitness, or a healthy lifestyle. The underlying message, however, is that controlling food intake, losing weight, and achieving a "perfect" body can resolve a myriad of social and emotional issues. For people who are struggling with an eating disorder, this message validates their unhealthy eating behaviors and makes their illness seem like an acceptable lifestyle choice.

Pro-ana and pro-mia websites offer praise, encouragement, and support for the "strength," "discipline," and "self-control" required to ignore the body's basic need for food and encourage readers to severely restrict or purge calories. Many sites also provide strategies or tips for eating less, purging more effectively, or hiding an eating disorder from concerned family members and friends. The sites may glorify extremely thin models and actresses and provide photos of emaciated people for "thinspiration," which has the effect of reinforcing negative, self-destructive body images.

A 2010 study showed that 83 percent of the websites that appeared in search results for such terms as "anorexia" and "support" included pro-ana/pro-mia ideas for dieting and staying thin. Research also indicates that exposure to such websites has a negative impact on the eating behaviors and self-esteem of people who view them. One study found that healthy college women with no history of eating disorders who were exposed to such sites for 1.5 hours reduced their caloric intake—most without even realizing it—during the week following their exposure. They also scored lower on measures of body image and feelings of attractiveness after viewing the pro-ED websites.

Counteracting Pro-Eating Disorders with Pro-Recovery

Given the dangers of pro-ED websites, eating-disorder experts argue that public education is needed to raise awareness of the sites and counteract their effects. The National Eating Disorder Association (NEDA) has worked with major online social networks, such as Facebook and Tumblr, to block pro-ana/pro-mia content, monitor Internet communities dedicated to eating disorders, and provide support and recovery resources for people who need help. NEDA also launched its own social media campaign, Proud2BMe, with a website dedicated to promoting healthy attitudes about food, weight, and body image.

Some eating-disorder experts claim that banning pro-ED websites, blogs, forums, and images may be counterproductive. Since many of these sites are operated by people who have eating disorders, they believe that maintaining an open dialogue and providing support is a better response. The pro-recovery movement aims to counteract the effects of pro-ED materials online by offering an alternative source of understanding and community for people struggling with eating disorders. They work to expose the dangers of websites that make eating disorders seem glamorous or encourage people to employ harmful weight-loss methods. They also combat these negative messages with positive information about treatment, recovery, health, fitness, and self-esteem.

References

1. Bond, Emma. "Virtually Anorexic—Where's the Harm?" Nominet Trust, November 28, 2012.

2. Ekern, Jacquelyn, and Crystal Karges. "The Pro-Recovery Movement Fights the Pro-Ana and Pro-Mia Websites," Eating Disorder Hope, August 14, 2013.

3. Klimek, Amy M. "The Dangers of Pro-ED Websites," Eating Disorder Hope, November 11, 2014.

Part Four

Medical Complications of Eating Disorders

Chapter 25

Overview of Medical Complications of Eating Disorders

Eating disorders have among the highest mortality rates of all mental disorders, killing up to ten percent of their victims. Individuals with eating disorders who use drugs to stimulate vomiting, bowel movement, or urination are in the most danger, as this practice increases the risk of heart failure.

In patients with anorexia, starvation can damage vital organs such as the heart and brain. To protect itself, the body shifts into "slow gear": monthly menstrual periods stop, breathing, pulse, and blood pressure rates drop, and thyroid function slows. Nails and hair become brittle; the skin dries, yellows, and becomes covered with soft hair called "lanugo." Excessive thirst and frequent urination may occur. Dehydration contributes to constipation, and reduced body fat leads to lowered body temperature and the inability to withstand cold.

Mild anemia, swollen joints, reduced muscle mass, and lightheadedness also commonly occur in anorexia. If the disorder becomes severe, patients may lose calcium from their bones, making them brittle and prone to breakage. They may also experience irregular heart rhythms

This chapter includes text excerpted from "Eating Disorders," Western Regional Center (WRC), National Oceanic and Atmospheric Administration (NOAA), May 8, 2017.

and heart failure. In some patients, the brain shrinks, causing personality changes. Fortunately, this condition can be reversed when normal weight is reestablished.

In research supported by the National Institute of Mental Health (NIMH), scientists have found that many patients with anorexia also suffer from other psychiatric illnesses. While the majority have co-occurring clinical depression, others suffer from anxiety, personality, or substance-abuse disorders, and many are at risk for suicide. Obsessive-compulsive disorder (OCD), an illness characterized by repetitive thoughts and behaviors, can also accompany anorexia. Individuals with anorexia are typically compliant in personality but may have sudden outbursts of hostility and anger or become socially withdrawn.

Bulimia nervosa patients—even those of normal weight—can severely damage their bodies by frequent binge eating and purging. In rare instances, binge eating causes the stomach to rupture; purging may result in heart failure due to loss of vital minerals, such as potassium. Vomiting causes other less deadly, but serious problems—the acid in vomit wears down the outer layer of the teeth and can cause scarring on the backs of the hands when fingers are pushed down the throat to induce vomiting. Further, the esophagus becomes inflamed and the glands near the cheeks become swollen. As in anorexia, bulimia may lead to irregular menstrual periods. Interest in sex may also diminish.

Some individuals with bulimia struggle with addictions, including abuse of drugs and alcohol, and compulsive stealing. Like individuals with anorexia, many people with bulimia suffer from clinical depression, anxiety, OCD, and other psychiatric illnesses. These problems, combined with their impulsive tendencies, place them at increased risk for suicidal behavior.

People with binge-eating disorder are usually overweight, so they are prone to the serious medical problems associated with obesity, such as high cholesterol, high blood pressure, and diabetes. Obese individuals also have a higher risk for gallbladder disease, heart disease, and some types of cancer. Research at NIMH and elsewhere has shown that individuals with binge-eating disorder have high rates of co-occurring psychiatric illnesses—especially depression.

Security Concerns

Eating disorders are primarily a medical problem, but anorexia and bulimia do have security overtones. As discussed, both are frequently accompanied by other mood, anxiety, and personality disorders that may be a security concern. According to the American Psychiatric Association (APA), for example, about one-third of those with bulimia also have a substance-abuse problem. From one-third to one-half also have one or more personality disorders, most frequently borderline personality disorder.

Those who suffer from bulimia are typically ashamed of their eating problems and attempt to conceal them. Their binge eating usually occurs in secrecy. Any out-of-control behavior that a person is ashamed of and seeks to conceal is a potential vulnerability of security concern.

Chapter 26

Symptoms and Complications of Binge-Eating Disorder and Bulimia

Chapter Contents

Section 26.1

Complications Associated with Binge-Eating Disorder

This section contains text excerpted from the following sources: Text under the heading "What Is Binge-Eating Disorder?" is excerpted from "Eating Disorders: About More Than Food," National Institute of Mental Health (NIMH), January 24, 2018; Text beginning with the heading "Who Is More Likely to Develop Binge-Eating Disorder?" is excerpted from "Definition and Facts for Binge Eating Disorder," National Institute of Diabetes and Digestive and Kidney Diseases (NIDDK), June 2016.

What Is Binge-Eating Disorder?

People with binge-eating disorder (BED) lose control over their eating. Unlike bulimia nervosa (BN), periods of binge eating are not followed by purging, excessive exercise, or fasting. As a result, people with binge-eating disorder are often overweight or obese.

Symptoms include:

- Eating unusually large amounts of food in a specific amount of time, such as a two-hour period

- Eating fast during binge episodes

- Eating even when full or not hungry

- Eating until uncomfortably full

- Eating alone or in secret to avoid embarrassment

- Feeling distressed, ashamed, or guilty about eating

- Frequent dieting, possibly without weight loss

Who Is More Likely to Develop Binge-Eating Disorder?

Binge-eating disorder can occur in people of average body weight but is more common in people with obesity, particularly severe obesity. However, it is important to note that most people with obesity do not have binge-eating disorder.

Painful childhood experiences—such as family problems and critical comments about your shape, weight, or eating—also are associated with developing binge-eating disorder. Binge-eating disorder also runs in families, and there may be a genetic component as well.

What Other Health Problems Can You Have with Binge-Eating Disorder?

Binge-eating disorder may lead to weight gain and health problems related to obesity. Overweight and obesity are associated with many health problems, including type 2 diabetes, heart disease, and certain types of cancer. People with binge-eating disorder may also have mental-health problems such as depression or anxiety. Some people with binge-eating disorder also have problems with their digestive system, or joint and muscle pain.

Section 26.2

Medical Symptoms and Complications Associated with Bulimia

This section contains text excerpted from the following sources: Text under the heading "What Is Bulimia Nervosa?" is excerpted from "Eating Disorders: About More Than Food," National Institute of Mental Health (NIMH), January 24, 2018; Text beginning with the heading "Who Is at Risk for Bulimia?" is excerpted from "Bulimia Nervosa," Office on Women's Health (OWH), U.S. Department of Health and Human Services (HHS), August 28, 2018.

What Is Bulimia Nervosa?

People with bulimia nervosa (BN) have recurrent episodes of eating unusually large amounts of food and feeling a lack of control over these episodes. This binge eating is followed by behaviors that compensate for the overeating, such as forced vomiting, excessive use of laxatives or diuretics, fasting, excessive exercise, or a combination of these behaviors. Unlike those with anorexia nervosa (AN), people with bulimia nervosa may maintain a normal weight or be overweight.

Symptoms include:

- Chronically inflamed and sore throat

- Swollen salivary glands in the neck and jaw area

- Worn tooth enamel and increasingly sensitive and decaying teeth (a result of exposure to stomach acid)

- Acid reflux disorder and other gastrointestinal problems

- Intestinal distress and irritation from laxative abuse

- Severe dehydration from purging

- Electrolyte imbalance (too low or too high levels of sodium, calcium, potassium, and other minerals), which can lead to stroke or heart attack

Who Is at Risk for Bulimia?

Bulimia affects more women than men. It affects up to two percent of women and happens to women of all races and ethnicities.

Bulimia affects more girls and younger women than older women. On average, women develop bulimia at 18 or 19. Teen girls between 15 and 19 and young women in their early 20s are most at risk. But eating disorders are happening more often in older women. In a study, 13 percent of American women over 50 had signs of an eating disorder.

How Does Bulimia Affect a Woman's Health?

Purging through vomiting or taking laxatives can prevent your body from getting the important nutrients it needs from food. Over time, bulimia can affect your body in the following ways:

- Stomach damage from overeating

- Electrolyte imbalance (having levels of sodium, potassium, or other minerals that are too high or too low, which can lead to heart attack or heart failure)

- Ulcers and other damage to your throat from vomiting

- Irregular periods or not having periods, which can cause problems getting pregnant

- Tooth decay from vomiting

- Dehydration

- Problems having bowel movements or damage to the intestines from laxative abuse

Long-term studies of 20 years or more show that women who had an eating disorder in the past usually reach and maintain a healthy weight after treatment.

How Does Bulimia Affect Pregnancy?

Bulimia can cause problems getting pregnant and during pregnancy. Repeated purging and binging can make your menstrual cycle irregular (your period comes some months but not others) or your period may stop for several months. Irregular or missing periods mean you may not ovulate, or release an egg from the ovary, every month. This can make it difficult to get pregnant. However, if you do not want to have children right now and you have sex, you should use birth control.

Bulimia can also cause problems during pregnancy. Bulimia raises your risk for:

- Miscarriage (pregnancy loss)

- Premature birth (also called preterm birth), or childbirth before 37 weeks of pregnancy

- Delivery by cesarean section (C-section)

- Having a low-birth-weight baby (less than five pounds, eight ounces at birth)

- Having a baby with a birth defect

- Depression after the baby is born (postpartum depression)

Chapter 27

Eating Disorders and Pregnancy Complications

Hormones can affect a woman's emotions and moods in different ways throughout her lifetime. Sometimes the impact on mood can affect a woman's quality of life (QOL). This is true for most women. But women with a mental health condition may have other symptoms related to their menstrual cycles or menopause. Throughout all these stages, you can learn ways to help your mental and reproductive health.

How Does My Mental-Health Condition Affect My Menstrual Cycle?

Throughout your monthly menstrual cycle, levels of certain hormones rise and fall. These hormone levels can affect how you think and feel mentally and physically. Mental-health conditions can cause period problems or make some period problems worse:

- **Premenstrual syndrome (PMS).** Most women have some symptoms of PMS in the week or two before their period. PMS can cause bloating, headaches, and moodiness. Women with depression or anxiety disorders may experience worse symptoms

This chapter includes text excerpted from "Reproductive Health and Mental Health," Office on Women's Health (OWH), U.S. Department of Health and Human Services (HHS), August 28, 2018.

of PMS. Also, many women seeking treatment for PMS have depression or anxiety. Symptoms of these mental-health conditions are similar to symptoms of PMS and may get worse before or during your period. Talk to your doctor or nurse about ways to relieve PMS symptoms.

- **Premenstrual dysphoric disorder (PMDD).** PMDD is a condition similar to PMS but with more severe symptoms, including severe depression, irritability, and tension. Symptoms of PMDD can be so difficult to manage that your daily life is disrupted. PMDD is more common in women with anxiety or depression. Talk to your doctor about ways to help if you experience worse symptoms of depression or anxiety around your period.

- **Irregular periods.** Studies show that women with anxiety disorder or substance-use disorder are more likely to have shorter menstrual cycles (shorter than 24 days). Irregular cycles are also linked to eating disorders and depression. Women with bipolar disorder are also twice as likely to have irregular periods.

How Do Mental-Health Conditions Affect Pregnancy?

Changing hormones during pregnancy can cause mental-health conditions that have been treated in the past to come back (this is called a relapse). Women with mental-health conditions are also at higher risk of problems during pregnancy.

- **Eating disorders.** Women with eating disorders may experience relapses during pregnancy, which can cause miscarriage, premature birth (birth before 37 weeks of pregnancy), and low birth weight.

- **Depression.** Depression is the most common mental-health condition during pregnancy. How long symptoms last and how often they happen are different for each woman. Women who are depressed during pregnancy have a greater risk of depression after giving birth, called postpartum depression. If you take medicine for depression, stopping your medicine when you become pregnant can cause your depression to come back.

- **Bipolar disorder.** Women may experience relief from symptoms of bipolar disorder during pregnancy, but they are at very high risk of a relapse of symptoms in the weeks after pregnancy.

Women with anxiety disorders and obsessive-compulsive disorder (OCD) are more likely to have a relapse during and after pregnancy. Talk to your doctor or nurse about your mental-health condition and your symptoms. Do not stop any prescribed medicines without first talking to your doctor or nurse. Not using medicine that you need may hurt you or your baby.

Will My Mental-Health Condition Affect My Chances of Getting Pregnant?

Maybe. Certain mental-health conditions can make it harder to get pregnant:

- Eating disorders can affect your menstrual cycle. The extreme weight loss that happens with anorexia can cause you to miss your menstrual periods. If you have bulimia, your menstrual cycle may be irregular, or your period may stop for several months. Both of these period problems can affect whether you ovulate. Not ovulating regularly can make it harder to get pregnant. Also, the longer you have an eating disorder, the higher the risk that you will face some type of problem getting pregnant.

- Depression, anxiety, and stress can also affect the hormones that control ovulation. This could make it difficult for a woman to become pregnant.

If you are having problems getting pregnant, the stress, worry, or sadness can make your mental-health condition worse. Talk to your doctor or nurse about your feelings. Treatment for your mental-health condition helps both you and your chances of having a baby. During pregnancy, it can also lower your baby's chances of developing depression or other mental-health conditions later in life.

Can I Continue to Take My Medicine If I'm Trying to Get Pregnant?

Maybe. Some medicines, such as antidepressants, may make it more difficult for you to get pregnant. Also, some medicines may not be safe to take during pregnancy or when trying to get pregnant. Talk to your doctor or nurse about other treatments for mental-health conditions, such as depression, that don't involve medicine.

Women who are already taking an antidepressant and who are trying to get pregnant should talk to their doctor or nurse about the benefits and risks of stopping the medicine. Some women who have been diagnosed with severe depression may need to keep taking their prescribed medicine during pregnancy. If you are unsure whether to take your medicine, talk to your doctor or nurse.

Talk therapy is one way to help women with depression. This type of therapy has no risks for women who are trying to get pregnant. During talk therapy, you work with a mental-health professional to explore why you are depressed and train yourself to replace negative thoughts with positive ones. Certain mental-healthcare professionals specialize in depression related to infertility.

Regular physical activity is another safe and healthy option for most women who are trying to get pregnant. Exercise can help with symptoms such as depression, difficulty concentrating, and fatigue.

Is My Medicine Safe to Take during Pregnancy or Breastfeeding?

It depends on the medicine. Some medicines can be taken safely during pregnancy or while you are breastfeeding, but others are not safe. Your doctor or nurse can help you decide. It is best to discuss these medicines with your doctor or nurse before you ever become pregnant.

How Does the Time before Menopause (Perimenopause) Affect My Mental Health?

As you approach menopause, certain levels of hormones in your body begin to change. This initial transition to menopause when you still get a period is called perimenopause. During perimenopause, some women begin to feel symptoms such as intense heat and sweating ("hot flashes"), trouble sleeping, and changing moods.

As you get closer to menopause, you may notice other symptoms, such as pain during sex, urinary problems, and irregular periods. These changes can be stressful on you and your relationships and cause you to feel more extreme emotions.

Women with mental-health conditions may experience more symptoms of menopause or go through perimenopause differently than women who do not have mental health conditions.

- Women with depression are more likely to go through perimenopause earlier than other women. Studies show that women with depression have lower levels of estrogen.

- Bipolar disorder symptoms may get worse during perimenopause.

- Insomnia affects up to half of the women going through menopause. Insomnia may be more common in women with anxiety or depression.

- Menopause can cause a relapse of OCD or a change in symptoms.

What Steps Can I Take to Stay Mentally Healthy throughout Life?

Steps you can take to support good mental health include the following:

- **Choose healthy foods most of the time.** Getting the right nutrients, including enough fiber, and staying hydrated can help you feel better physically and can boost your mood.

- **Get enough sleep.** Good sleep helps you stay in good mental health. If pregnancy or your menopause symptoms, such as hot flashes, are keeping you awake at night, talk to a doctor or nurse about treatments that can help.

- **Get enough physical activity.** Exercise may help prevent or treat some mental-health conditions. Researchers know that physical activity or exercise can help many people with mental-health conditions, including depression, anxiety, schizophrenia, bipolar disorder, posttraumatic stress disorder (PTSD), eating disorders, and substance-abuse disorders. Exercise alone does not usually treat or cure mental-health conditions, but combined with other treatments like therapy or medicine, it can make your symptoms less severe.

- **Take your medicines.** If you take medicines for a mental-health condition, don't stop without first talking to your doctor or nurse. Once you go through menopause, medicines may work differently for you. They may not be as effective or may have different or worse side effects. Talk to your doctor or nurse about whether you need to switch medicines.

- **Keep a support network.** Whether you talk to friends, family, or a therapist, stay in good communication with people who know you well. Ask for help if you need it.

- **Stay involved as you get older.** Retirement can be a positive opportunity for change, but it can also be stressful. You may miss going to work each day. Having a chronic disease like diabetes or heart disease may change how much you see friends and family. Find opportunities for volunteering, social activities such as golf or community gardening, or even part-time work to stay connected to others and your community.

Chapter 28

Eating Disorders and Oral Health

Dental and oral health are important components of an individual's overall health and well-being. Eating disorders (EDs) can have deleterious consequences for dental and oral health. Individuals with eating disorders may experience several oral manifestations arising from nutritional deficiencies and resulting metabolic impairment. Oral manifestations of EDs may also be caused by drug use, poor personal hygiene, altered nutritional habits, and other psychological disturbances associated with EDs. The tissues usually affected include the oral mucosa, periodontium (the supporting tissues that anchor the teeth to the maxillary and mandibular bones [upper and lower jawbones]), teeth, salivary glands, and perioral area (the soft tissue around the mouth).

General Signs and Symptoms of Dental and Oral Implications of Eating Disorders

- Changes in color, size, and shape of teeth often resulting in brittle, translucent teeth

- Increased sensitivity to extreme temperatures

"Eating Disorders and Oral Health," © 2019 Omnigraphics. Reviewed December 2018.

- Exposed, infected pulp tissue, sometimes, leading to pulpitis (inflammation of dental pulp tissue) and finally to pulp death

Oral Sequelae of Bulimia and Anorexia Nervosa

Chronic self-induced vomiting, a classic symptom of bulimia and anorexia nervosa, is one of the most important etiologies of oral complications associated with the disorders. The severity of oral complications depends largely on the duration of the disease, the frequency of vomiting, and the fundamental quality of the dentition. Tooth erosion, or perimylolysis in medical parlance, is one of the most serious consequences of the binge–purge cycle. At the onset, there is a subtle loss of the tooth enamel—the hard, mineralized outer layer of a tooth that serves as a barrier against food, drinks, and microorganisms. Over time, regular exposure of the dentition to acidic content regurgitated from the stomach during purging begins to wear away the dentine—the dense and calcified bony tissue beneath the enamel.

Tooth erosion may manifest as early as six months following the onset of regular self-induced vomiting, but a definitive diagnosis confirming the lesions associated with EDs may take a year or more. These lesions typically occur in the maxillary teeth. They also occur on the mandibular teeth, albeit to a lesser degree since the tongue protects the lower jaw dentition from acid attack. In addition to acid exposure, mechanical degradation of the dentine is also present, resulting from the abnormal tongue movements and disrupted swallowing patterns characteristic of EDs.

Other oral complications of EDs include tooth decay, gingivitis (non-destructive gum disease), and xerostomia (drying of the oral cavity). Poor oral hygiene and ingestion of high-carbohydrate food and carbonated beverages characteristic of binge-eating episodes cause dental caries (tooth decay). Gum disease results from the exposure of gum tissue to the low-pH gastric content during purging. Volitional purging can also cause enlargement of the salivary glands. This manifests as a swelling of the area between the neck and jaw and is sometimes identifiable by what is commonly described as the "chipmunk cheeks." While this condition may be intermittent during the initial days of purging, it often becomes persistent after a considerable period of purging and results in reduced salivary secretion and xerostomia. While the exact mechanism of salivary-gland enlargement is not clear, this condition presents in over 50 percent of patients with self-induced vomiting, and is seen to regress spontaneously with cessation of the purging. Rapid ingestion of large amounts of food and forced regurgitation may also injure the oral mucosa (the mucous membranes that line the inside of the mouth) and the pharynx. In some cases, the soft palate may be injured by fingers or other objects used to induce vomiting.

Awareness of the fact that volitional purging strongly associated with bulimia nervosa has serious oral and dental implications is evident, but the fact that anorexia nervosa can be just as detrimental to dental health is less widely known. Individuals suffering from anorexia may also engage in inappropriate compensatory methods such as self-induced purging to prevent weight gain. In this subtype of anorexia, individuals may purge after binge eating, or even following ingestion of small amounts of food. In addition to purging, most people with an anorexia disorder also engage in restrictive eating in an effort to maintain their abnormally low body weight. Nutritional deficiencies associated with the semi-starvation that is typical of anorexia can also have devastating consequences on health in general. Anorexics may develop osteoporosis and experience weakening of the jawbone, which could lead to weakening of teeth and subsequent tooth loss. Studies also show a correlation between osteoporosis and progression of periodontal (gum) disease in EDs. Periodontitis is a chronic inflammatory condition involving the soft tissues surrounding the teeth. It usually begins as gingivitis a mild inflammation of the gums caused by a bacterial infection. Over time, those bacterial toxins work together with the body's natural immune response to infection to break down the bone and connective tissue that hold the teeth in place. This may progress at an accelerated pace if the density of bone affected by periodontitis is already suboptimal as a result of the effect of osteoporosis in EDs.

Dental Management in Eating Disorders

Dentists and dental hygienists are among the first healthcare professionals to detect clinical signs of EDs. If oral healthcare professionals suspect oral manifestations of EDs, it is recommended that they subject their patients to a preliminary screening in a nonconfrontational manner. Discussing the patient's eating habits and recommending weight-management strategies after creating an environment conducive to patient–physician interaction is paramount. This may help open up a line of communication with the patient during subsequent visits and may lead to referrals.

Ideally, individuals with EDs require continuous care and support for managing their oral health. Diagnosis of dental and oral complications are based on external examination and imaging studies of the hard and soft tissues of the oral cavity. Patients should also be encouraged to return for further evaluation and follow-up treatment. Regarding dental treatment involving complex restorative or prosthodontic procedures, clinical authorities recommend that it is initiated only after the cessation of the binge–purge cycle and after the underlying psychiatric components of the disorder have been adequately stabilized. This, however, does not include pain palliation.

Interim measures to arrest further destruction of the tooth structure include:

- Professional dental care on a regular basis and topical fluoride application to reduce thermal hypersensitivity and prevent further erosion

- Rigorous hygiene and home care, including daily application of fluoride gel or prescription fluoride dental paste to promote remineralization of enamel

- Gum or lozenges to stimulate saliva secretion; or artificial saliva, to treat severe xerostomia

- Mouthwash immediately after vomiting to neutralize acids and protect tooth surfaces

Role of Dental Professionals in Identifying Eating Disorders

Pediatric dentists and orthodontists usually monitor their patients throughout childhood and adolescence and, therefore, play an important role in the early detection of EDs—a crucial factor in aiding recovery and reducing the morbidity and mortality associated with EDs. Hence, it is very important for these dental professionals to pick up clinical clues of EDs from dental examination and radiographs and then utilize them to make referrals for appropriate healthcare services. These service providers can facilitate management of the underlying psychiatric condition.

It is widely perceived that dental professionals are the first to observe the overt health effects of EDs. Yet studies show that this does not always lead to early diagnosis and intervention for EDs. A lack of knowledge about the scope and severity of EDs among oral-health professionals, lack of skilled training in patient communication, and lack of practice protocol are often seen as barriers to the identification and referral treatment of EDs.

References

1. "Oral Health Fact Sheet for Dental Professionals—Adults with Eating Disorders," University of Washington School of Dentistry, August 17, 2010.

2. "Eating Disorders and Oral Health: A Review of the Literature," *Australian Dental Journal*, 2005.

Chapter 29

Anorexia Nervosa and Osteoporosis

What Is Anorexia Nervosa?

Anorexia nervosa (AN) is an eating disorder characterized by an irrational fear of weight gain. People with anorexia nervosa believe that they are overweight even when they are extremely thin.

Individuals with anorexia become obsessed with food and severely restrict their dietary intake. The disease is associated with several health problems and, in rare cases, even death. The disorder may begin as early as the onset of puberty. The first menstrual period is typically delayed in girls who have anorexia when they reach puberty. For girls who have already reached puberty when they develop anorexia, menstrual periods are often infrequent or absent.

What Is Osteoporosis?

Osteoporosis is a condition in which the bones become less dense and more likely to fracture. Fractures from osteoporosis can result in significant pain and disability. In the United States, more than 53 million people either already have osteoporosis or are at high risk due to low bone mass.

This chapter includes text excerpted from "What People with Anorexia Nervosa Need to Know about Osteoporosis," NIH Osteoporosis and Related Bone Diseases ~ National Resource Center (NIH ORBD~NRC), April 2016.

Risk factors for developing osteoporosis include:

- Thinness or small frame
- Family history of the disease
- Being postmenopausal and particularly having had early menopause
- Abnormal absence of menstrual periods (amenorrhea)
- Prolonged use of certain medications, such as those used to treat lupus, asthma, thyroid deficiencies, and seizures
- Low calcium intake
- Lack of physical activity
- Smoking
- Excessive alcohol intake

Osteoporosis often can be prevented. It is known as a silent disease because, if undetected, bone loss can progress for many years without symptoms until a fracture occurs. Osteoporosis has been called a childhood disease with old age consequences because building healthy bones in youth helps prevent osteoporosis and fractures later in life. However, it is never too late to adopt new habits for healthy bones.

The Link between Anorexia Nervosa and Osteoporosis

Anorexia nervosa has significant physical consequences. Affected individuals can experience nutritional and hormonal problems that negatively impact bone density. Low body weight in females can cause the body to stop producing estrogen, resulting in a condition known as amenorrhea, or absent menstrual periods. Low estrogen levels contribute to significant losses in bone density.

In addition, individuals with anorexia often produce excessive amounts of the adrenal hormone cortisol, which is known to trigger bone loss. Other problems, such as a decrease in the production of growth hormone and other growth factors, low body weight (apart from the estrogen loss it causes), calcium deficiency, and malnutrition, may contribute to bone loss in girls and women with anorexia. Weight loss, restricted dietary intake, and testosterone deficiency may be responsible for the low bone density found in males with the disorder.

Studies suggest that low bone mass is common in people with anorexia and that it occurs early in the course of the disease. Girls with anorexia may be less likely to reach their peak bone density, and therefore, may be at increased risk for osteoporosis and fracture throughout life.

Osteoporosis-Management Strategies

Up to one-third of peak bone density is achieved during puberty. Anorexia is often identified during mid to late adolescence, a critical period for bone development. The longer the duration of the disorder, the greater the bone loss and the less likely it is that bone mineral density will ever return to normal. The primary goal of medical therapy for individuals with anorexia is weight gain and, in females, the return of normal menstrual periods. However, attention to other aspects of bone health is also important.

Nutrition: A well-balanced diet rich in calcium and vitamin D is important for healthy bones. Good sources of calcium include low-fat dairy products; dark green, leafy vegetables; and calcium-fortified foods and beverages. Supplements can help ensure that people get adequate amounts of calcium each day, especially in people with a proven milk allergy. The Institute of Medicine (IOM) recommends a daily calcium intake of 1,000 mg (milligrams) for men and women up to age 50. Women over age 50 and men over age 70 should increase their intake to 1,200 mg daily.

Vitamin D plays an important role in calcium absorption and bone health. Food sources of vitamin D include egg yolks, saltwater fish, and liver. Many people may need vitamin D supplements to achieve the recommended intake of 600 to 800 international units (IU) each day.

Exercise: Like muscle, bone is living tissue that responds to exercise by becoming stronger. The best activity for your bones is weight-bearing exercise that forces you to work against gravity. Some examples include walking, climbing stairs, lifting weights, and dancing.

Although walking and other types of regular exercise can help prevent bone loss and provide many other health benefits, these potential benefits need to be weighed against the risk of fractures, delayed weight gain, and exercise-induced amenorrhea in people with anorexia and those recovering from the disorder.

Healthy lifestyle: Smoking is bad for bones as well as the heart and lungs. In addition, smokers may absorb less calcium from their diets. Alcohol also can have a negative effect on bone health. Those who drink heavily are more prone to bone loss and fracture, because of both poor nutrition and increased risk of falling.

Bone density test: A bone mineral density (BMD) test measures bone density in various parts of the body. This safe and painless test can detect osteoporosis before a fracture occurs and can predict one's chances of fracturing in the future. The BMD test can help determine whether medication should be considered.

Medication: There is no cure for osteoporosis. However, medications are available to prevent and treat the disease in postmenopausal women, men, and both women and men taking glucocorticoid medication.

Part Five

Recognizing and Treating Eating Disorders

Chapter 30

Physiological Symptoms and Warning Signs

Anorexia Nervosa

The major symptoms of anorexia nervosa are:

- Emaciation (extremely thin from lack of nutrition)
- Relentless pursuit of thinness; unwilling to maintain a normal or healthy weight
- Distorted body image; intense fear of gaining weight
- Lack of menstruation among girls and women
- Repeatedly weighing her- or himself
- Portioning food carefully, eating only small amounts of only certain foods
- Excessive exercise, self-induced vomiting, misuse of laxatives, diuretics, or enemas

Other symptoms that may develop over time:

- Thinning bones
- Brittle hair and nails

This chapter includes text excerpted from "Symptoms and Warning Signs," MedlinePlus, National Institutes of Health (NIH), 2008. Reviewed December 2018.

- Dry, yellowish skin
- Growth of fine hair over the body
- Mild anemia and muscle weakness and loss
- Severe constipation
- Low blood pressure, slowed breathing, and pulse
- Feeling cold all the time
- Lethargy

Bulimia Nervosa

The major symptoms of bulimia nervosa are:

- Frequently eating large amounts of food (binge eating)
- Feeling a lack of control over the eating
- Compensating for binge eating with self-induced vomiting, misuse of laxatives and diuretics, fasting, and excessive exercise
- Binging and purging in secret; feelings of shame and disgust
- Intensely unhappy with body size and shape despite normal height and weight

Other symptoms include:

- Chronically inflamed and sore throat
- Swollen glands in neck and below jaw
- Worn tooth enamel from exposure to stomach acids
- Gastroesophageal reflux disorder
- Intestinal distress from laxative abuse
- Kidney problems from diuretic abuse
- Severe dehydration from purging

Binge-Eating Disorder

The symptoms of binge-eating disorder are:

- Frequently eating large amounts of food (binge eating)
- Feeling unable to control the eating behavior
- Feelings of guilt, shame, and/or distress about the behavior, which can lead to more binge eating

Chapter 31

Confronting a Person with an Eating Disorder

Chapter Contents

Section 31.1

How to Approach a Loved One You Suspect May Have an Eating Disorder

"How to Approach a Loved One You Suspect May Have an Eating Disorder," © 2019 Omnigraphics. Reviewed December 2018.

Eating disorders are serious mental issues that need to be addressed promptly. Every year, thousands of teens and adults develop some sort of disordered-eating behavior—either by eating too much or too little—and for various reasons. Such abnormal eating behaviors, left untreated, can affect the physical, mental, and social health of the person. Sometimes, the consequences may even be fatal. So, if you suspect that someone is suffering from an eating disorder, approach the person immediately and take all the necessary steps to get her or him help.

Signs and Symptoms of Eating Disorders

Eating disorders can strike anyone irrespective of age, gender, and race. People with eating problems often fail to realize or refuse to accept that they have a problem. However, certain behavioral changes may suggest that a person has an eating disorder. These include:

- Talking too much about food, diet, calories, and weight loss
- Following highly restrictive diet patterns such as having only raw vegetables, oats, clear soup, and so on
- Always coming up with an excuse for skipping meals
- Avoiding having meals with or in front of others
- Cutting food into small pieces and moving it around on the plate while eating
- Exercising too often, even when feeling tired or unwell
- Taking pride in eating too little and being too skinny
- Gaining a lot of weight in spite of eating too little
- Going to bathroom very often
- Vomiting or having a vomiting sensation soon after the meals
- Taking laxatives or diet pills frequently

- Being very sensitive and defensive about his or her eating habits

- Wearing overly large and baggy clothes to hide the body

You may also look for the following signs and symptoms in the person you suspect may have an eating disorder:

- Fear and anxiety

- Stress

- Sleeping problems

- Dizziness

- Dry skin and hair

- Thinning of hair

- Dental problems such as cavities and discoloration of teeth

- Muscle weakness

- Stomach cramps

- Irregular menstrual cycles in women

Strategies for Approaching a Loved One with an Eating Disorder

People with eating disorders may not open up about their problems because they tend to feel a lot of shame and embarrassment. They may respond to you with anger or denial when you approach them. So, handling someone you suspect may have an eating disorder requires a high level of patience and sensitivity. It is better to approach than to confront them.

Here are some do's and don'ts for approaching your loved one with eating disorders.

Do's

- Educate yourself about eating disorders before you approach the person.

- The person may respond in a harsh way. Be prepared to face it.

- Choose a calm and caring environment in which to start the conversation.

- Provide enough time and space for the person to open up.

- Listen patiently when your loved one speaks.

- Let your loved one pour her or his heart out. This will allow your loved one to get rid of the stress and feel better.

- Ask comforting questions such as:

  - How can I help you?

  - What would make you feel better?

- Encourage the person to seek help/treatment.

- Assure the person that you will be happy to help her or him at any time.

- Know your limits.

- Respect the privacy of the person.

Don'ts

- Do not judge the person based on their eating behaviors.

- Do not blame or shame the person. Having an eating disorder is not completely their fault.

- Avoid approaching the person while having meals. She or he may already be stressed at that time.

- Avoid food policing. Giving instructions regarding what to eat and when to eat it can make the person feel guilty and depressed.

- Do not be watchful of the food habits and choices of the person.

- Do not comment on her or his body weight, shape, and appearance.

- Do not try to get the person out of the problem forcefully. Resolving eating disorders usually takes time and your pressure may increase stress and prolong the issue.

How to Help

Eating disorders are complex mental issues. Their causes and symptoms may vary from person to person and they rarely get better on their own. Hence, professional and individualized treatments are required to cure eating disorders. When you are aware that your loved one is suffering from an eating disorder, convince the person to seek the help of a medical doctor. The doctor may provide references to other professionals such as counselors, psychologists, or psychiatrists who can help with overcoming the disorder. Also, help the person join support groups in which she or he can network with other people experiencing eating disorders and share their experiences.

References

1. "About Eating Disorders," TeensHealth, September 2014.

2. "I Think My Friend Has an Eating Disorder," Newbridge, October 14, 2008.

3. Hamel, Sarah-Eve. "Some Do's and Don'ts for Confronting a Loved One with Suspected Binge Eating Disorder," Walden, September 10, 2018.

4. "What to Say and Do," National Eating Disorders Collaboration (NEDC), April 10, 2014.

Section 31.2

How to Approach Your Student: A Guide for Teachers

"How to Approach Your Student: A Guide for Teachers,"
© 2019 Omnigraphics. Reviewed December 2018.

Since children and young teens spend much of their day in schools, a teacher may be the first person to notice the warning signs of eating disorders among students. So, it is important for every teacher to be aware of the different signs and symptoms of eating disorders. A teacher should also be able to approach students with abnormal eating behaviors in the right way and provide them proper support to overcome the problem.

School-Specific Signs and Symptoms of Eating Disorders

Eating disorders can be identified by various physical and behavioral changes. If a student consistently exhibits some of the following symptoms, this may be a matter of concern.

- Change in attitude
- Lack of focus in the classroom
- Difficulty in sitting still in the classroom
- Depreciation in academic performance and grades
- Avoiding friends and staying isolated
- Making excuses to avoid having food with friends
- Pretending to be busy during lunch breaks
- Sudden weight loss or weight gain
- Exercising for long periods
- Wearing large or baggy clothes to hide her or his body
- Avoiding activities such as swimming that involve undressing
- Complaining about abdominal pain, bloating, and nausea
- Frequent bathroom use
- Visiting the school nurse too often

Strategies to Approach Students with Eating Disorders

Here is a list of strategies and approaches that teachers may use to handle students with eating disorders.

- Have a good and friendly rapport with the student
- Make the student feel comfortable in your presence
- Encourage the student to share his or her fears and anxieties
- Be in constant touch with the parents and inform the activities of the student

- Be flexible with the student in terms of completing homework and academic performance.

- Motivate the student constantly and offer positive feedback.

- Appreciate every little achievement of the student. Discuss the concerns of the student in private and not in front of the class.

- Do not comment on the student's food habits, body image, or appearance.

- Also, do not allow other students to do so.

- Do not let other students tease or shame students with eating disorders.

- Encourage the student to mingle with peers.

- Teach the student about realistic body images.

- Be aware of any hyper risk-taking behavior and make sure your student is not involved in such risk-taking activities.

How to Help Students with Eating Disorders

- Arrange a comfortable eating location for the student in the school so that she or he can have food alone.

- Provide an extended time period in which the student can eat.

- Allow the student to have food between classes, if required.

- Provide the student with a comfortable classroom seating arrangement near supportive peers.

- Allow the student to have supportive peer partners during group activities.

- Give advance notice of tests, assignments, and projects

- Have frequent discussions about the activities of the student with the students' parents and the school nurse.

- Provide opportunities for the student to join support groups in which the student can network with other people experiencing eating disorders and share their experiences.

References

1. Vargas, Erika. "Helping Your Students in Eating Disorder Recovery Thrive at School," Walden, September 10, 2018.

2. "Eating Disorder Strategies," Ontario Teachers' Federation (OTF), November 3, 2013.

3. Alexander, June. "A Lesson for Teachers in Addressing the Eating Disorder Bully," National Eating Disorders Association (NEDA), July 8, 2013.

Chapter 32

Diagnosing Eating Disorders

Chapter Contents

Section 32.1

Diagnostic Criteria for Eating Disorders

This section includes text excerpted from "DSM-5
Changes: Implications for Child Serious Emotional
Disturbance," Substance Abuse and Mental Health
Services Administration (SAMHSA), June 2016.

Anorexia nervosa (AN) is an eating disorder characterized by an intense fear of gaining weight and the refusal to maintain a minimally normal body weight. Individuals with anorexia also exhibit a misperception of body shape and/or size. There have been several *Diagnostic and Statistical Manual of Mental Disorders, 5th Edition* (DSM-5) criteria changes. In *Diagnostic and Statistical Manual of Mental Disorders, 4th Edition* (DSM-IV), a diagnosis of anorexia nervosa was excluded if the patient maintained bodyweight at or above the 85th percentile for her or his height/age. In DSM-5 this criterion is similar, but adds sex, developmental norms, and physical health and uses body mass index data. The DSM-5 adds "persistent behavior that interferes with weight gain" as an added way to meet a criterion. The DSM-5 does not include criteria on menstruating females' absence of three consecutive menses, as the DSM-IV does. The restrictive type and binge-eating/purging types differ in that DSM-IV specifies "during the current episode" and DSM-5 specifies "during the past three months." The DSM-5 adds criteria for partial and full remission, while the DSM-IV does not include this information. Data from a United States sample of 215 youth 8 to 21 years enrolled as new patients with eating disorders in six clinics showed an increase from 30 to 40 percent in anorexia nervosa when comparing DSM-IV and DSM-5 criteria. Table 32.1 shows a comparison between DSM-IV and DSM-5 for anorexia nervosa.

Bulimia nervosa is an eating disorder characterized by binge eating followed by inappropriate compensatory behaviors designed to prevent weight gain. In addition, the self-evaluation of individuals with bulimia nervosa is excessively influenced by weight and body shape. The major change in criteria for diagnosis of bulimia nervosa is reducing the binge frequency threshold from twice per week in DSM-IV to once per week in DSM-5. The other differences include the DSM-IV differentiating between purging and nonpurging type (the DSM-5 does not) and the DSM-5 specifying criteria for partial remission, full remission, and severity, while the DSM-IV does not. DSM-IV to DSM-5 criteria changes may increase the prevalence rate.

Table 32.1. DSM-IV to DSM-5 Anorexia Nervosa Comparison

DSM-IV	DSM-5
Disorder Class: Eating Disorders	Disorder Class: Feeding and Eating Disorders
A. Refusal to maintain bodyweight at or above minimally normal weight for height/age (less than 85th percentile).	A. Restriction of energy intake relative to requirements, leading to a significant low body weight in the context of the age, sex, developmental trajectory, and physical health(less than minimally normal/expected[1]).
B. Intense fear of gaining weight or becoming obese, even though underweight.	B. Intense fear of gaining weight or becoming fat or persistent behavior that interferes with weight gain.
C. Disturbed by one's body weight or shape, self-worth influenced by body weight or shape, or persistent lack of recognition of seriousness of low bodyweight.	SAME
D. In menstruating females, absence of at least 3 consecutive nonsynthetically induced menstrual cycles.	DROPPED
Specify type: Restricting type: During the current episode, has not regularly engaged in binge-eating or purging.	Specified whether: Restricting type: During the last 3 months…SAME.
Binge-eating/purging type: During the current episode, has regularly engaged in binge-eating or purging[2].	Binge-eating/purging type: During the last 3 months…SAME. Partial remission: After full criteria met, low bodyweight has not been met for sustained period, BUT at least one of the following two criteria still met: Intense fear of gaining weight/ becoming obese or behavior that interferes with weight gain OR Disturbed by weight and shape. Full remission: After full criteria met, none of the criteria met for sustained period of time.

[1]*Severity is based on body mass index (BMI) derived from World Health Organization (WHO) categories for thinness in adults; corresponding percentiles should be used for children and adolescents: Mild: BMI greater than or equal to 17 kg/m2, Moderate: BMI 16 to 16.99 kg/m2, Severe: BMI 15 to 15.99 kg/m2, Extreme: BMI less than 15 kg/m2. [2]Purging is self-induced vomiting or misuse of laxatives, diuretics, or enemas.*

Data from an Australian cohort study of 2,822 adolescents and young adults (57.0 percent female) whose parents were recruited from ante-natal clinics at a single hospital and followed through age 20, indicate that rates of bulimia nervosa are higher when applying the DSM-5 criteria versus the DSM-IV. Similarly, data from a United States sample of 215 youth 8 to 21 years enrolled as new patients with eating disorders in six clinics showed an increase in bulimia nervosa from 7.3 percent to 11.8 percent when comparing DSM-IV and DSM-5 criteria. Table 32.2 shows a comparison between DSM-IV and DSM-5 for bulimia nervosa.

Table 32.2. DSM-IV to DSM-5 Bulimia Nervosa Comparison

DSM-IV	DSM-5
Disorder Class: Eating Disorders	Disorder Class: Feeding and Eating Disorders
A. Recurrent episodes of binge eating, as characterized by both: 1. Eating, within any 2-hour period, an amount of food that is definitively larger than what most individuals would eat in a similar period of time under similar circumstances. 2. A feeling that one cannot stop eating or control what or how much one is eating.	SAME
B. Recurrent inappropriate compensatory behaviors in order to prevent weight gain such as self-induced vomiting; misuse of laxatives, diuretics, or other medications; fasting or excessive exercise.	SAME
C. The binge eating and inappropriate compensatory behaviors occur, on average, at least twice a week for three months.	C. The binge eating and inappropriate compensatory behaviors occur, on average, at least once a week for three months.
D. Self-evaluation is unjustifiability influenced by body shape and weight.	SAME

Table 32.2. Continued

DSM-IV	DSM-5
E. The disturbance does not occur exclusively during episodes of anorexia nervosa.	SAME.
Specify type: Purging type: During the current episode, the person has regularly engaged in self-induced vomiting or the misuse of laxatives, diuretics, or enemas. Nonpurging Type: During the current episode, the person has used inappropriate compensatory behaviors, such as fasting or excessive exercise, but has not regularly engaged in self-induced vomiting or the misuse of laxatives, diuretics, or enemas.	Not a criterion.
Not a criterion.	Specify if: Partial remission: After full criteria were previously met, some but not all of the criteria have been met for a sustained period of time. Full remission: After full criteria were previously met, none of the criteria have been met for a sustained period of time.
Not a criterion.	Current severity Mild: An average of 1–3 episodes of inappropriate compensatory behaviors per week. Moderate: An average of 4–7 episodes of inappropriate compensatory behaviors per week. Severe: An average of 8–13 episodes of inappropriate compensatory behaviors per week. Extreme: An average of 14 or more episodes of inappropriate compensatory behaviors per week.

The level of severity may be increased to reflect other symptoms and the degree of functional disability.

Binge-eating disorder had been included in DSM-IV as a "criteria set provided for further study," and has been included in DSM-5 as a disorder. This disorder is characterized by binge or out of control eating accompanied by significant distress about eating.

Binge-eating disorder is differentiated from bulimia nervosa in that there are no inappropriate compensatory behaviors (e.g., purging or excessive exercise) seen in binge-eating disorder. As noted previously, this disorder was added into DSM-5 because a significant subset of people presenting with an eating disorder had exhibited binge-eating behaviors that were not accompanied by any behaviors intended to compensate for the binge eating. Changes between the criteria enumerated in DSM-IV and those in DSM-5 are minimal. The only change, which represents a less stringent requirement in DSM-5, reduces the minimum frequency/duration of the binge-eating behavior to at least once a week for three months (it had been at least two days a week for six months). Table 32.3 shows a comparison between DSM-IV and DSM-5 for binge-eating disorder.

Table 32.3. DSM-IV to DSM-5 Binge-Eating Disorder Comparison

DSM-IV	DSM-5
Disorder Class: Criteria Sets and Axes Provided for Further study	Disorder Class: Feeding and Eating Disorders

A. Recurrent episodes of binge eating. An episode of binge eating is characterized by both of the following:
  1. Eating, in a discrete period of time (e.g., within any 2-hour period), an amount of food that is definitely larger than most people would eat in a similar period of time under similar circumstances.
  2. A sense of lack of control over eating during the episode (e.g., a feeling that one cannot stop eating or control what or how much one is eating)
	SAME

B. The binge-eating episodes are associated with three (or more) of the following:
  1. Eating much more rapidly than normal
  2. Eating until feeling uncomfortably full
  3. Eating large amounts of food when not feeling physically hungry
  4. Eating alone because of feeling embarrassed by how much one is eating
  5. Feeling disgusted with oneself, depressed, or very guilty after overeating
	SAME

Table 32.3. Continued

DSM-IV	DSM-5
C. Marked distress regarding binge eating is present.	SAME
D. The binge eating occurs, on average, at least 2 days a week for 6 months. Note: The method of determining frequency differs from that used for bulimia nervosa; future research should address whether the preferred method of setting a frequency threshold is counting the number of days on which binges occur or counting the number of episodes of binge eating.	D. The binge eating occurs, on average, at least once a week for 3 months.
E. The binge eating is not associated with the regular use of inappropriate compensatory behaviors (e.g., purging, fasting, excessive exercise) and does not occur exclusively during the course of anorexia nervosa or bulimia nervosa.	SAME
	Specify if: In partial remission: After full criteria for binge-eating disorder were previously met, binge eating occurs at an average frequency of less than one episode per week for a sustained period of time. In full remission: After full criteria for binge-eating disorder were previously met, none of the criteria have been met for a sustained period of time. Specify current severity: Severity is also noted in the diagnosis, from mild to extreme: Mild: 1–3 binge-eating episodes per week Moderate: 4–7 binge-eating episodes per week Severe: 8–13 binge-eating episodes per week Extreme: 14 or more binge-eating episodes per week

DSM-IV feeding disorder of infancy or early childhood has been renamed avoidant/restrictive food intake disorder, and the criteria have been significantly expanded. The DSM-IV disorder was rarely used, and limited information is available on its course and outcome or the characteristics of children with this disorder. A large number of children and adolescents substantially restrict their food intake and experience significant associated physiological or psychosocial problems but do not meet criteria for any DSM-IV eating disorder. Avoidant/restrictive food intake disorder is a broad category intended to capture this range of presentations. In the DSM-5 field trials in the United States and Canada based on child clinical populations (general child psychiatry outpatient services), avoidant/restrictive food intake disorder prevalence was described for one site and it was 11 percent using DSM-5 (not applicable for DSM-IV). Table 32.4 shows a comparison between DSM-IV and DSM-5 for avoidant/restrictive food-intake disorder.

Table 32.4. DSM-IV to DSM-5 Avoidant/Restrictive Food Intake Disorder

DSM-IV	DSM-5
Name: Feeding Disorder of Infancy or Early Childhood	Name: Avoidant/Restrictive Food Intake Disorder
Disorder Class: Feeding and Eating Disorders of Infancy or Early Childhood	Disorder Class: Feeding and Eating Disorders
A. Feeding disturbance as manifested by persistent failure to eat adequately with significant failure to gain weight or significant loss of weight over at least one month.	A. An eating or feeding disturbance (e.g., apparent lack of interest in eating or food; avoidance based on the sensory characteristics of food; concern about aversive consequences of eating) as manifested by persistent failure to meet appropriate nutritional and/or energy needs associated with one (or more) of the following: 1. Significant weight loss (or failure to achieve expected weight gain or faltering growth in children)

Table 32.4. Continued

DSM-IV	DSM-5
	2. Significant nutritional deficiency 3. Dependence on enteral feeding or oral nutritional supplements 4. Marked interference with psychosocial functioning
B. The disturbance is not due to an associated gastrointestinal or other general medical condition (e.g., esophageal reflux).	B. The disturbance is not better explained by lack of available food or by an associated culturally sanctioned practice.
C. The disturbance is not better accounted for by another mental disorder (e.g., Rumination Disorder) or by lack of available food.	C. The eating disturbance does not occur exclusively during the course of anorexia nervosa or bulimia nervosa, and there is no evidence of a disturbance in the way in which one's body weight or shape is experienced.
D. The onset is before age 6 years.	DROPPED
	Specify if: In remission: After full criteria for avoidance/restrictive food intake disorder were previously met, the criteria have not been met for a sustained period of time.

Section 32.2

Screening for Eating Disorders

This section contains text excerpted from the following sources:
Text in this section begins with excerpts from "Integrated Care for
Eating Disorder Evaluation, Diagnosis, and Treatment," Agency
for Healthcare Research and Quality (AHRQ), February 17, 2015.
Reviewed December 2018; Text beginning with the heading "Body
Mass Index" is excerpted from "Body Mass Index," Substance Abuse
and Mental Health Services Administration (SAMHSA),
February 2011. Reviewed December 2018.

Eating disorders (EDs) are serious, life-threatening conditions that
are often associated with additional physical and mental illnesses.
Depressive symptoms, suicide, obsessive-compulsive disorder (OCD),
anxiety, and substance use disorders are common in people with eating disorders. In particular, anorexia nervosa is associated with over-
use injuries and stress fractures, osteoporosis, and potentially fatal
arrhythmias. Family physicians and multidisciplinary care teams
play an important role in addressing eating disorders. Annual health
examinations and sports physicals provide an opportunity for physicians to screen patients for eating disorders.

Screening for Eating Disorders along with Other Behavioral Health Disorders

Little is known about ideal screening for eating disorders in substance-use disorder (SUD) treatment programs. Researchers recommend that SUD treatment programs screen for EDs, along with other
behavioral health disorders, at intake and intermittently during treatment of all patients in SUD treatment. An analysis of National Treatment Center Study (NTCS) data notes that programs that screen for
EDs do so during intake and assessment.

About half these programs screen all admissions for EDs, and half
screen only when an ED is suspected. Screening for EDs only when one
is suspected can be complex, because signs and symptoms of EDs can
overlap with those of SUDs or with those of other behavioral health
problems. For example, weight loss, lethargy, changes in eating habits,
and depressed mood can indicate an SUD or an affective disorder. In
addition, signs may not be readily observable to counselors, because
people with EDs often go to great lengths to disguise and hide their
disorder.

However, counselors should be aware of common red flags for EDs that tend not to overlap with those of other behavioral health disorders. Given below are some indications (in addition to DSM criteria) that an ED may be present.

Screening all patients for EDs will likely result in identification of more patients in need of further assessment and treatment. SUD treatment counselors can easily (and unobtrusively) incorporate some ED screening into the SUD assessment in a number of ways:

- As part of the drug use assessment, ask patients about their use of over-the-counter (OTC) and prescription laxatives, diuretics, and diet pills.

- As part of taking a medical history, ask patients about past hospitalizations and behavioral health treatment history, including for EDs.

- As part of assessing daily activities, ask patients how often and for how long they exercise.

- Ask patients, "Other than those we've discussed so far, are there any health issues that concern you?"

Counselors also can use a standardized screening instrument. The SCOFF questionnaire discussed later in this section is a screening tool that was originally developed and validated in the United Kingdom and has been validated for use in the United States. Other validated brief screening instruments include:

- Eat-26 (The Eating Attitudes Test, a 26-item version of the original 40-question Eating Attitudes Test)

- The Bulimia Test—Revised (BULIT—R)

Patients in SUD treatment may be confused or defensive about being asked questions regarding their eating and body image. Counselors can prepare patients by:

- Explaining that EDs commonly co-occur with SUDs

- Explaining that it is important to have a clear picture of the patient's overall health status

- Asking the patient for permission to pursue ED screening (e.g., "May I ask you some questions about your eating habits?")

Screening does not end at intake. Counselors should remain alert for signs of EDs, including changes in weight that may appear later in treatment or recovery.

The SCOFF Questionnaire

1. Do you make yourself Sick [induce vomiting] because you feel uncomfortably full?

2. Do you worry you have lost Control over how much you eat?

3. Have you recently lost more than One stone (14 pounds) in a 3-month period?

4. Do you believe yourself to be Fat when others say you are too thin?

5. Would you say that Food dominates your life?

Two or more "yes" responses indicate that an ED is likely.

Body Mass Index

Body mass index (BMI) is a number derived from a calculation based on a person's weight and height. For most people, BMI correlates with their amount of body fat. Measuring BMI is an inexpensive and easy alternative to a direct measurement of body fat percentage and is a useful method of screening for weight categories that may lead to health problems. BMI categories are:

Underweight: BMI score of less than 18.5

Table 32.5. BMI Score for Underweight

Severe thinness	BMI score of less than 16
Moderate thinness	BMI score between 16.00 and 16.99
Mild thinness	BMI score between 17.00 and 18.49

Normal range: BMI score between 18.5 and 24.9
Overweight: BMI score between 25.0 and 29.9
Obese: BMI score of 30.0 or more

Section 32.3

Suggested Medical Tests in Diagnosing Eating Disorders

"Suggested Medical Tests in Diagnosing Eating Disorders,"
© 2016 Omnigraphics. Reviewed December 2018.

Many people with eating disorders either deny that a problem exists or try to hide it from friends, family members, and medical professionals. As a result, diagnosing an eating disorder can be a difficult process, and such conditions as anorexia nervosa, bulimia nervosa, and binge-eating disorder often go undetected for long periods of time. However, doctors have a variety of assessment tools and medical tests available to aid in the diagnosis of eating disorders. If an eating disorder is suspected, the diagnostic process is likely to include the following:

- A full medical history, including information about both physical and emotional health

- A mental-health screening to look for underlying psychological problems, evaluate eating habits, and assess attitudes about food and body image

- A complete physical examination to check for signs of eating disorders as well as health problems related to malnutrition

- additional medical tests—including X-rays and chemical analysis of blood and urine—to look for evidence of damage to the heart, kidneys, gastrointestinal tract, and other organs.

In the process of diagnosing eating disorders, doctors must rule out other health conditions that may present similar symptoms, such as hyperthyroidism, inflammatory bowel syndrome, immunodeficiency, chronic infection, diabetes, and cancer. In addition, doctors must look for evidence of diseases that often coexist with eating disorders, such as depression, anxiety, obsessive-compulsive disorder, schizophrenia, and substance abuse.

Commonly Used Medical Tests

The initial step in diagnosing eating disorders usually involves administering questionnaires and conducting interviews to gather information about the patient's eating history, body image, and attitudes about food. Interviews are often conducted by a psychologist or psychiatrist in the presence of a supportive friend or family member of the patient. Medical professionals may also administer psychometric tests that are specifically designed to elicit information about eating disorders, such as the Eating Disorders Examination (EDE), the Eating Disorders Examination-Questionnaire (EDE-Q), and the SCOFF questionnaire. The results of these screening assessments help doctors determine whether further testing and evaluation is appropriate.

The next step in diagnosing eating disorders may involve administering a number of different medical tests to detect and rule out physical symptoms and health complications related to eating disorders. Some of the most commonly used tests include:

- A complete blood count, including levels of cholesterol, protein, and electrolytes

- A urinalysis to evaluate kidney function

- An oral glucose tolerance test (OGTT) to assess the body's ability to metabolize sugar

- An enzyme-linked immunosorbent assay (ELISA) to check for antibodies to various viruses and bacteria

- A Secretin-CCK test to evaluate pancreas and gallbladder function

- A blood urea nitrogen (BUN) test to evaluate protein metabolism and kidney function

- A BUN-to-creatinine ratio to check for evidence of severe dehydration, kidney failure, congestive heart failure, cirrhosis of the liver, and other serious conditions

- A serum cholinesterase test to assess liver function and check for signs of malnutrition

- A luteinizing hormone (Lh) response to gonadotropin-releasing hormone (GnRH) to evaluate pituitary gland function

- Thyroid-stimulating hormone (TSH) and parathyroid hormone (PTH) tests to assess thyroid function

- A creatine kinase test to evaluate enzyme levels in the heart, brain, and muscles

- An echocardiogram or electrocardiogram (EKG) to assess heart function

- An electroencephalogram (EEG) to measure electrical activity in the brain

- An upper GI series to look for problems in the upper gastrointestinal tract

- X-rays or a barium enema to assess issues in the lower gastrointestinal tract

Making a Diagnosis

The results of these various medical tests can help medical professionals diagnose an eating disorder as well as pinpoint the specific type of disorder in order to provide effective treatment. To receive a diagnosis of anorexia nervosa, a patient typically has a distorted self-image and an intense fear of gaining weight, which translates into an inability or refusal to maintain a healthy weight for their age, height, and body type. Severely restricting food intake, abusing laxatives or diuretics in an effort to eliminate calories, and exercising excessively are common symptoms of anorexia. In females, the loss of menstrual function for at least three months is another key indicator.

The criteria for diagnosing bulimia nervosa include patterns of purging food from the body through self-induced vomiting or other methods at least twice a week for three months. Bulimia can be difficult to diagnose because patients usually binge and purge secretly and deny that they have a problem. In addition, most people with bulimia fall within their normal weight range. Dental and gum problems, stomach and digestive issues, dehydration, fatigue, and other symptoms related to repeated vomiting are key factors in the diagnosis of bulimia.

The diagnosis of binge-eating disorder often occurs when a patient seeks medical help with losing weight or dealing with an obesity related health problem. Medical tests aid in the diagnosis by ruling out physical illnesses and detecting health consequences of the eating disorder. With all types of eating disorders, early diagnosis is important to reduce the patient's risk of long-term health problems and improve the chances of successful treatment and recovery.

References

1. "Anorexia Nervosa—Exams and Tests," WebMD, November 14, 2014.

2. "Bulimia Nervosa—Exams and Tests," WebMD, November 14, 2014.

3. "Diagnosing Binge Eating Disorder," WebMD, 2016.

4. Mandal, Ananya. "Eating Disorders Diagnosis," News Medical, 2016.

Chapter 33

Determining the Type of Treatment Needed

Chapter Contents

Section 33.1

Determining Level of Care for Eating Disorder

"Determining Level of Care for Eating Disorder,"
© 2016 Omnigraphics. Reviewed December 2018.

There is no effective "one size fits all" approach to the treatment of eating disorders. Even though different people may suffer from the same type of disorder, they will often respond favorably to different types of treatment, and therefore, prescribed therapies may employ a combination of various kinds of interventions and levels of care tailored to suit individual requirements.

The phrase "level of care" refers to the intensity of services provided for a patient undergoing treatment for an eating disorder. The level of care prescribed for an individual primarily depends on the severity of the illness and the degree of functional loss resulting from the condition. More serious illnesses and greater loss of functionality will require more intensive levels of care to meet the individual's clinical needs and treatment goals.

While treatment settings are required to be the least restrictive possible, the level of care is decided on the basis of the patient's initial diagnosis. For instance, an adult patient whose weight is less than 80 percent of his or her estimated ideal body weight may require a highly structured program in a restrictive setting—such as inpatient care—to gain weight.

That being said, inpatient care may be deemed appropriate even for those whose weight is above 80 percent of their healthy body weight. For example, this could be prescribed when psychosocial parameters, such as behavior and co-occurring psychological issues, are taken into consideration. Therefore, regular evaluation of the patient's condition and needs is necessary to determine whether the patient is ready to be moved to a different level of care, clinically appropriate with his or her current nutritional and medical status.

Broadly, the two traditional levels of care include the outpatient setting and the inpatient setting. However, in reality, these settings form the two ends of a continuum of services, which includes both distinctive and overlapping components aimed at providing the best type of treatment and rehabilitative options based on individual needs.

Outpatient Treatment for Eating Disorders

The least restrictive level of care, outpatient treatment is particularly useful for those who do not want the therapy to interfere with their occupation or school. This is also suitable for those who cannot afford higher levels of care but require assistance to stay in recovery. The duration of treatment in an outpatient setting may depend on the severity of the eating disorder, as well as the prognosis, and it may range from a few weeks to a few months, during which the visits may be reduced in frequency. Outpatient settings can offer intensive care in the form of supervised meals and a structured treatment plan provided by a professional team, which may include a primary-care physician, a psychotherapist, and a registered nutritionist or dietician.

Partial Hospitalization

Partial hospitalization is a type of outpatient care in which the level of intensity falls somewhere between 24-hour care and an outpatient setting. This means the patient may require hospitalization for a few hours per day at a hospital or a residential facility. Often referred to as a "day hospital," these settings offer a range of ambulatory services that can compare with acute inpatient settings. The treatment team in a day hospital usually comprises a primary-care physician, a psychotherapist/family therapist, and a nutrition counselor, and this type of setting also offers ample opportunity for group therapies. Partial hospitalization may take anywhere from a week to a few months, and based on the progress made, the patient may be moved to an outpatient setting.

Inpatient/Hospital Treatment

Inpatient settings offer intensive care for eating disorders and may include hospitals or treatment facilities offering different levels of specialization. While hospitals offer 24-hour acute care services, residential-care facilities focus less on clinical treatment and more on rehabilitation. Inpatient settings provide a wide range of services, and the duration of treatment may range from a few days to several months, depending on the patient's physical and psychological treatment goals.

Hospitals generally offer a structured treatment program for eating disorders, which may start with stabilizing the patient's physical symptoms. Some of the symptoms that could require immediate medical attention include electrolyte imbalance, hypotension, hypothermia, osteoporosis, and edema, among others. Regular laboratory tests are performed to regulate and monitor metabolic functions. The patient receives one-on-one psychotherapy, which motivates them to participate actively in the treatment program and also work towards developing healthy patterns of behavior. Nutritionists formulate a diet plan for the patient based on individual needs, and nursing staff supervise the patient's meal time and snacks. Hospitals also may provide group therapy sessions and family support groups.

Residential Care

Residential care is usually recommended for children and adolescents who require 24-hour support to treat their eating disorders and other associated behavioral and psychosocial conditions. Residential care offers a comfortable and informal setting and is less restrictive than a hospital. Treatment is based on a predefined time limit, individual needs, and clear goals and is supervised by a team of professionals, including medical physicians, psychiatrists, psychologists, nurses, dieticians, and occupational therapists. Residential-care facilities also may bring in registered therapists to offer art-based psychotherapies, such as painting, sculpting, music, dance, and drama. And some also offer academic support to help children with eating disorders continue their academic pursuits while in active therapy or rehabilitation.

Reference

"Types of Treatment and Therapy," Eating Disorder Hope, June 12, 2012.

Section 33.2

Types of Therapy

"Types of Therapy,"
© 2016 Omnigraphics. Reviewed December 2018.

Eating disorders are health conditions with serious physical, psychological, and social consequences. What starts out as an urge to eat less or more in response to a distorted perception of body image, may spiral out of control and become a debilitating or chronic medical illness. Early intervention is key to successful treatment outcomes and may avoid the fatal or life-threatening conditions often associated with eating disorders, such as anorexia nervosa. Studies have shown that multiple factors—genetic, biological, psychological, and social—determine the cause of eating disorders, and efforts are underway to develop specific psychotherapies and medications that can control eating behavior by targeting specific centers in the brain.

Typically, treatment goals involve formulating a healthy nutrition plan, restoring body weight to a prescribed level, and stopping such behaviors as binge eating and purging. Treatment plans are tailored to meet individual requirements and also treat coexisting conditions, such as depression, substance abuse, or personality disorders. While some types of psychotherapy can be provided on an outpatient basis, others may require hospitalization to treat the more severe effects of malnutrition.

The treatment protocol for eating disorders is highly dependent on the type and severity of the disorder and any associated conditions. It may include one or a combination of the following:

- Individual, family, or group psychotherapy

- Medical care and monitoring

- Nutritional counseling

- Medications (for example, antidepressants)

Some Common Types of Therapy Available for Eating Disorders
Cognitive Behavioral Therapy

Cognitive behavioral therapy (CBT) is one of the most widely practiced forms of psychological intervention for treating eating disorders. Developed by psychotherapist Aaron Beck, M.D., in the 1960s, CBT combines two therapies, cognitive therapy (CT) and behavioral therapy, and is based on the theory that negative thoughts and negative behavior are interlinked. This kind of therapy focuses on helping individuals recognize the irrational thinking patterns associated with food and body image, then develop positive and healthy behavior patterns.

The treatment plan usually includes three phases and requires the active participation of both patient and therapist. The first phase is called the behavioral phase, in which the therapist and the patient devise a plan to stabilize eating behavior, treat symptoms, and learn coping mechanisms with the help of in-session activities. The second phase, the cognitive phase, involves restructuring techniques intended to change harmful and problematic thinking patterns and replace them with new perspectives and ideas. This phase also assesses other psychological and social factors, such as relationship problems or low self-esteem, that may underlie the eating problem. The final phase of CBT is the relapse prevention phase. Here the focus is on eliminating triggers and maintaining the progress made thus far. CBT is almost always incorporated into the treatment plan for eating disorders because of its adaptability in creating individualized therapy to achieve personal goals and promote holistic healing.

Medical Nutrition Therapy

This type of treatment, an essential part of the treatment plan for eating disorders, focuses on helping patients normalize their eating patterns. Creating a healthy eating regimen includes maintaining a nutritious and balanced diet, promoting a harmonious and sustainable relationship with food devoid of negative or harmful rationale, and learning to trust the body's natural response to feelings of hunger or fullness.

Medical nutrition therapy (MNT) can be implemented in all kinds of treatment settings, including inpatient, outpatient, and residential care facilities. In all cases, a registered dietician formulates a structured meal plan on the basis of the patient's medical history, as well as his or her dietary and laboratory evaluations, and supervises the implementation of the dietary plan. The dietitian also educates the patient on the importance of following the prescribed diet plan and avoiding dysfunctional eating behavior and may also modify the plan to address specific deficiencies or medical conditions.

Dialectical Behavioral Therapy

Dialectical behavior therapy (DBT) is a form of CBT originally developed to treat people with borderline personality disorder. The term "dialectical" refers to a discussion that takes place between two people holding opposing views until they find common ground or achieve a balance between the two extreme views. In a treatment setting, the therapist engages in a philosophical exercise with the patient and tries to make her or him therapy responsible for disruptive behavior, while at the same time assuring the patient that illogical thoughts and actions are understandable and not necessarily destructive.

In recent years, DBT has often been incorporated into treatment plans for eating disorders—in both individual and group therapy sessions—and is known to have better outcomes than CBT, which is based more on the premise that the patient's thoughts have to be controlled or changed. In contrast, DBT is based more on acceptance of the patient's extreme behavior and gradual progress toward recognizing triggers, learning to perceive when boundaries are overstepped, and acquiring skills to deal with conflict and stress.

This form of psychotherapy accepts the fact that the patient has spent months—even years—developing eating-disorder patterns and would find it difficult to switch them off in a day. For instance, an anorexic's "I am fat" mindset is not something she or he can unlearn quickly, but developing a heightened awareness of thought processes can help control negative emotions and shift focus to healthy and positive emotions. DBT relies greatly on a close relationship between patient and therapist, and while patients learn new skills during individual sessions, they get an opportunity to practice their newly acquired skills at group sessions.

Expressive or Creative Arts Therapy

Expressive or creative arts therapy uses the creative process to help people treat depression and eating disorders. Used in conjunction with other traditional therapies, this approach has been particularly beneficial in people with a history of trauma.

Art therapy is based on developing self-awareness and centers on the experiences and perceptions of the individual. The process of creating an image of one's thoughts, emotions, and conflicts through the medium of art—say sculpting or painting—is often called "concretization.," which can help the patient accept and recognize his or her inner self through the use of symbols. These symbols of self-expression may also help the therapist in diagnosis, in addition to providing research material for this relatively new field.

Art provides a creative outlet for self-expression and offers a coping mechanism for self-destructive behavior, such as bingeing or purging. A licensed creative-arts therapist can assess, evaluate, and provide therapeutic intervention for the treatment of eating disorders through the use of such activities as drawing, painting, sculpting, photography, music, dance, and drama.

Animal-Assisted Therapy

Although early studies have shown that companion animals contribute significantly to mental and emotional well-being, it is only recently that animal-assisted therapy has begun to be used in conjunction with established therapies to treat many types of mental disorders. Working or playing with animals, such as cats, dogs, or horses, is increasingly being incorporated into the treatment of behavioral problems, particularly in pediatric settings.

For example, equine-assisted psychotherapy is being used as an effective treatment for such disorders as anxiety, attention deficit hyperactivity disorder (ADHD), depression, eating disorders, and post-traumatic stress disorder (PTSD). Caring for animals has been shown to improve self-image in people with eating disorders, and patients also forge an emotional bond with animals, which provides them with a means of self-expression while also teaching them coping mechanisms to deal with self-injurious thoughts and emotions.

Play Therapy

Play therapy is commonly used as a therapeutic intervention, particularly in children and adolescents, as it provides them with an opportunity to express and communicate at their own pace. Toys and games help children make developmentally appropriate responses and also allows the therapist to gain insight into the child's inner world.

Studies have shown that each child's personal experience plays a role in determining the child's self-image as well as the behavioral tendencies that she or he develops to function in the world. Play therapy helps focus on the child's effort to develop coping mechanisms to resolve social or emotional conflict, both in the present and the future. More recently, play therapy has gained momentum as an effective treatment tool for behavioral disorders, including binge-eating and anorexia nervosa, as it offers a safe environment in which children can work toward finding their sense of emotional stability without having to relive past traumas.

Family-Based Therapy

Family-based therapy was developed from the premise that involving family and improving relationships between family members increases the likelihood of a positive treatment outcome. Therapists work at resolving conflicts within the family, educating relatives about the patient's condition and early signs of problems, and charting out an action plan to manage the condition effectively.

Studies have shown favorable outcomes with family-focused therapy in terms of both stabilizing treatment and preventing relapse. Moreover, this kind of therapy builds better understanding and communication and has been effective in preventing "burn out" in family caregivers, which could in turn result in apathy to the patient's condition.

The Maudsley Approach

One type of family-based therapy, called the Maudsley approach for its development at Maudsley Hospital in London, has proven to be effective in the long-term improvement of anorexia nervosa and bulimia nervosa, particularly in adolescents. This approach is characterized by three distinct procedural stages:

- Weight restoration

- Returning control over eating to the teen

- Establishing healthy adolescent identity

In the first phase, the parents are made responsible for helping the teen adopt a healthy eating plan. They are also counseled on the child's condition and how to refrain from criticism. The second phase involves getting the patient to assume responsibility for his or her eating habits. Here, there is a gradual shift away from parental control, and the patient is encouraged to develop the cognitive processes required to take responsibility for healthy nutrition. The third stage begins after the patient reaches and maintains a healthy body weight. During this stage, the therapist helps the patient develop a healthy identity and resolve adolescent and family issues that may underlie the eating disorder. The therapist also helps the patient develop autonomy while helping caregivers cope with high anxiety and stress, which may be counterproductive to the success of family-based therapies.

Despite this method gaining popularity as a treatment regime for binge eating and anorexia, Maudsley studies have shown that the model has had mixed outcomes with older adolescents, adults, and the chronically ill. Moreover, the high degree of parental involvement in the treatment and recovery process may sometimes further exacerbate dysfunctional patterns in adolescents and make it difficult for the patient to gain autonomy, something crucial to the recovery phase. And yet, notwithstanding these issues, the Maudsley approach continues to be a popular therapeutic modality studied by researchers across the United States and Europe.

Photo Therapy

Bright light therapy has traditionally been used in the treatment of seasonal affective disorder (SAD), a form of depression associated with imbalances of melatonin, a hormone that regulates the sleep and wake cycles, often referred to as the circadian rhythm. SAD may also be attributed to a fall in the levels of serotonin, a neurotransmitter responsible for maintaining mood, sleep, and appetite.

Melatonin is produced nocturnally by the pineal gland, and its production stops with exposure to sunlight. It has been proven that exposure to bright light or natural sunlight during the day triggers early nocturnal production of melatonin, thereby enhancing sleep cycle, appetite, and mood. Serotonin is a precursor of melatonin and is also influenced by sunlight. Although it is produced during the day, the conversion of serotonin to melatonin occurs at night. Short days and long nights in winter not only lower serotonin production during the day, but also causes delayed nighttime melatonin production, both of which negatively impact energy levels, sleep, and sense of well-being.

Light therapy is administered by exposing the patient to bright light for prescribed periods of time. In recent years, light therapy has been used to treat eating disorders, in conjunction with other established therapies. Disorders such as bulimia nervosa or binge eating share certain features with SAD, in that symptoms are seasonal and depression is a coexisting condition. Although more studies are needed before drawing definitive conclusions on the efficacy of light therapy, it is being used to treat eating disorders, particularly in cases where antidepressants and established psychotherapies fail to be effective.

References

1. "Psychotherapies," National Institute of Mental Health (NIMH), October 2008.

2. Sholt, Michal and Gavron, Tami. "Therapeutic Qualities of Clay-work in Art Therapy and Psychotherapy: A Review" *Journal of the American Art Therapy Association*, 2006.

3. "Eating Disorder Treatment," Eating Disorder Hope, November 2015.

4. Wilson, George F. and Philips, Kelley L. "Concepts and Definitions Used in Quality Assurance and Utilization Review" *Manual of Psychiatric Quality Assurance*, American Psychiatric Association (APA), 2005.

Chapter 34

Psychotherapy and Eating Disorders

Psychotherapy (sometimes called "talk therapy") is a term for a variety of treatment techniques that aim to help a person identify and change troubling emotions, thoughts, and behavior. Most psychotherapy takes place with a licensed and trained mental-healthcare professional and a patient meeting one on one or with other patients in a group setting.

Someone might seek out psychotherapy for different reasons:

- You might be dealing with severe or long-term stress from a job or family situation, the loss of a loved one, or relationship or other family issues. Or you may have symptoms with no physical explanation: changes in sleep or appetite, low energy, a lack of interest or pleasure in activities that you once enjoyed, persistent irritability, or a sense of discouragement or hopelessness that won't go away.

- A health professional may suspect or have diagnosed a condition such as depression, bipolar disorder, posttraumatic stress,

This chapter contains text excerpted from the following sources: Text in this chapter begins with excerpts from "Psychotherapies," National Institute of Mental Health (NIMH), November 2016; Text under the heading "Psychotherapy for Eating Disorder" is excerpted from "Eating Disorders," Substance Abuse and Mental Health Services Administration (SAMHSA), May 12, 2017; Text under the heading "Interpersonal Psychotherapy" is excerpted from "Mental Health," U.S. Department of Veterans Affairs (VA), December 9, 2015. Reviewed December 2018.

or other disorder and recommended psychotherapy as a first treatment or to go along with medication.

- You may be seeking treatment for a family member or child who has been diagnosed with a condition affecting mental health and for whom a health professional has recommended treatment.

An exam by your primary care practitioner can ensure there is nothing in your overall health that would explain your or a loved one's symptoms.

What to Consider When Looking for a Therapist

Therapists have different professional backgrounds and specialties. There are resources at the end of this material that can help you find out about the different credentials of therapists and resources for locating therapists.

There are many different types of psychotherapy. Different therapies are often variations on an established approach, such as cognitive behavioral therapy. There is no formal approval process for psychotherapies as there is for the use of medications in medicine. For many therapies, however, research involving large numbers of patients has provided evidence that treatment is effective for specific disorders. These "evidence-based therapies" have been shown in research to reduce symptoms of depression, anxiety, and other disorders.

The particular approach a therapist uses depends on the condition being treated and the training and experience of the therapist. Also, therapists may combine and adapt elements of different approaches. The health information pages for specific disorders on the National Institute of Mental Health (NIMH) list some of the evidence-based therapies for those disorders.

One goal of establishing an evidence base for psychotherapies is to prevent situations in which a person receives therapy for months or years with no benefit. If you have been in therapy and feel you are not getting better, talk to your therapist, or look into other practitioners or approaches. The object of therapy is to gain relief from symptoms and improve quality of life (QOL).

Once you have identified one or more possible therapists, a preliminary conversation with a therapist can help you get an idea of how treatment will proceed and whether you feel comfortable with the therapist. Rapport and trust are important. Discussions in therapy are deeply personal and it's important that you feel comfortable and trusting with the therapist and have confidence in his or her expertise. Consider asking the following questions:

- What are the credentials and experience of the therapist? Does she or he have a specialty?

- What approach will the therapist take to help you? Does she or he practice a particular type of therapy? What can the therapist tell you about the rationale for the therapy and the evidence base?

- Does the therapist have experience in diagnosing and treating the age group (for example, a child) and the specific condition for which treatment is being sought? If a child is the patient, how will parents be involved in treatment?

- What are the goals of therapy? Does the therapist recommend a specific time frame or number of sessions? How will progress be assessed and what happens if you (or the therapist) feel you aren't starting to feel better?

- Will there be homework?

- Are medications an option? How will medications be prescribed if the therapist is not an M.D.?

- Are our meetings confidential? How can this be assured?

Psychotherapies and Other Treatment Options

Psychotherapy can be an alternative to medication or can be used along with other treatment options, such as medications. Choosing the right treatment plan should be based on a person's individual needs and medical situation and under a mental health professional's care.

Even when medications relieve symptoms, psychotherapy and other interventions can help a person address specific issues. These might include self-defeating ways of thinking, fears, problems with interactions with other people, or dealing with situations at home and at school or with employment.

Elements of Psychotherapy

A variety of different kinds of psychotherapies and interventions have been shown to be effective for specific disorders. Psychotherapists may use one primary approach, or incorporate different elements depending on their training, the condition being treated, and the needs of the person receiving treatment.

Here are examples of the elements that psychotherapies can include:

- Helping a person become aware of ways of thinking that may be automatic but are inaccurate and harmful. (An example might be someone who has a low opinion of his or her own abilities.) The therapist helps the person find ways to question these thoughts, understand how they affect emotions and behavior, and try ways to change self-defeating patterns. This approach is central to cognitive behavioral therapy (CBT).

- Identifying ways to cope with stress

- Examining in depth a person's interactions with others and offering guidance with social and communication skills, if needed

- Relaxation and mindfulness techniques

- Exposure therapy for people with anxiety disorders. In exposure therapy, a person spends brief periods, in a supportive environment, learning to tolerate the distress certain items, ideas, or imagined scenes cause. Over time, the fear associated with these things dissipates.

- Tracking emotions and activities and the impact of each on the other

- Safety planning to help a person recognize warning signs, and thinking about coping strategies, such as contacting friends, family, or emergency personnel

- Supportive counseling to help a person explore troubling issues and provide emotional support

Taking the First Step

The symptoms of mental disorders can have a profound effect on someone's quality of life (QOL) and ability to function. Treatment can address symptoms as well as assist someone experiencing severe or ongoing stress. Some of the reasons that you might consider seeking out psychotherapy include:

- Overwhelming sadness or helplessness that doesn't go away

- Serious, unusual insomnia or sleeping too much

- Difficulty focusing on work, or carrying out other everyday activities

- Constant worry and anxiety

- Drinking to excess or any behavior that harms self or others

- Dealing with a difficult transition, such as a divorce, children leaving home, job difficulties, or the death of someone close

- Children's behavior problems that interfere with school, family, or peers

Seeking help is not an admission of weakness, but a step towards understanding and obtaining relief from distressing symptoms.

Psychotherapy for Eating Disorder

Psychotherapy can help people change their eating and deal with emotions related to the eating disorder. Psychotherapy involves working with a professional one-on-one or in a group. Several therapies are helpful for treating eating disorders. Some target symptoms directly. Others focus on changing a person's thoughts, environment, or problems that affect their actions and ability to change their actions.

Cognitive behavioral therapy helps adults with bulimia and binge-eating disorder (BED). The person learns skills to help stop binge eating or using compensatory behaviors to control weight. This therapy can reduce unhealthy eating and negative thoughts the person may have about their body.

The Maudsley approach is a family-based therapy. It helps people with anorexia or bulimia achieve a normal weight, address problem behaviors, and function better. Parents learn to manage their child's dieting, exercising, binging, and purging.

Interpersonal Psychotherapy

Interpersonal psychotherapy (IPT) is a treatment for depression that focuses on relationship issues that may be the cause or the result of depression. Many studies have been done that support the usefulness of IPT for depression. Also, studies have shown IPT to be useful in the treatment of other issues such as anxiety, bipolar disorder, eating disorders, and borderline personality disorder.

IPT is typically delivered during 16 weekly sessions over three phases of treatment (initial sessions, intermediate sessions, and termination). During the initial sessions, the therapist will provide

237

you with education about depression, how your life situations may be contributing to depression, and how depression may affect your daily life. The intermediate sessions focus on one or two problem areas that are most concerning to you and may be contributing to your depression. These areas include dealing with major life changes, conflict with others, grief related to the death of a significant person, or problems making or keeping social connections. During Termination, the therapist will work with you to review progress, explore possible stressors that may contribute to depression, discuss how skills learned in IPT can continue to be used, and evaluate the need for further treatment.

Goals are established early in treatment. One of the most important factors in the success of therapy is a commitment to participating in treatment and regularly attending sessions. In IPT, you would typically meet one-on-one with your therapist for 12 to 16 sessions. Sessions are generally held on a weekly basis and last approximately 50 minutes. The information you learn during the therapy sessions will be important to you as you apply it to everyday life in order to feel better.

If you decide to participate in IPT, you will be asked to:

- Attend sessions regularly

- Work with your therapist to set therapy goals

- Discuss relationship issues during each session

- Practice new skills—both in and outside of session

Chapter 35

Encountering Treatment Resistance

Patients with eating disorders usually fail to accept that they have a problem. They often tend to resist and drop out of their treatment. This makes handling eating-disorder patients very difficult and the relapse rate is much higher among such people. Their resistance to treatment may either be a conscious or an unconscious act and it may differ based on the methods of diagnosis and treatment. Hence, a professional who treats people with eating disorders needs a high level of patience and sensitivity.

How People with Eating Disorders Might React

Many people with eating disorders fail to admit that they have a problem and tend to experience a lot of shame and embarrassment. When someone tries to approach the person about the disorder, it is very common that she or he will deny it and respond with anger. These people mostly try to end the conversation by saying something along the lines of "I'm all right," or "Mind your own business," and so on. Some may also try to conceal their disorder by:

- Eating slowly

- Hiding food

- Taking very little food from the plate

- Drinking too much water

- Avoiding having food with others

- Giving excuses for skipping meals

- Wearing large and baggy clothes

One should understand that a patient with an eating disorder behaves in this manner in an effort to keep themselves safe and protect themselves from being shamed.

Reasons for Treatment Resistance

Here are some of the common reasons why people with eating disorders resist treatment.

- Many people with disordered-eating behaviors do not realize that they have a problem. Even if they do realize it, they fail to understand the seriousness of the problem.

- People with eating disorders are afraid that they may be shamed, bullied, or judged by others if they reveal their problem.

- Some people might be terrified of gaining weight and will adopt very strict diet rules. They will also exercise a lot. The anxiety of weight gain will restrict them from getting out of such practices.

- Some patients view the disorder as a part of their personality and daily life. They take immense pride in dieting, exercising, and being so thin. They consider their behavior an ability rather than a disorder and avoid getting treated for it. This kind of behavior is more common among anorexia nervosa patients.

How to Respond to Treatment Resistance

If anyone is resisting treatment for eating disorders, here is how you can help the person.

- First try to understand the fear and anxiety with which a person with eating disorder deals. Give them hope and help them come out of the fear.

- Start a friendly conversation. However, do not expect them to open up too soon. Give them enough space and time to open up.

- Say motivating words and let them know that you will be consistently supportive.

- Do research on the various treatment options available for eating disorders. Explain that there are ways to cope with their issue.

- Be prepared to answer their questions about the treatment options. If you are unable to answer, seek the help of professionals.

- Encourage them to get treated, but do not force them.

- Allow them to choose the treatment option that they believe will suit them best.

- Assist them as they navigate treatment centers.

- Support them throughout the recovery process.

References

1. Vandana Aspen, Alison M. Darcy, and James Lock. "Patient Resistance in Eating Disorders," Psychiatric Times, September 24, 2014.

2. "How to Help a Loved One That Resists Treatment for an Eating Disorder," Magnolia Creek, April 3, 2017.

3. "Self-Denial, Secrecy and Deliberate Lying in Eating Disorders," Science of Eating Disorders (SEDs), November 23, 2012.

Chapter 36

Online Interventions for Eating Disorders

Eating disorders (EDs) have the highest rate of mortality of any mental illness. ED age of onset coincides with the undergraduate years (ages 18 to 25). As such, colleges provide access to a large, epidemiologically vulnerable population and present a unique opportunity for intervention. On college campuses, 14 percent of female and 4 percent of male students screen positive for clinically significant EDs. An estimated 80 percent of these students do not receive treatment. Left untreated EDs typically become more severe and refractory to treatment. Help-seeking interventions typically focus on minimizing stigma, improving knowledge, and addressing other barriers emphasized by classic theories of health behavior. On the whole, these interventions have failed to increase treatment utilization for the vast

This chapter contains text excerpted from the following sources: Text in this chapter begins with excerpts from "A Novel Intervention Promoting Eating Disorder Treatment among College Students," ClinicalTrials.gov, National Institutes of Health (NIH), May 28, 2015. Reviewed December 2018; Text under the heading "Study on Effectiveness of Internet-Based Intervention for Women in College" is excerpted from "Internet-Based Program Can Help Women with Eating Disorders," National Institutes of Health (NIH), August 11, 2006. Reviewed December 2018; Text under the heading "Self-Monitoring Apps for Eating Disorders" is excerpted from "Evaluating and Implementing a Smartphone Application Treatment Program for Bulimia Nervosa and Binge Eating Disorder," ClinicalTrials. gov, National Institutes of Health (NIH), January 26, 2018.

majority of students with ED symptoms. Innovative approaches are urgently needed to narrow the ED treatment gap on college campuses.

Study on Effectiveness of Internet-Based Intervention for Women in College

A study has found that an eight-week, Internet-based intervention may help college-age women at risk. Previous studies have shown that an Internet-based intervention can be effective in reducing body dissatisfaction and excessive weight concerns. Dr. C. Barr Taylor of Stanford University and his colleagues set out to do the first long-term, large-scale study of such a program. Funded by National Institutes of Health's (NIH) National Institute of Mental Health (NIMH), the researchers recruited women between 18 and 30 years of age in the San Francisco Bay area and San Diego. During preliminary interviews, they identified 480 as being at risk for developing an eating disorder.

Half the women completed an eight-week, Internet-based, structured program called "Student Bodies," which was effective in previous small-scale short-term studies. The program included reading and other assignments such as keeping an online body-image journal. The participants also took part in an online discussion group moderated by clinical psychologists. Participants were interviewed immediately following the end of the online program and then annually for up to three years to determine their attitudes toward their weight and shape, and to measure the onset of any eating disorders.

The results, published in the *Archives of General Psychiatry*, show that the Internet-based intervention significantly reduced weight and shape concerns in women who were at high risk for developing an eating disorder. Among the women in the intervention group who were overweight, none developed an eating disorder after two years, while 11.9 percent of the women in the control group who were overweight developed an eating disorder. Of those with symptoms of an eating disorder at the start of the program (such as self-induced vomiting, laxative use, diuretic use, diet pill use, or driven exercise) 10.1 percent in the intervention group developed an eating disorder within two years, compared to 19 percent of those in the control group.

The authors caution, however, that the study was limited by the need for participants to report their own history and progress. Further testing of the Internet-based intervention also needs to be completed in a more diverse group, to include women from different geographical regions, age groups and motivation levels.

Self-Monitoring Apps for Eating Disorders

The prevalence of bulimia nervosa (BN) is approximately 1.0 to 1.5 percent among women. With consistently higher prevalence rates, binge-eating disorder (BED) affects up to 3.5 percent of women and 1.5 percent of men. These eating disorders represent a public health concern due to the high comorbidity of BN and BED with other psychiatric disorders and the association with poor physical health outcomes.

Given this public health impact, it is concerning that less than half of BN and BED patients seek treatment for their eating disorder. This is especially concerning since a greater duration of untreated illness is associated with a poorer prognosis. Individuals' reluctance to seek treatment is likely due to factors such as an avoidance of disclosing symptoms to family members or clinicians. For example, one study reported that 27 percent of adolescents with BN declined participation because they did not want their families involved. Even for those who do wish to engage, treatment is often inaccessible due to the geographic centralization of eating disorder specialists and a low ratio of specialists to patients.

Given the ubiquity of smartphone devices among adults and adolescents, one possible way to improve treatment accessibility and privacy is to offer it through a smartphone app. In recent development, evidence-based smartphone apps have been conceived for use by people suffering from eating disorders as an adjunct to clinical treatment. These tools allow patients to self-monitor eating behaviors, and connect directly with their clinician. The app also provides other therapeutic features (e.g., coping skill cues).

One study demonstrated that 26 percent of app users in a clinically severe range at baseline demonstrated clinically significant reductions in eating disorder symptoms at least 28 days later, which is consistent with other forms of self-help for BN. Moreover, 89 percent of users reported that using the app helped their condition from getting worse and a majority reported improvements to the frequency of disordered behaviors, reported urges, and mood.

App developers have outfitted some of the apps with an adaptive program that automatically uses patient data to tailor treatment for individual users (i.e., an automated pure self-help course of treatment). Although pure self-help is efficacious for BN and BED, self-help augmented by coaching (from a healthcare profession) has been associated with even better outcomes.

Chapter 37

Pharmacotherapy: Medications for Eating Disorders

Although medication alone cannot cure eating disorders, pharmaco therapy often plays a role in the treatment and recovery process. When used along with psychotherapy and nutritional guidance, medications such as antidepressants can help patients with eating disorders stabilize their mental and physical condition and control their symptoms. Prescription drugs may help people with bulimia suppress their urges to binge and purge, for instance, and may help people with anorexia manage their obsessive thinking about food and weight. A medication that benefits one patient might not work effectively for another, however, so it is important to consider different options. In addition, all medications involve side effects, so patients must weigh the risks of each drug against its possible health benefits.

There are three main categories of medications that are commonly used in the treatment of eating disorders:

- Medications to restore body chemistry and manage the physical damage done by severe caloric restriction or repeated bingeing and purging episodes

"Pharmacotherapy: Medications for Eating Disorders," © 2016 Omnigraphics. Reviewed December 2018.

- Medications to treat physical and mental health conditions that frequently coexist with eating disorders and complicate treatment

- Psychiatric medications to treat the underlying depression, anxiety, obsessive-compulsive disorder (OCD), and other mental health conditions that often affect people with eating disorders

Medications to Manage Physical Damage

Several types of medication may be prescribed to help manage the harmful physical effects of severe food restriction. To prevent health complications involving the kidneys, heart, and brain, for instance, patients with anorexia and bulimia may need medication to restore the proper electrolyte balance in their bodies. Medications commonly used to replenish electrolytes include potassium chloride, potassium phosphate, and calcium gluconate. For patients with binge-eating disorder who experience health complications related to obesity, medications may be prescribed to promote weight loss. Examples include appetite suppressants like sibutramine (Meridia) and fat blockers like orlistat (Xenical). These medications may involve side effects, however, such as increases in blood pressure, insomnia, dry mouth, and loose, oily stools.

Medications to Address Coexisting Conditions

A variety of physical and mental health conditions often coexist with eating disorders and complicate the treatment process. Many people with eating disorders also have clinical psychiatric disorders such as depression, anxiety, bipolar, obsessive-compulsive, attention deficit, and posttraumatic stress. Medications are available to help patients manage the symptoms of these conditions in order to improve their ability to recover from eating disorders. Physical health conditions such as diabetes and celiac disease may also coexist with eating disorders. The special nutritional requirements associated with these conditions may impede the treatment of eating disorders. Medication can help patients manage their symptoms and eat a normal diet.

Psychiatric Medications for Eating Disorders

Antidepressants, mood stabilizers, and other psychiatric medications are often prescribed to treat eating disorders. Eating disorders are considered a form of psychiatric illness, and many people with eating disorders also have symptoms of depression, anxiety, and other psychiatric conditions. The most common types of psychiatric medications used in the treatment of eating disorders include:

- **Selective serotonin reuptake inhibitors (SSRIs):** This category of antidepressant drugs works by increasing the level of serotonin (a chemical that affects mood) in the brain. SSRIs are commonly used to treat depression, anxiety, and obsessive-compulsive disorder. Fluoxetine (Prozac) is the only medication approved by the U.S. Food and Drug Administration (FDA) for the treatment of bulimia. Research suggests that fluoxetine may also help people with anorexia overcome underlying depression and maintain a healthy weight once they have brought their eating under control. Other commonly prescribed SSRIs include sertraline (Zoloft), fluvoxamine (Luvox), citalopram (Celexa), and paroxetine (Paxil). Although SSRIs well-tolerated by most people, some experience such side effects as drowsiness, weight gain, agitation, and loss of interest in sex.

- **Tricyclic antidepressants (TCAs) and monoamine oxidase inhibitors (MAOIs):** These categories of antidepressant drugs have long been used to treat depression, panic disorder, and chronic pain. There is also some evidence that they may be effective in treating eating disorders, especially bulimia. They have more side effects than SSRIs, however, including dry mouth, headaches, blurred vision, dizziness, nausea, drowsiness, and insomnia. Examples include imipramine (Tofranil) and desipramine (Norpramin).

- **Other antidepressants:** Other types of antidepressants that are not related to SSRIs, TCAs, and MAOIs are also prescribed in the treatment of eating disorders. Medications like bupropion (Wellbutrin) and trazodone (Desyrel) work by increasing the levels of certain neurotransmitters, like norepinephrine, serotonin, and dopamine.

- **Mood stabilizers:** Mood stabilizers, such as lithium, are typically used in treating manic-depressive and bipolar disorders. Some research has indicated that they may also be helpful for patients with bulimia. Since these medications may cause weight loss, however, they are not usually considered for patients with anorexia.

- **Antipsychotics:** Olanzapine (Zyprexa) is an antipsychotic drug that is often prescribed for schizophrenia. Research has shown that it can also help some anorexia patients gain weight and overcome their obsessive thinking about food. Although many people tolerate olanzapine well, there is a risk of lightheadedness, dizziness, drowsiness, weakness, and tardive dyskinesia (a movement disorder).

- **Anticonvulsants:** The antiseizure medication topiramate (Topamax) has been shown to help some people with bulimia suppress their urge to binge and purge and reduce their preoccupation with eating and weight. It can involve side effects, however, such as nausea, constipation or diarrhea, dizziness, drowsiness, insomnia, loss of appetite, and weight loss.

- **Central nervous system stimulants:** Lisdexamfetamine dimesylate (Vyvanse), a medication that was developed to treat attention deficit hyperactivity disorder (ADHD), received FDA approval for the treatment of binge-eating disorder in 2015. It has been shown to help adults who compulsively overeat to manage their urge to binge. However, Vyvanse is not approved as a medication to promote weight loss.

References

1. Marks, Hedy. "How Medication Treats Eating Disorders," Everyday Health, May 10, 2010.

2. "Medications/Drugs to Treat Eating Disorders," Eating Disorder Referral and Information Center, n.d.

3. Tracy, Natasha. "Medications for Eating Disorders," Healthy Place, January 10, 2012.

Chapter 38

Nutritional Support: A Key Component of Eating-Disorders Treatment

Nutrition therapy is an integral component of the therapeutic modalities used to treat eating disorders (EDs). The primary role of nutrition therapy is to normalize eating behavior and nutritional status. Provided by a registered dietitian trained in the area of EDs, nutrition therapy is offered at all levels of care, including inpatient or outpatient programs and individual or group therapy. Nutrition professionals work on the guidelines provided by the diagnostic criteria for EDs and provide appropriate nutritional interventions along a range of disorders from restrictive eating to diagnosed EDs to unspecified EDs. Disruptions in eating behavior and imbalance in macro- and micro-nutrient intake, and unhealthy compensatory behaviors (purging, laxative abuse, or excessive exercise) are important components of the etiology of EDs. Therefore, dietetic treatment focuses on:

- Achievement of a safe rate of weight restoration

- Reinstatement of normal eating patterns or behavior

- Nutrition education/counseling for maintaining healthy eating patterns to ensure recovery

"Nutritional Support: A Key Component of Eating Disorders Treatment," © 2019 Omnigraphics. Reviewed December 2018.

Components of Medical Nutrition Therapy

1. **Nutrition assessment:** This involves identifying nutrition-related problems, including eating disorder symptoms and core attitudes toward eating and body image. This also involves assessing unhealthy behaviors, such as purging, excessive exercise, food restriction, binge eating, ritualistic/secretive eating, and obsessions. Growth patterns, particularly in younger patients, are assessed on the basis of anthropometric measurements (height, weight history, and growth chart), and evaluation of the physiological effects of EDs is done on the basis of biochemical data.

2. **Nutrition intervention:** This involves applying nutrition diagnosis to create a refeeding plan to resolve nutrition problems and restore weight by prescribing appropriate macro- and micro-nutrient intake. Patients are given goals to normalize eating patterns and achieve normal weight and nutritional status. Both patients and caregivers are counseled on food plans and meal schedules. The most important element of nutrition intervention is nutrition counseling. Patients are assisted in normalizing perceptions about food, hunger, and satiety. This takes into account the patient's health history, individual preferences, and psychological and social factors.

3. **Nutrition monitoring and evaluation:** This involves monitoring nutrition intake and making necessary adjustments throughout the course of treatment in order to bring about the expected rates of weight change necessary to meet age-appropriate body composition and health goals. After achieving a safe rate of weight restoration, food intake is adjusted to maintain the weight achieved.

4. **Care coordination:** This involves working in tandem with the treatment team to optimize tolerance to feeding regimens. This also involves prescribing supplements to ensure maximum absorption of nutrients; preventing, or minimizing nutrient–drug interaction; and taking long-term measures to prevent relapse of unhealthy eating behavior.

Nutrition Professionals

Nutrition professionals are an important component of the multidisciplinary clinical team that provides treatment to individuals suffering from EDs. Nutrition professionals participate in all levels of the care continuum in EDs, and therefore, must possess competency in assessing the nutritional status of the individual and offering appropriate interventions tailored to specific patient needs. These professionals understand the complexities of EDs, such as physiological complications and comorbid mental disorders. They also understand how patients live in denial of their EDs and how they would need to negotiate personal boundary issues with patients—both of which are major deterrents to the effective diagnosis and treatment of EDs. In recent years, the knowledge and expertise provided by nutrition therapy in association with specific eating disorder has shown themselves to important factors for positive treatment outcomes.

Nutrition Therapy for Anorexia Nervosa

Nutritional rehabilitation is the core component of anorexia nervosa because the need to restore normal body weight and reduce the severe metabolic impairment that results from the prolonged starvation typical of the disorder is paramount. Nutritional rehabilitation and weight restoration also improve cognition and physiological functions that lead to better outcomes for psychiatric interventions for EDs. Patients incapable of oral feeding are prescribed enteral nutrition—also called tube feeding—which involves delivering a part of the calorie requirement directly into the stomach or small intestine of the patient via a tube. This process is used to stabilize fluid and electrolyte balances in patients with severe illness. An increased risk of medical complications, infection, and patient distress are associated with enteral feeding; it is, therefore, used as an emergency procedure only in life-threatening situations.

Nutrition Therapy in Bulimia Nervosa

As in anorexia nervosa, adequate nourishment and replacement of nutrient losses in the body are the key objectives of nutrition therapy. Weight stabilization is achieved through minimizing the binge–purge cycles typical of bulimia. The patient is also helped to develop intuitive eating. This involves helping patients to reconnect with their internal wisdom, which enables them to trust their body to recognize hunger or satiety signs and let them know what, when, and how much to eat. Nutritional plans are formulated to reverse malnutrition based on individual requirements, and measures are taken to restore blood-sugar levels and correct fluid and electrolyte imbalances.

Goals in Nutrition Therapy for Binge-Eating Disorder

Nutrition therapy—as in other EDs—is an important component of a multidisciplinary response to binge-eating disorder (BED), and is usually employed with other therapeutic domains, such as psychotherapy or medical therapy, to normalize eating behavior and nutritional status. Individuals with BED often tend to have a higher body-mass index (BMI) than those with other EDs. Obesity can be both an outcome or a facilitator for BED. Controlling binge-eating episodes is the first step in nutrition therapy, and this is followed up with weight control, if necessary. This is important because a restrictive diet is known to be a major trigger for binge eating and weight gain. Nutrition counseling also plays a key role in therapy and involves educating patients about the importance of nutrition; helping patients identify triggers for emotional eating, or loss-of-control eating; and teaching them to acquire healthy coping mechanisms to replace unhealthy eating behavior.

Refeeding Syndrome: A Side Effect of Nutritional Therapy in Eating Disorders

Although not very common, refeeding syndrome is a risk among patients who are put under rapid feeding regimens after chronic starvation. Because a loss of over 50 percent of normal body weight carries a high risk of fatality, particularly among anorexics, it is important to restore normal nutritional status in a slow manner to avoid refeeding syndrome. Initially observed during the nutritional rehabilitation of concentration-camp survivors following World War II, refeeding syndrome is usually associated with dangerously low levels of minerals (phosphorous, magnesium, and sodium) in blood, glucose intolerance, and a deficiency of thiamine (vitamin B1). The levels of minerals in blood fall because refeeding increases synthesis of glycogen, fat, and proteins in the body, a process that requires minerals whose levels are already depleted from prolonged starvation. The fall in serum electrolyte can have serious neurological, cardiac, and hematological complications. The patient could have a heart failure, develop respiratory distress, or become comatose. Therefore, close monitoring of blood biochemistry to diagnose any electrolyte imbalance is extremely important to prevent refeeding syndrome, particularly in the early days of weight restoration for EDs.

References

1. "Nutrition Therapy at the Center for Eating Disorders," The Center for Eating Disorders at Sheppard Pratt, n.d.

2. "Nutritional Rehabilitation in Anorexia Nervosa: Review of the Literature and Implications for Treatment," National Center for Biotechnology Information (NCBI), November 7, 2013.

3. "A Review of Feeding Methods Used in the Treatment of Anorexia Nervosa," National Center for Biotechnology Information (NCBI), September 2, 2013.

Chapter 39

Recovering and Overcoming Negative Thoughts

Chapter Contents

Section 39.1

Principles of Recovery

This section includes text excerpted from "SAMHSA's Working Definition of Recovery," Substance Abuse and Mental Health Services Administration (SAMHSA), 2012. Reviewed December 2018.

Ten Guiding Principles of Recovery

1. **Recovery emerges from hope.** The belief that recovery is real provides the essential and motivating message of a better future—that people can and do overcome the internal and external challenges, barriers, and obstacles that confront them. Hope is internalized and can be fostered by peers, families, providers, allies, and others. Hope is the catalyst of the recovery process.

2. **Recovery is person-driven.** Self-determination and self-direction are the foundations for recovery as individuals define their own life goals and design their unique path(s) towards those goals. Individuals optimize their autonomy and independence to the greatest extent possible by leading, controlling, and exercising choice over the services and supports that assist their recovery and resilience. In so doing, they are empowered and provided the resources to make informed decisions, initiate recovery, build on their strengths, and gain or regain control over their lives.

3. **Recovery occurs via many pathways.** Individuals are unique with distinct needs, strengths, preferences, goals, culture, and backgrounds—including trauma experience—that affect and determine their pathway(s) to recovery. Recovery is built on the multiple capacities, strengths, talents, coping abilities, resources, and inherent value of each individual. Recovery pathways are highly personalized. They may include professional clinical treatment; use of medications; support from families and in schools; faith-based approaches; peer support; and other approaches. Recovery is nonlinear, characterized by continual growth and improved functioning that may involve setbacks. Because setbacks are a natural, though not inevitable, part of the recovery process, it is essential to foster resilience for all individuals and families.

In some cases, recovery pathways can be enabled by creating a supportive environment. This is especially true for children, who may not have the legal or developmental capacity to set their own course.

4. **Recovery is holistic.** Recovery encompasses an individual's whole life, including mind, body, spirit, and community. This includes addressing: self-care practices, family, housing, employment, transportation, education, clinical treatment for mental disorders and substance-use disorders, services and supports, primary healthcare, dental care, complementary and alternative services, faith, spirituality, creativity, social networks, and community participation. The array of services and supports available should be integrated and coordinated.

5. **Recovery is supported by peers and allies.** Mutual support and mutual aid groups, including the sharing of experiential knowledge and skills, as well as social learning, play an invaluable role in recovery. Peers encourage and engage other peers and provide each other with a vital sense of belonging, supportive relationships, valued roles, and community. Through helping others and giving back to the community, one helps one's self. Peer-operated supports and services provide important resources to assist people along their journeys of recovery and wellness. Professionals can also play an important role in the recovery process by providing clinical treatment and other services that support individuals in their chosen recovery paths. While peers and allies play an important role for many in recovery, their role for children and youth may be slightly different. Peer supports for families are very important for children with behavioral health problems and can also play a supportive role for youth in recovery.

6. **Recovery is supported through relationship and social networks.** An important factor in the recovery process is the presence and involvement of people who believe in the person's ability to recover; who offer hope, support, and encouragement; and who also suggest strategies and resources for change. Family members, peers, providers, faith groups, community members, and other allies form vital support networks. Through these relationships, people leave unhealthy and/or unfulfilling life roles behind and engage in new roles (e.g., partner, caregiver, friend, student, employee) that lead

to a greater sense of belonging, personhood, empowerment, autonomy, social inclusion, and community participation.

7. **Recovery is culturally based and influenced.** Culture and cultural background in all of its diverse representations—including values, traditions, and beliefs—are keys in determining a person's journey and unique pathway to recovery. Services should be culturally grounded, attuned, sensitive, congruent, and competent, as well as personalized to meet each individual's unique needs.

8. **Recovery is supported by addressing trauma.** The experience of trauma (such as physical or sexual abuse, domestic violence, war, disaster, and others) is often a precursor to or associated with alcohol and drug use, mental health problems, and related issues. Services and supports should be trauma-informed to foster safety (physical and emotional) and trust, as well as promote choice, empowerment, and collaboration.

9. **Recovery involves individual, family, and community strengths and responsibility.** Individuals, families, and communities have strengths and resources that serve as a foundation for recovery. In addition, individuals have a personal responsibility for their own self-care and journeys of recovery. Individuals should be supported in speaking for themselves. Families and significant others have responsibilities to support their loved ones, especially for children and youth in recovery. Communities have responsibilities to provide opportunities and resources to address discrimination and to foster social inclusion and recovery. Individuals in recovery also have a social responsibility and should have the ability to join with peers to speak collectively about their strengths, needs, wants, desires, and aspirations.

10. **Recovery is based on respect.** Community, systems, and societal acceptance and appreciation for people affected by mental health and substance use problems—including protecting their rights and eliminating discrimination—are crucial in achieving recovery. There is a need to acknowledge that taking steps towards recovery may require great courage. Self-acceptance, developing a positive and meaningful sense of identity, and regaining belief in one's self are particularly important.

Section 39.2

Overcoming Negative Thoughts

This section includes text excerpted from "Changing Negative Thinking Patterns," U.S. Department of Veterans Affairs (VA), August 2013. Reviewed December 2018.

When bad things happen in our lives, it's normal to have negative thoughts—like expecting the worst, or seeing the worst in people or situations. Negative thoughts like these can be useful during a traumatic or stressful event. But after the event has passed, continuing to have negative thoughts may no longer be helpful. Always having negative thoughts can make you feel bad. And it can stress your body. If you can identify thinking patterns you may have, and challenge the ones that are not helpful, you can open yourself up to new and different ways of looking at the situation, which can help you feel better.

Negative Thinking Styles

Indicate which of these negative thinking styles sometimes apply to you:

- **All-or-nothing thinking:** People who engage in this kind of thinking see the world in all-or-nothing terms. Things are either black or white, but never (or rarely) gray.

- **Emotional thinking:** This thinking happens when what you feel controls what you think. Feelings are important, but your feelings can play tricks on you. In fact, if you are anxious most of the time, your feelings are almost certainly sending you the wrong message.

- **Overestimating risk:** This happens when you assess the risk associated with a situation as higher than it really is. This way of thinking can lead to feeling a lot of anxiety.

- **"Must" or "Should" thinking:** These are unwritten rules or expectations for how you ought to behave that are based on myths rather than facts. They are standards that you feel you must or should live up to.

- **Self-blame:** People who engage in this style of thinking blame themselves when bad things happen. They take responsibility for things they often had little or no control over.

- **Expecting the worst:** Some people always expect the worst to happen. Many times their fears are triggered by "what if" thoughts.

- **Overgeneralization:** People who over-generalize believe that because something happened once it will happen again and again.

A Negative, Trauma-Related Thought

Identify the negative thinking pattern(s) this thought falls into. Choose as many as you think apply.

- All-or-nothing thinking

- Emotional thinking

- Overestimating risk

- "Must" or "Should" thinking

- Self-blame

- Expecting the worst

- Overgeneralization

Combat Negative Thinking

Here are some questions you can ask yourself any time you need to combat negative thinking:

- Is there any other way of looking at the situation?

- Is there any other explanation?

- How would someone else, like a friend, think about the situation? Or what would you tell a friend who had the thought?

- Am I using all or nothing thinking? Is there a middle ground?

- Am I expecting more of myself than I do of other people?

- Am I overestimating (or underestimating) how much control and responsibility I have in this situation?

- What is the most realistic thing that would happen if my thought came true?

- Do I have other ways of handling the problem?

- Am I overestimating the risk involved?

- Am I predicting the future as if I have a crystal ball?

Chapter 40

Insurance Coverage for Eating Disorders Treatment

Eating disorders are serious, life-threatening illnesses, but studies have shown that early intervention and a full course of treatment can lead to recovery for many patients. Despite these promising results, however, many health insurance providers deny coverage for eating disorder treatment. Some insurance policies exclude psychiatric conditions in general, while some exclude eating disorders specifically. Other health insurance policies only cover a small portion of expenses for procedures that are deemed "medically necessary" or establish low daily payment limits that are insufficient for inpatient treatment. The denial of insurance coverage leaves countless eating disorder patients not only fighting for recovery, but also battling with insurance companies to obtain reimbursement for medical costs.

Why Eating Disorder Treatment Should Be Covered

Advocates for people with eating disorders make a number of arguments for covering treatment costs in health insurance policies. They point out, for instance, that federal mental health parity laws require insurance plans to provide the same coverage limits for mental health benefits as for other medical conditions. Anorexia nervosa is one of

"Insurance Coverage for Eating Disorders Treatment," © 2016 Omnigraphics. Reviewed December 2018.

the deadliest forms of mental illness, with a mortality rate of up to 10 percent, so denying patients access to treatment can affect their very survival.

Advocates also note that early diagnosis and intervention can significantly reduce the long-term cost of treatment and improve the chances of recovery for people with eating disorders. Studies of patients with bulimia nervosa have shown that 80 percent of patients recover when they begin treatment within five years of symptoms appearing, while only 20 percent recover when they begin treatment after experiencing fifteen years of symptoms. Insurance coverage increases the likelihood that people with eating disorders will seek medical treatment promptly.

Eating disorder treatment is a long, intensive process that must be administered in stages to address the complex medical and psychiatric components of the illness. Yet research has shown that a full course of specialized treatment is cost-effective in the long run, because shortening the length of treatment reduces successful outcomes and increases readmissions. Some insurance providers insist that patients be discharged from inpatient treatment programs as soon as their weight or body mass index (BMI) reaches a certain target figure, even though many other factors determine the severity of an eating disorder and the effectiveness of treatment.

Although the costs associated with treating eating disorders are high, effective treatment helps patients avoid many indirect costs associated with long-term health complications and disabilities. Eating disorders can compromise patients' physical and emotional health to the point that they cannot hold jobs or be productive members of society. In addition, untreated eating disorders can contribute to the development of expensive, ongoing medical problems such as depression, substance abuse, dehydration, electrolyte imbalance, osteoporosis, organ damage, cognitive losses, gastrointestinal problems, and cardiac arrest.

Tips for Obtaining Insurance Coverage

Obtaining insurance coverage for eating disorder treatment, or contesting the denial of coverage, can be a complicated and frustrating process. But it is vital for patients to receive all the healthcare benefits to which they are entitled in order to gain access to life-saving treatments and make a full recovery. The following tips can help patients and their advocates navigate the process of obtaining insurance coverage:

- Read your health insurance policy and understand the coverage and benefits it provides before beginning treatment. Employers and insurance providers are required to provide subscribers with copies of their policy upon request. Get advice from a doctor's office or an attorney if you have trouble understanding what is covered. It may also be helpful to become familiar with applicable federal and state laws relating to health insurance coverage and mental health parity.

- Keep records of all communication with doctors, therapists, treatment centers, and insurance representatives, including detailed notes on every telephone conversation and copies of all email messages, written correspondence, and receipts. Ask healthcare professionals to provide reports or letters explaining why specific treatments are medically necessary and why specific facility choices are appropriate.

- Follow the medical advice of your treatment team and do not allow the insurance provider to make healthcare determinations for you. Although eating disorder treatment can be very costly, it is important to remain in treatment even if your insurance company denies coverage. In order to pursue legal action to recover unpaid benefits, you must continue treatment and pay out of pocket. Some treatment providers are willing to negotiate a reduction in fees during the insurance appeal process.

- If your insurance company denies coverage, find out the reason for the denial and get it in writing. Appeal the decision immediately by phone and by sending a letter to the provider's medical director. Explain the medical necessity of treatment and provide documentation to support your claims. Although the appeal process can be complicated and stressful, remember that a denial of coverage is not the final word.

- If your appeal is not resolved to your satisfaction, seek assistance from an attorney. Sometimes a letter from a law firm is enough to get the attention of an insurance company. Also consider contacting the state insurance or consumer rights commission, your legislators, or the local media and asking for support.

- If no health insurance coverage is available, seek treatment from alternative sources that may offer services at a reduced cost, such as community mental health agencies, university medical schools, or government-funded clinics. Also inquire about free clinical trials and research programs available through such organizations as the National Institute of Mental Health, the Academy of Eating Disorders, or the American Academy of Child and Adolescent Psychiatry.

References

1. Andersen, Arnold. "How to Fight Insurance Discrimination," National Association of Anorexia Nervosa and Associated Disorders (ANAD), 2016.

2. Teicher, Rachel. "What You Should Know about Insurance Coverage and Eating Disorder Treatment," Eating Disorder Hope, June 5, 2013.

Part Six

Preventing Eating Disorders and Achieving a Healthy Weight

Chapter 41

Eatlng-Disorder Prevention

Important Role of Prevention

In addition to pushing for treatment for those currently suffering from eating disorders it is equally important to offer prevention programs for youth. Primary efforts are designed to prevent the occurrence of eating disorders before they begin by promoting healthy development.

Experts on optimal prevention programs for eating disorders conclude that successful programs are designed to promote healthy development, thus are multidimensional and comprehensive. Successful curricula include not only information about nutritional content but also information about responding to hunger and satiety, positive body image development, positive self-esteem development, and learning life skills, such as stress management, communication skills, and problem-solving and decision-making skills. Successful interventions are tailored to the developmental and cultural needs of the target population and include family, school, and community involvement.

This chapter contains text excerpted from the following sources: Text beginning with the heading "Important Role of Prevention" is excerpted from "Testimony of the Eating Disorders Coalition for Research, Policy and Action," U.S. Senate Committee on Health, Education, Labor, and Pensions, April 25, 2002. Reviewed December 2018; Text beginning with the heading "Improving Your Eating Habits" is excerpted from "Improving Your Eating Habits," Centers for Disease Control and Prevention (CDC), May 15, 2015. Reviewed December 2018.

Basic Principles for the Prevention of Eating Disorders

Eating-disorder prevention experts, Margo Maine, Ph.D., and Michael Levine, Ph.D., outline a number of important principles for prevention efforts here.

1. Given that eating disorders are serious and complex problems we need to avoid thinking of them in simplistic terms, like "anorexia is just a plea for attention," or "bulimia is just an addiction to food." Eating disorders arise from a variety of physical, emotional, social, and familial issues, all of which need to be addressed for effective prevention and treatment.

2. The objectification and other forms of mistreatment of women by others contribute directly to two underlying features of an eating disorder: obsession with appearance and shame about one's body.

3. Eating disorders are not just a "woman's problem" or "something for the girls." Males who are preoccupied with shape and weight can also develop eating disorders as well as dangerous shape control practices like steroid use.

4. Prevention efforts will fail, or worse, inadvertently encourage disordered eating, if they concentrate solely on warning the public about the signs, symptoms, and dangers of eating disorders. Effective prevention programs must also address:

   • Our cultural obsession with slenderness as a physical, psychological, and moral issue

   • The roles of men and women in our society

   • The development of people's self-esteem and self-respect in a variety of areas (school, work, community service, hobbies) that transcend physical appearance

5. Whenever possible, prevention programs for schools, community organizations, etc. should be coordinated with opportunities for participants to speak confidentially with a trained professional with expertise in the field of eating disorders, and, when appropriate, receive referrals to sources of competent, specialized care.

Promoting a Healthy Environment for Youth

In addition to inoculating the individual from developing disordered eating, effective prevention efforts should also create positive environments for youth in which they may flourish. Such environments would emphasize the value of each child, promote a sense of self-efficacy and confidence, be free from harassment and violence, respond appropriately to teasing and bullying, separate a child's worth from beauty and body weight, offer nutritional and tasty food options, offer opportunities for exercise and play, encourage youth to value their uniqueness and the uniqueness of others, and other factors that promote the healthy development of youth.

Efforts designed to promote healthy eating must be done in such a way as to not inadvertently create new problems. Focusing on body weight and urging youth to be thin has not helped reduce the prevalence of overweight. Instead it has resulted in a host of new health problems such as widespread body dissatisfaction, poor body image, low self-esteem, pathogenic weight-control practices, and eating disorders. Therefore, effective interventions for promoting healthy eating with youth should promote a healthy lifestyle and not promote unhealthy weight-management techniques.

Improving Your Eating Habits

When it comes to eating, we have strong habits. Some are good ("I always eat breakfast"), and some are not so good ("I always clean my plate"). Although many of our eating habits were established during childhood, it doesn't mean it's too late to change them.

Making sudden, radical changes to eating habits such as eating nothing but cabbage soup, can lead to short-term weight loss. However, such radical changes are neither healthy nor a good idea, and won't be successful in the long run. Permanently improving your eating habits requires a thoughtful approach in which you Reflect, Replace, and Reinforce.

- **REFLECT** on all of your specific eating habits, both bad and good; and, your common triggers for unhealthy eating.

- **REPLACE** your unhealthy eating habits with healthier ones.

- **REINFORCE** your new, healthier eating habits.

Reflect, Replace, Reinforce: A Process for Improving Your Eating Habits

1. **Create a list of your eating habits.** Keeping a food diary for a few days, in which you write down everything you eat and

the time of day you ate it, will help you uncover your habits. For example, you might discover that you always seek a sweet snack to get you through the mid-afternoon energy slump. It's good to note how you were feeling when you decided to eat, especially if you were eating when not hungry. Were you tired? Stressed out?

2. **Highlight the habits on your list that may be leading you to overeat.** Common eating habits that can lead to weight gain are:

   - Eating too fast

   - Always cleaning your plate

   - Eating when not hungry

   - Eating while standing up (may lead to eating mindlessly or too quickly)

   - Always eating dessert

   - Skipping meals (or maybe just breakfast)

3. **Look at the unhealthy eating habits you've highlighted.** Be sure you've identified all the triggers that cause you to engage in those habits. Identify a few you'd like to work on improving first. Don't forget to pat yourself on the back for the things you're doing right. Maybe you almost always eat fruit for dessert, or you drink low-fat or fat-free milk. These are good habits! Recognizing your successes will help encourage you to make more changes.

4. **Create a list of "cues"** by reviewing your food diary to become more aware of when and where you're "triggered" to eat for reasons other than hunger. Note how you are typically feeling at those times. Often an environmental "cue," or a particular emotional state, is what encourages eating for nonhunger reasons.

5. Common triggers for eating when not hungry are:

   - Opening up the cabinet and seeing your favorite snack food

   - Sitting at home watching television

   - Before or after a stressful meeting or situation at work

   - Coming home after work and having no idea what's for dinner

- Having someone offer you a dish they made "just for you!"
- Walking past a candy dish on the counter
- Sitting in the break room beside the vending machine
- Seeing a plate of doughnuts at the morning staff meeting
- Swinging through your favorite drive-through every morning
- Feeling bored or tired and thinking food might offer a pick-me-up

1. **Circle the "cues" on your list that you face on a daily or weekly basis.** Going home for the Thanksgiving holiday may be a trigger for you to overeat, and eventually, you want to have a plan for as many eating cues as you can. But for now, focus on the ones you face more often.

2. **Ask yourself** these questions for each "cue" you've circled:

   Is there anything I can do to avoid the cue or situation? This option works best for cues that don't involve others. For example, could you choose a different route to work to avoid stopping at a fast food restaurant on the way? Is there another place in the break room where you can sit so you're not next to the vending machine?

   For things I can't avoid, can I do something differently **that would be healthier?** Obviously, you can't avoid all situations that trigger your unhealthy eating habits, like staff meetings at work. In these situations, evaluate your options. Could you suggest or bring healthier snacks or beverages? Could you offer to take notes to distract your attention? Could you sit farther away from the food so it won't be as easy to grab something? Could you plan ahead and eat a healthy snack before the meeting?

3. **Replace unhealthy habits with new, healthy ones.** For example, in reflecting upon your eating habits, you may realize that you eat too fast when you eat alone. So, make a commitment to share a lunch each week with a colleague, or have a neighbor over for dinner one night a week. Other strategies might include putting your fork down between bites or minimizing other distractions (i.e., watching the news during dinner) that might keep you from paying attention to how quickly—and how much—you're eating.

Eat more slowly. If you eat too quickly, you may "clean your plate" instead of paying attention to whether your hunger is satisfied.

Eat only when you're truly hungry instead of when you are tired, anxious, or feeling an emotion besides hunger. If you find yourself eating when you are experiencing an emotion besides hunger, such as boredom or anxiety, try to find a noneating activity to do instead. You may find a quick walk or phone call with a friend helps you feel better.

Plan meals ahead of time to ensure that you eat a healthy well-balanced meal.

4. **Reinforce your new, healthy habits and be patient with yourself.** Habits take time to develop. It doesn't happen overnight. When you do find yourself engaging in an unhealthy habit, stop as quickly as possible and ask yourself: Why do I do this? When did I start doing this? What changes do I need to make? Be careful not to berate yourself or think that one mistake "blows" a whole day's worth of healthy habits. You can do it! It just takes one day at a time!

Chapter 42

Promoting Positive Self-Esteem

Chapter Contents

Section 42.1

What Is Self-Esteem?

This section contains text excerpted from the following sources:
Text in this section begins with excerpts from "Self-Esteem," Mental
Illness Research, Education and Clinical Centers (MIRECC), U.S.
Department of Veterans Affairs (VA), July 2013. Reviewed December
2018; Text under the heading "Boost Your Self-Esteem and Self-
Confidence" is excerpted from "Boost Your Self-Esteem and Self-
Confidence," girlshealth.gov, Office on Women's Health (OWH),
January 7, 2015. Reviewed December 2018.

Self-esteem is a way of thinking, feeling, and acting that implies
that you accept, respect, and believe in yourself.

- When you accept yourself, you are okay with both the good and
  not so good things about yourself

- When you respect yourself, you treat yourself well in much the
  same way you would treat someone else you respect

- To believe in yourself means that you feel you deserve to have
  the good things in life. It also means that you have confidence
  that you can make choices and take actions that will have a
  positive effect on your life.

Part of self-esteem is knowing that you are important enough to
take good care of yourself by making good choices for yourself. For
example, choosing nutritious food for your body, exercising, giving
yourself time to relax, etc. Self-esteem doesn't mean you think you
are better or more important than other people are, it means that you
respect and value yourself as much as other people. Self-esteem needs
to come from within and not be dependent on external sources such
as material possessions, your status, or approval from others. Having
self-esteem also means you don't have to put other people down to feel
good about yourself.

Signs of Low and High Self-Esteem
Signs of Low Self-Esteem

- Lack of confidence

- Negative view of life

- Perfectionistic attitude

- Mistrusting others inappropriately
- Blaming behavior
- Fear of taking appropriate risks
- Feelings of being unloved and unlovable
- Dependence on others to make decisions
- Fear of being ridiculed
- Distorted view of self and others

Signs of High Self-Esteem

- Confidence
- Self-direction
- Nonblaming behavior
- Awareness of personal strengths
- Ability to make mistakes and learn from them
- Ability to accept mistakes from others
- Optimism
- Ability to solve problems
- Independent and cooperative attitude
- Feeling comfortable with a wide range of emotions
- Ability to appropriately trust others
- Good sense of personal limitations
- Ability to set boundaries and say no
- Good self-care

Causes of Low Self-Esteem

- Nobody is born with low self-esteem; it's something that is learned. It is the result of filtering opinions, comments, looks, suggestions, and actions of those around us through a person's own feelings and self-image.
- Some possible early causes of low self-esteem:
  - Overly critical parents (never good enough, feelings of inferiority or self-criticism)

- Significant childhood losses (abandonment, insecurity)

- Parental abuse, alcoholism, neglect, or rejection (unreliable family atmosphere resulting in lack of trust, insecurity, inadequacy or worthlessness, anger, guilt, denying feelings)

- Parental overprotectiveness (lack of confidence)

- Parental overindulgence (feelings of being cheated and insecure because life does not continue to provide what they learned to expect as a child)

- Some possible later contributors to low self-esteem:

  - Negative or controlling personal relationships

  - Negative experiences on the job

  - Messages from society

- Even if low self-esteem had its roots in childhood, you can learn to identify and challenge the assumptions you consciously or unconsciously have about yourself.

  - Take notice of and become more consciously aware of your needs

  - Acknowledge the importance of self-nurturing and self-care activities and take appropriate steps in that direction

  - Recognize and take pride in your accomplishments

  - Focus on problem-solving

Boost Your Self-Esteem and Self-Confidence

Do you want to feel better about yourself? You can learn how to build self-esteem and raise your self-confidence. Try these tips:

- **Check out new activities.** You'll feel proud for stretching your wings. Does trying something new on your own seem too scary? Maybe see if a friend will go along.

- **Be your own BFF.** Make a list of things you love about you. Are you friendly, funny, creative, or hard-working, for example?

- **Celebrate your successes.** Try to really enjoy your achievements. Record them in a journal, tell your friends, or hang up pictures or other reminders.

- **Tell your inner critic to be quiet.** If you have a mean thought about yourself, see if you can change it to something positive instead. For example, if you think, "I'm dumb," try remembering a time you did something smart.

- **Don't compare yourself to others.** Someone else may have tons of online friends or a "great" body. But everyone has strengths and weaknesses.

- **Practice being assertive.** Try to express your thoughts, opinions, and needs. It feels great to know you can speak up for yourself! (Of course, you want to do this without stomping on other people's feelings.)

- **Find ways to feel like you're contributing.** It feels great to help. You might do chores at home or volunteer in your community.

- **Set realistic goals.** Aim for a goal that you think you can reach. Then make a plan for how to get there. If you pick something very hard, you may get frustrated and quit.

- **Forgive yourself when you fail.** Nobody is perfect. The important thing is to learn from your mistakes. And it's good to know you can pick yourself up and keep going!

- **Find true friends.** Hang out with people who make you feel good about yourself. Real friends like you for you.

- **Honor your background.** It can be great to feel proud of who you are and where you come from. Read about exploring your culture and what girls have to say about their unique identities.

If you try working on your self-esteem for a while and still don't feel good about yourself, reach out for help. Talk to a parent or guardian, doctor, school counselor, school nurse, teacher, or other trusted adult. An adult may be able to suggest other things you can try, and it may help just to talk about how you're feeling. Also, sometimes low self-esteem can increase your risk for depression and other emotional problems. An adult you trust could help you get treatment if you need it.

279

Section 42.2

Building Self-Esteem: A Self-Help Guide

This section includes text excerpted from "Ways to Build Self-Esteem," girlshealth.gov, Office on Women's Health (OWH), December 22, 2015. Reviewed December 2018.

Having healthy or high self-esteem means that you feel good about yourself and are proud of what you can do. Having high self-esteem can help you to think positively, deal better with stress, and boost your drive to work hard. Having high self-esteem can also make it easier to try new things. Before you try something new, you think, "I can do this," and not, "This is too hard. I'll never be able to do this."

If you have an illness or disability, how does it affect your self-esteem? Do you find your self-esteem is affected by how you think others see you? Do people put you down or bully you? This can put your self-esteem at risk. If you need a self-esteem boost, take these steps:

- **Ask yourself what you are really good at and enjoy doing.** Everyone is good at something. When you're feeling bad about yourself, just think, "I'm good at art" (or computers or playing an instrument or whatever you're good at). You might make a list of your great traits and talents, too. And remember that it's okay not to be great at everything.

- **Push yourself to try new things.** If you try something new and fail, that's okay. Everyone fails sometime. Try to figure out what went wrong, so you can try again in a new way. Keep trying, and don't give up. In time, you'll figure out how to succeed.

- **Always give your best effort, and take pride in your effort.** When you accomplish a goal, celebrate over a family meal or treat yourself to a fun outing.

- **If you need help, ask for it.** Talking to a parent, teacher, or friend can help you come up with different ways to solve a problem. This is called brainstorming. Make a list of your possible solutions. Put the ones that you think will work the best at the top. Then rehearse them ahead of time so that you'll know exactly what you're going to do or say when the problem comes up. If your first plan doesn't work, then go on to Plan B. If Plan B doesn't work, go on to Plan C, and so on.

- **Join a support group.** Finding out how other kids deal with illnesses or disabilities can help you cope. Ask your doctor, teachers, or parents for help finding a support group in your community or online. Check out these options for chatting with other kids online. Make sure to get your parent's permission first.

- **Volunteer to do something at school or in your community.** For instance, you could tutor a younger child or take care of the plants in the community center lobby. You might also volunteer to do some chores at home.

- **Look for ways to take more control over your life.** For instance, every student who has needs related to an illness or disability in school must have an Individualized Education Plan (IEP). Your IEP describes your goals during the school year and any support that you'll need to help achieve those goals. Get involved with the development of your IEP. Attend any IEP meetings. Tell your parents, teachers, and others involved in your IEP what you think your goals at school should be and what would help you achieve them. It's your education, and you get a say in what happens!

- **Speak up for yourself.** This can be difficult if you're shy. But it can get easier with practice. Learn to communicate your needs and don't hesitate to ask for something.

- **Work on trying to feel good about how you look.** Everyone has some things they like and don't like about their bodies. It pays to focus on the positives since your body image, or how you feel about your looks, can affect your self-esteem. And remember that real beauty comes from the inside! If you like makeup and clothes, ask for help dealing with any obstacles your illness or disability might present.

- **If you still find that you are not feeling good about yourself, talk to your parents, a school counselor, or your doctor because you may be at risk for depression.** You can also ask the school nurse if your school offers counseling for help through tough times.

Chapter 43

Promoting a Healthy Body Image

Chapter Contents

Section 43.1

What Is Body Image?

This section includes text excerpted from "Body Image,"
Office on Women's Health (OWH), U.S. Department of
Health and Human Services (HHS), August 28, 2018.

A healthy body image means you feel comfortable in your body
and you feel good about the way you look. This includes what you
think and feel about your appearance and how you judge your own
self-worth. A negative body image can put you at higher risk of
certain mental-health conditions, such as eating disorders and
depression.

Your body image is what you think and how you feel when you look
in the mirror or when you picture yourself in your mind. This includes
how you feel about your appearance; what you think about your body
itself, such as your height and weight; and how you feel within your
own skin. Body image also includes how you behave as a result of your
thoughts and feelings. You may have a positive or negative body image.
Body image is not always related to your weight or size.

Why Is a Healthy Body Image Important?

Women with a positive body image are more likely to have good
physical and mental health. Girls and women with negative thoughts
and feelings about their bodies are more likely to develop certain
mental health conditions, such as eating disorders and depression.
Researchers think that dissatisfaction with their bodies may be part
of the reason more women than men have depression.

A negative body image may also lead to low self-esteem, which can
affect many areas of your life. You may not want to be around other
people or may obsess constantly about what you eat or how much you
exercise. But you can take steps to develop a healthier body image.

Are Some People More Likely to Develop a Negative Body Image?

Yes. Girls are more likely than boys to have a negative body image.
This may be because many women in the United States feel pressured
to measure up to strict and unrealistic social and cultural beauty ideals, which can lead to a negative body image.

White girls and young women are slightly more likely to have a negative body image than African-American or Hispanic girls and young women. However, cultural beauty ideals change over time, and it can be difficult to correctly measure a complicated idea like body image among women from different backgrounds. Children of parents who diet or who have a negative body image are also more likely to develop unhealthy thoughts about their own bodies.

Why Are Women so Focused on Body Image?

In the United States, girls and women hear and see messages about how they look from the first moments they are alive, throughout much of their childhood, and into adulthood. Young girls and teens are more likely to be praised for how they look than for their thoughts or actions. The media focuses on showing women who are thin, attractive, and young. Images of these women are often edited using computer technology. As a result, girls and young women often try to reach beauty and body ideals that do not exist in the real world.

What Causes a Negative Body Image

Past events and circumstances can cause you to have a negative body image, including:

- Being teased or bullied as a child for how you looked
- Being told you're ugly, too fat, or too thin, or having other aspects of your appearance criticized
- Seeing images or messages in the media (including social media) that make you feel bad about how you look
- Being underweight, overweight, or obese

In rare cases, people can have such a distorted view of their bodies that they have a mental health condition called body dysmorphic disorder (BDD). BDD is a serious illness in which a person is preoccupied with minor or imaginary physical flaws.

How Does Overweight or Obesity Affect Body Image?

In the United States, two out of every three women have overweight or obesity. Women with obesity are more likely to have a negative body image, but not all women who have obesity or overweight are dissatisfied with their bodies. Women with a healthy weight can also have a negative body image, although obesity can make a woman's negative body image more severe.

Weight is not the only part of a person's body that determines body image. Self-esteem, past history, daily habits such as grooming, and the particular shape of your body all contribute to body image. Weight is an important part of body image, but it is not the only part.

How Does Underweight Affect Body Image?

In the United States, 1.6 percent of women are underweight. Women of all age groups are more likely to be underweight than men are. Women who are underweight due to a health condition like an eating disorder, cancer, or Crohn's disease may have a negative body image due to the effects of their condition. Women who are underweight without another health condition may also have a negative body image if others comment negatively on their weight or express other negative attitudes.

Weight is not the only part of a person's body that determines body image. Self-esteem, past history, daily habits such as grooming, and the particular shape of your body all contribute to body image. Weight is an important part of body image, but it is not the only part.

How Can I Have a Healthy Body Image?

Research shows that if you have overweight or obesity, your body image may improve if you participate in a weight-loss program, even if you don't lose as much weight as you hoped. The weight-loss program should include a focus on healthy eating and physical activity.

If you are underweight and have a negative body image, you can work with a doctor or nurse to gain weight in a healthy way and treat any other health problems you have. If you are eating healthy and getting enough exercise, your weight may matter less in your body image.

The more you practice thinking positive thoughts about yourself and the fewer negative thoughts you have about your body, the better you will feel about who you are and how you look. While very few people are 100 percent positive about every aspect of their body, it can help to focus on the things you do like. Also, most people realize as they get older that how you look is only one part of who you are. Working on accepting how you look is healthier than constantly working to change how you look.

How Can I Help My Kids Have a Healthy Body Image?

Your body image plays a role in how your kids see themselves. Studies show that daughters are twice as likely to have ideas about dieting when their mothers diet. If you want to lose weight to get healthy, pay attention to the language that you use with your kids. Rather than talking about "dieting," explain that you are eating healthy foods. Together with your family, cook healthy meals, order healthy meals at restaurants, and get more physical activity. Teach your children about smart food choices and help them develop healthy eating and exercise habits.

You can help your children develop healthy body images by:

- Making sure your children understand that weight gain and growth are normal parts of development, especially during puberty

- Not making negative statements about food, weight, and body size and shape—yours, your children's, or anyone else's

- Allowing your children to make decisions about food while making sure that plenty of healthy and nutritious meals and snacks are available

- Complimenting your children more on their efforts, talents, accomplishments, and personal values and less on their looks

- Limiting screen time. In addition to getting less exercise, kids who watch television shows or movies or play online games often see unrealistic female bodies. Talk with kids about the media images you see.

- Encouraging your children's school to create policies against bullying

- Talking to your children often and showing them that you're always there to listen

You may be teaching your kids harmful habits if you:

- Often complain about your weight or your body shape

- Often try new "miracle" diets

- Tell your kids they would be more attractive if they lost weight

Are Some Children More at Risk of Body Image Problems?

Yes. Many things can trigger weight concerns for girls or boys and affect their eating habits in potentially unhealthy ways:

- Having mothers who are very worried about their own weight
- Having mothers who are very worried about their kids' weight and looks
- Natural weight gain and other body changes during puberty
- Peer pressure to look a certain way
- Struggles with self-esteem
- Media images showing the ideal female body as thin

Many teenage girls of average weight think they have overweight and are not satisfied with their bodies. Having extreme weight concerns—and acting on those concerns—can harm girls' social, physical, and emotional growth. Skipping meals or taking diet pills can lead to poor nutrition and difficulty learning. For some teens, extreme efforts to lose weight can lead to eating disorders such as anorexia or bulimia. For others, the pressure to be thin can lead to binge-eating disorder (BED)—overeating that is followed by extreme guilt. Girls are also more likely than boys to risk their health by trying to lose weight in unhealthy ways, such as smoking.

Is Cosmetic Surgery Good or Bad for a Healthy Body Image?

It depends. If you are considering cosmetic surgery, you must be honest with yourself. Why do you want surgery, and what do you expect surgery to do for you? It is never a good idea to have cosmetic surgery to try to impress someone other than yourself. If a partner or spouse insists on you having cosmetic surgery, that is a type of abuse, and you should tell a doctor, a family member, or someone else who can help you think through the decision.

Because the changes resulting from cosmetic surgery are often dramatic and permanent, it's important to have a clear understanding of how surgery might make you feel—before you have the surgery.

Section 43.2

Parental and Peer Factors Associated with Body Image

This section includes text excerpted from "Parental and Peer Factors Associated with Body Image: Discrepancy among Fifth-Grade Boys and Girls," Centers for Disease Control and Prevention (CDC), April 2018.

Many young adolescents are dissatisfied with their body weight and shape. One reason for their dissatisfaction with their bodies might be a discrepancy between their ideal and actual body size. Young adolescents with a discrepancy are at a higher risk for low self-esteem and poor self-concept. Furthermore, such adolescents are at higher risk for chronic body image problems, which can contribute to weight cycling, eating disorders, depression, and obesity.

Researchers often use the terms "body image," "body dissatisfaction," and "body image discrepancy" interchangeably, regardless of how they are measured. In general, body image is the subjective concept of one's physical appearance based on self-perceptions and self-attitudes, including thoughts, beliefs, and feelings. Body image is composed of two components: perceptions of the appearance of one's body (cognitive/rational) and emotional responses to those perceptions (affective/emotional). Some researchers examine these components as one index called body dissatisfaction. However, other researchers examine these components separately as body image discrepancy, which is defined as the difference between individuals' self-perceived body size and the size they believe a person their age and sex should be (cognitive/rational). Although research of body dissatisfaction and body image discrepancy might yield similar findings, it is important to be able to articulate which parental, peer, and psychological factors contribute uniquely to these two outcomes, so that researchers can develop targeted prevention and intervention programs.

Research suggests that children and adolescents learn from their families and friends that they should be thin and that being overweight is unappealing. Much of the research examines the role of family and peer relationships and psychological well-being as they relate to body dissatisfaction. For example, studies have shown that a lack of social support from parents and peers has been associated with body dissatisfaction in young adolescents. Researchers also have examined the association between adolescent self-beliefs (e.g., global self-esteem and self-worth) and body dissatisfaction, demonstrating that higher levels of self-esteem are associated with lower levels of body dissatisfaction.

Parental Factors

Research has shown that when parents are emotionally warm, affectionate, and available, and balance these qualities with high expectations and a firm but fair disciplinary style, they create an emotional context in which children and adolescents tend to be more secure, well adjusted, healthier, and safer than peers raised in other settings. Specifically, parental nurturance is important throughout the developmental process and appears to be an especially significant factor in the positive development of young adolescents. Researchers have found positive associations between young adolescents who are satisfied with their bodies and parents who are nurturing and supportive, whereas young adolescents dissatisfied with their bodies are associated with parents who are less nurturing and warm. These findings are consistent for boys and girls.

Nurturing parents also have a lasting effect on their children's body image. Studies show that boys and girls with positive and supportive parents have more consistent body image satisfaction over time. These associations rarely have been examined for body image discrepancy; however, the few studies that have examined these associations have shown that low social and emotional support received from parents was associated with higher levels of body image discrepancy.

Parents also might indirectly affect how young adolescents view their bodies by affecting their perceptions of self-worth. For example, research suggests that parents who are critical and unsupportive (e.g., who express dissatisfaction with their own, or their children's weight, or tease them about it) can have a negative impact on their children's beliefs about themselves. These findings are consistent for boys and girls.

Peer Factors

Young adolescents who feel that they are accepted and well-connected to their peer group have more positive perceptions of themselves and their bodies. Researchers have also found that children's perception that being thin is related to popularity among peers predicted children's body dissatisfaction and eating-related concerns, especially for girls.

However, much of the research examining associations between peers and body image has focused on peer criticism about weight and shape, peer conversations about appearance, and peer weight-loss habits. Peers also might influence body image discrepancy by affecting young adolescents' beliefs about themselves. For example, young adolescents who worry about what others think of them or how they may be treated at school tend to have negative perceptions of themselves. In addition, peer criticism and teasing contribute negatively to young adolescents' beliefs about their physical appearance and are correlated with lower levels of self-worth.

Fostering Positive Peer and Parental Influences

Research shows that both self-esteem/self-worth and body image satisfaction decrease from childhood to adolescence, especially for girls. Future studies are needed to explore other mechanisms (e.g., parental and peer beliefs, self-efficacy beliefs) through which social and cultural influences affect the body image discrepancy of young adolescents. A greater understanding of the development of body image discrepancy will lead to more appropriate and effective educational programs targeting young adolescents at risk for developing body discrepancies, as well as the negative health outcomes that are associated with body dissatisfaction, such as depression or eating disorders. These findings have important prevention and intervention implications. Prevention efforts to consider include developing targeted resources that educate mothers and fathers about how they influence their children's self-worth and perception of their body size, including their beliefs, thoughts, feelings, and behaviors. Resources also can be developed that could be integrated into the school curriculum. School programs can be based on a collaborative approach with school counselors, teachers, and parents to help reinforce key messages. These resources can include information on how to have a high self-worth, resist social pressures to be thin, deal with peer norms about body image, prevent body image problems, and get help if they have a body-image issue.

Section 43.3

Creating a Positive Body Image

This section includes text excerpted from "Body Positivity,"
Smokefree Women, U.S. Department of Health and
Human Services (HHS), September 6, 2018.

Feeling good about your body can be difficult. But learning to have a positive body image can improve your self-esteem and increase your chances of quitting for good.

How You See Yourself

Body image is how you think and feel about your body. Many people feel badly about their bodies from time to time—even people who you may think have a "perfect" body. There are many things that might cause you to have a negative body image, such as:

- Comparing yourself to other people

- Worrying if people think you're attractive

- Comments about your appearance from family, friends, or strangers

- Messages from movies, television, magazines, and social media

Having a negative body image can hurt your confidence and can keep you from living the life you want to live. You may avoid parties, dating, going to the gym, or meeting new people. You may also start or continue unhealthy activities to help you feel better about your body, like smoking. If this sounds familiar, you're not alone.

Creating a Positive Body Image

Having a positive body image means being comfortable and confident in your body. It's seeing yourself as a whole person, instead of focusing on how you look or how much you weigh. It's learning to accept, appreciate, and even love the parts of you that are different. This can be difficult. And it can be a lifelong process because your body goes through changes throughout your life.

Becoming body positive doesn't happen overnight. It takes some practice to appreciate your body. Here are some things you can do to feel good about yourself:

- **Think of what's important:** The next time you want to smoke because you feel badly about yourself, try thinking about the things that are important to you. What do you value? What do you want in your future? Then ask yourself how smoking could negatively affect these things. This can help you stay motivated and avoid smoking again.

- **Stay positive:** Try to be aware of when you have a negative thought about your body. When it happens, think of a positive quality about yourself. You can even make a list and read it to yourself in the mirror. This can help you begin to change negative thoughts. Surround yourself with positive people. They can support your quit and help you see all the great things about yourself.

- **Find fun things to do:** Try a new dance workout. Volunteer with a local charity. Or start a book club with a group of close friends. Do fun activities to create a positive environment for yourself. When you're enjoying life, you will have less time to focus on your appearance.

- **Help others:** Help your loved ones see their beauty, inside and out. Try saying nice things, focusing on health instead of weight, and not criticizing other people's physical appearance (including your own). This can help create a positive environment for you and the other women in your life. Plus, doing something nice for someone else can lift your mood and keep you distracted when a cigarette craving hits.

- **Stress less:** When you're feeling down or stressed, you're more likely to slip. Use relaxation exercises, like deep breathing or muscle relaxation, to handle nicotine withdrawal or help a food craving pass.

- **Focus on your superpowers:** Think about the powerful and amazing things your body can do. You're able to get around and do things, heal yourself when you're injured or sick, or comfort others with the power of touch.

293

Section 43.4

Body Image during Pregnancy: Loving Your Body at All Stages

This section includes text excerpted from "Pregnancy and Body Image," Office on Women's Health (OWH), U.S. Department of Health and Human Services (HHS), August 28, 2018.

Pregnancy and Body Image

Pregnancy causes many changes in your body. Some of these changes can be difficult to deal with or very uncomfortable. Also, after giving birth, your body may take a while to get back to the way it was before, or it may never completely return to the way it looked before pregnancy. Although these changes are natural, some women may struggle with keeping a positive body image during and after pregnancy. You can learn ways to cope with feelings about your body's changes during and after pregnancy.

How Does Pregnancy Affect Body Image?

For some women, pregnancy can cause body image problems they did not have before or make body image problems worse. During pregnancy, your body goes through several changes, including weight gain. Hormonal changes will cause your stomach and breasts to get larger as the baby grows and your body prepares for breastfeeding. You might develop stretch marks where your body gets larger. Sometimes your skin will break out with acne. You may also be much more tired than usual and have mood swings more often. A negative mood may make you more likely to have unhealthy or negative thoughts about your body.

Being comfortable with your body before pregnancy can help you get through the physical and emotional changes during pregnancy.

How Can I Love and Accept My Pregnant Body?

Women's bodies are amazing for the ability to nourish and deliver a baby. Some of the body changes that come with pregnancy are uncomfortable, but they all support your growing child. Pregnancy does not last forever.

- **Focus on the positive work your body is doing.** Your body is changing to help your baby grow and develop. This is normal.

- **Express your feelings.** Talk with your partner, family, or friends about how you are feeling. Keeping your feelings bottled up will only make you feel worse.

- **Get regular physical activity.** A light swim or walk can help you clear your mind and get the focus off your body image.

- **Try prenatal yoga (if your doctor, nurse, or midwife is okay with it).** Yoga* helps you focus less on how your body looks and more on the link between your body and your mind.

A mind and body practice with origins in ancient Indian philosophy. The various styles of yoga typically combine physical postures, breathing techniques, and meditation or relaxation.

- **Try a massage (if your doctor, nurse, or midwife is okay with it).** Massage can relieve stress and anxiety and help you feel more comfortable in your own skin.

- **Learn as much as you can about pregnancy.** By educating yourself, you will know what to expect and feel more in control.

- **Seek mental health support if you need it.** There is no shame in reaching out for help. Do it for yourself and your baby. Talk to your doctor or nurse about where to find support.

How Can I Get My Prebaby Body Back?

Pregnancy changes your body in many ways. After your baby is born, your body has to adjust to being in a nonpregnant state. This will take time. Some women find that their bodies never completely return to the way they were before getting pregnant. That's OK too. All women, whether they have children or not, experience changes in their bodies as they get older.

Breastfeeding as much as possible after childbirth will help produce the hormone oxytocin. One of the effects of oxytocin is that it helps shrink your uterus back to a smaller size. Choosing healthy foods and getting regular physical activity are the best ways to lose weight you put on during pregnancy. Join a gym that offers child care, or take your baby for a walk through the neighborhood. If you are breastfeeding, you will also burn more calories than usual.

Chapter 44

Determining a Healthy Weight

Chapter Contents

Section 44.1

How to Assess Your Weight

This section contains text excerpted from the following sources:
Text in this section begins with excerpts from "Calculate Body
Mass Index," National Heart, Lung, and Blood Institute (NHLBI),
February 13, 2013. Reviewed December 2018; Text beginning with
the heading "What Are the BMI Trends for Children and Teens in
the United States?" is excerpted from "About Child and Teen BMI,"
Centers for Disease Control and Prevention (CDC), October 24, 2018.

For adults, a healthy weight is defined as the appropriate body
weight in relation to height. Body mass index (BMI) is calculated from
your height and weight and is a useful measure of overweight and
obesity. People who are overweight (BMI of 25 to 29.9) have too much
body weight for their height.

People who are obese (BMI of 30 or above) almost always have a
large amount of body fat in relation to their height. There are excep-
tions, of course. Big athletes with lots of muscle might have a BMI over
30, but may still have a healthy body composition. They would not be
considered obese from the perspective of health risk.

Use a BMI calculator for adults and learn your BMI by entering
your height and body weight.

What Are the Body Mass Index Trends for Children and Teens in the United States?

The prevalence of children and teens who measure in the 95th percentile or greater on the Centers for Disease Control and Prevention (CDC)
growth charts has greatly increased over the past 40 years. However,
this trend has leveled off and has even declined in certain age groups.

How Can I Tell If My Child Is Overweight or Obese?

The CDC and the American Academy of Pediatrics (AAP) recommend the use of BMI to screen for overweight and obesity in children
and teens age 2 through 19 years. For children under the age of two
years old, consult the World Health Organization (WHO) standards.
Although BMI is used to screen for overweight and obesity in children
and teens, BMI is not a diagnostic tool. To determine whether the child
has excess fat, further assessment by a trained health professional
would be needed.

Can I Determine If My Child or Teen Is Obese by Using an Adult Body Mass Index Calculator?

In general, it's not possible to do this.

The adult calculator provides only the BMI value (weight/height^2) and not the BMI percentile that is needed to interpret BMI among children and teens. It is not appropriate to use the BMI categories for adults to interpret the BMI of children and teens.

However, if a child or teen has a BMI of $\geq$ 30 kg/m^2, the child is almost certainly obese. A BMI of 30 kg/m^2 is approximately the 95th percentile among 17-year-old girls and 18-year-old boys.

My Two Children Have the Same Body Mass Index Values, but One Is Considered Obese and the Other Is Not. Why Is That?

The interpretation of BMI varies by age and sex. So if the children are not the same age and the same sex, the interpretation of BMI has different meanings. For children of different age and sex, the same BMI could represent different BMI percentiles and possibly different weight status categories.

See the following graphic for an example for a 10-year-old boy and a 15-year-old boy who both have a BMI-for-age of 23. (Note that two children of different ages are plotted on the same growth chart to illustrate a point. Normally the measurement for only one child is plotted on a growth chart.)

What Are the Health Consequences of Obesity during Childhood?
Health Risks Now

Childhood obesity can have a harmful effect on the body in a variety of ways.

- High blood pressure and high cholesterol, which are risk factors for cardiovascular disease (CVD). In one study, 70 percent of obese children had at least one CVD risk factor, and 39 percent had two or more.

- Increased risk of impaired glucose tolerance, insulin resistance and type 2 diabetes

- Breathing problems, such as sleep apnea, and asthma

- Joint problems and musculoskeletal discomfort

- Fatty liver disease, gallstones, and gastro-esophageal reflux (i.e., heartburn)

- Psychological stress such as depression, behavioral problems, and issues in school

- Low self-esteem and low self-reported quality of life (QOL)

- Impaired social, physical, and emotional functioning

Health Risks Later

- Obese children are more likely to become obese adults. Adult obesity is associated with a number of serious health conditions including heart disease, diabetes, and some cancers.

- If children are overweight, obesity in adulthood is likely to be more severe.

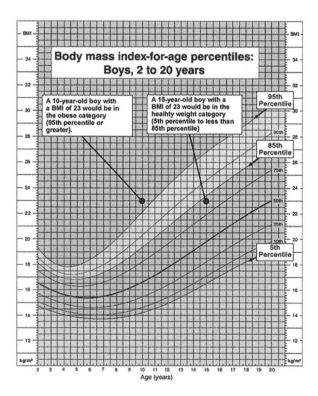

Figure 44.1. *Body Mass Index for Age Percentile*

Section 44.2

Are You Overweight?

This section includes text excerpted from "Overweight and Obesity Statistics," National Institute of Diabetes and Digestive and Kidney Diseases (NIDDK), August 2017.

Defining Overweight and Obesity

A person whose weight is higher than what is considered as a normal weight adjusted for height is described as being overweight or having obesity.

Fast Facts

According to data from the National Health and Nutrition Examination Survey (NHANES), 2013–2014:

- More than one in three adults were considered to be overweight

- More than two in three adults were considered to be overweight or have obesity

- More than one in three adults were considered to have obesity

- About 1 in 13 adults were considered to have extreme obesity

- About one in six children and adolescents ages 2 to 19 were considered to have obesity

Using Body Mass Index to Estimate Overweight and Obesity

Body mass index (BMI) is the tool most commonly used to estimate and screen for overweight and obesity in adults and children. BMI is defined as weight in kilograms divided by height in meters squared. For most people, BMI is related to the amount of fat in their bodies, which can raise the risk of many health problems. A healthcare professional can determine if a person's health may be at risk because of his or her weight. The tables below show BMI ranges for overweight and obesity.

Adults

Table 44.1. BMI of Adults Ages 20 and Older

Body Mass Index	Classification
18.5 to 24.9	Normal weight
25 to 29.9	Overweight
30+	Obesity (including extreme obesity)
40+	Extreme obesity

An online tool for gauging the BMIs of adults can be found at: www.cdc.gov

Children and Adolescents

Table 44.2. BMI of Children and Adolescents Ages 2 to 19

Body Mass Index	Classification
At or above the 85th percentile on the CDC growth charts	Overweight or obesity
At or above the 95th percentile on the CDC growth charts	Obesity (including extreme obesity)
At or above 120 percent of the 95th percentile on the CDC growth charts	Extreme obesity

Children grow at different rates at different times, so it is not always easy to tell if a child is overweight. The Centers for Disease Control and Prevention (CDC) BMI growth charts are used to compare a child's BMI with other children of the same sex and age. It is important that a child's healthcare provider evaluates a child's BMI, growth, and potential health risks due to excess body weight.

Causes and Health Consequences of Overweight and Obesity

Factors that may contribute to weight gain among adults and youth include genes, eating habits, physical inactivity, television, computer, phone, and other screen time, sleep habits, medical conditions or medications, and where and how people live, including their access to healthy foods and safe places to be active.

Overweight and obesity are risk factors for many health problems such as type 2 diabetes, high blood pressure, joint problems, and gallstones, among other conditions.

Prevalence of Overweight and Obesity

The data presented on prevalence are from the 2013–2014 NHANES survey of the National Center for Health Statistics (NCHS) unless noted otherwise. NCHS is part of the CDC.

Adults
Estimated (Age-Adjusted) Percentage of U.S. Adults with Overweight and Obesity by Sex, 2013–2014 NHANES Data

Table 44.3. Percentage of U.S. Adults with Overweight and Obesity

	All (Men and Women)	Men	Women
Overweight or obesity	70.2	73.7	66.9
Overweight	32.5	38.7	26.5
Obesity (including extreme obesity)	37.7	35	40.4
Extreme obesity	7.7	5.5	9.9

As shown in the above table:

- More than 2 in 3 adults (70.2%) were considered to be overweight or have obesity

- About 1 in 3 adults (32.5%) were considered to be overweight

- More than 1 in 3 adults (37.7%) were considered to have obesity

- About 1 in 13 adults (7.7%) were considered to have extreme obesity

- More than 1 in 3 (38.7%) of men, and about 1 in 4 (26.5%) of women were considered to be overweight

- Obesity was higher in women (about 40%) than men (35%)

- Extreme obesity was higher in women (9.9%) than men (5.5%)

- Almost 3 in 4 men (73.7%) were considered to be overweight or have obesity; and about 2 in 3 women (66.9%) were considered to be overweight or have obesity.

Estimated (Age-Adjusted) Percentage of U.S. Adults with obesity by Race/Ethnicity, 2013–2014 NHANES Data

- Among non-Hispanic white adults, more than 1 in 3 (36.4%) were considered to have obesity, and about 1 in 13 (7.6%) were considered to have extreme obesity.

- Among non-Hispanic black adults, almost half (48.4%) were considered to have obesity, and about 1 in 8 (12.4%) were considered to have extreme obesity.

- Among Hispanic adults, about 1 in 2 (42.6%) were considered to have obesity, and about 1 in 14 (7.1%) were considered to have extreme obesity.

- Among non-Hispanic Asian adults, about 1 in 8 (12.6%) were considered to have obesity.

Children and Adolescents (Youth)

Estimated (Age-Adjusted) Percentage of U.S. Adults with obesity by Race/Ethnicity, 2013–2014 NHANES Data

- Among children and adolescents ages 2 to 19, about 1 in 6 (17.2%) were considered to have obesity, about 1 in 17 (6%) were considered to have extreme obesity.

- Young children ages 2 to 5 had a lower prevalence of obesity than older youth, about 1 in 11 (9.4%).

- Less than 2 percent of young children were considered to have extreme obesity.

- Among children and youth ages 6 to 11, about 1 in 6 (17.4%) were considered to have obesity, and about 1 in 23 (4.3%) were considered to have extreme obesity.

- Among adolescents, ages 12 to 19, about 1 in 5 (20.6%) were considered to have obesity, and about 1 in 11 (9.1%) were considered to have extreme obesity.

The prevalence of obesity increased significantly among adult men and women between 1980–2000.

- Between 2005–2014, the prevalence of overall obesity and extreme obesity increased significantly among women, however, there were no significant increases for men.

Trends in Overweight and Obesity among Adults and Youth in the United States

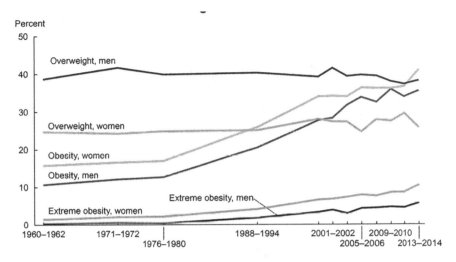

Figure 44.2. *Trends in Adult Overweight, Obesity and Extreme Obesity among Men and Women Aged 20 to 74; United States 1960–1962 through 2013–2014*

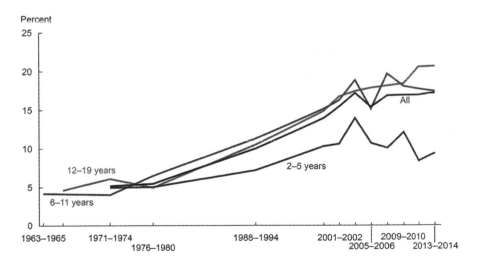

Figure 44.3. *Trends in Obesity among Children and Adolescents Aged 2 to 19 Years by Age; United States 1963–1965 through 2013–2014*

- The prevalence of obesity among children and adolescents 2 to 19 years increased between 1988–1994 and 2003–2004. Since this time there has been no significant change in prevalence. Among children ages 2 to 5, the prevalence of obesity increased between 1988–1994 and 2003–2004 and then decreased.

- Among children ages 6 to 11, the prevalence of obesity increased between 1988–1994 and 2007–2008, and then did not change.

- Among adolescents, ages 12 to 19, the prevalence of obesity increased between 1988–1994 and 2013–2014.

Section 44.3

Signs That You Are Underweight

This section includes text excerpted from "Underweight,"
Office on Women's Health (OWH), U.S. Department of
Health and Human Services (HHS), December 27, 2018.

In today's world, thinness is often praised. But being underweight, when your weight is lower than what is considered healthy for your height, can be a sign of a serious health problem. Many different things can cause women to be underweight, including eating habits, health problems, and medicines. Underweight can cause other health problems and problems getting pregnant. You can work with your doctor or nurse to help you reach a healthy weight.

How Do I Know If I'm Underweight?

You can use the body mass index (BMI) to find out whether your weight is in a healthy or unhealthy range. BMI is a tool to estimate body fat. Type your height and weight into this BMI calculator.

Women with a BMI of less than 18.5 are considered underweight. The average woman's height is 5 feet, 4 inches. If you weigh 107 pounds or less at this height, you are considered underweight with a BMI of 18.4. A healthy weight range for that woman would be 108 to 145 pounds.

BMI is just one way to measure healthy weight. Some women have a low, but still healthy weight. Talk to your doctor or nurse about what is a healthy weight for you.

Who Is at Risk for Underweight?

In the United States, 1.6 percent of women are underweight. Women of all age groups are more likely to be underweight than men are.

What Causes Women to Be Underweight or to Lose Weight Suddenly

Some women are naturally thinner than others. But certain health problems, certain medicines, or other serious problems can lead to chronic (long-term) underweight or sudden weight loss. These include:

- Health problems that affect the metabolism, such as overactive thyroid or diabetes

- Health problems that affect the digestive system, such as celiac disease or Crohn disease

- Other health problems, such as viral hepatitis, cancer, chronic obstructive pulmonary disease (COPD), or Parkinson disease (PD)

- A lack of appetite due to stress, illness, or substance use

- Medicines that may cause nausea or lack of appetite

- Eating disorders, such as anorexia

- Overexercising, such as for athletic training

- Age. Underweight can especially be a problem for older women who may have loss of appetite, problems chewing, or a health problem.

- Genes. Underweight can run in families.

Also, there may be a link between underweight in childhood and developing an eating disorder in adolescence.

How Does Underweight Affect a Woman's Health?

Underweight raises your risk for serious health problems. Some women have a low, but still healthy weight. But if you have experienced sudden weight loss or are not eating enough to keep your body working, you may develop serious health problems, including:

- **Problems with your menstrual cycle.** A regular period is a sign of good health. Losing too much weight can cause periods to be less regular or stop completely. This can happen if your body fat drops so low that you stop ovulating, or releasing an egg from an ovary each month. This is especially true if you are losing weight because you are not eating enough or because you are exercising too much, which may be signs of an eating disorder like anorexia nervosa.

- **Problems getting pregnant.** Problems with your menstrual cycle can make it harder to get pregnant, especially if your period stops completely. If you do not get a period, then you are probably not ovulating, or releasing an egg from an ovary each month.

- **Osteoporosis.** Underweight increases your risk of osteoporosis later in life. Osteoporosis is a condition that causes bones to become weak and break easily.

- **Malnutrition.** Malnutrition means your body is not getting enough vitamins and minerals to do what it needs to do. This can cause serious health problems, such as a weaker immune system and anemia. Anemia happens when your blood cannot carry enough oxygen to your body because of a lack of iron. If you have anemia, you may feel dizzy, lightheaded, weak, or tired.

- **Depression.** Studies show that depression is more common in women who are underweight than women who are at a healthy weight.

Women who are underweight may also be more likely to die early than people of normal weight. Women who are underweight earlier in adulthood may also experience menopause sooner than women who stayed a normal weight.

How Can I Gain Weight in a Healthy Way?

Talk to your doctor or nurse about an eating plan that can help you gain weight in a healthy way. To gain weight in a healthy way, you should focus on getting enough nutrients—calories, vitamins, and minerals—for your body to work correctly. To reach a healthy weight, you should eat foods from all of the food groups with a calorie amount that is healthy for your current weight. Your doctor or nurse can tell you how quickly to gain weight in a safe and healthy way. Gaining weight suddenly, or by eating a lot of sweet or fatty foods, is not healthy.

If you need to gain weight because of an eating disorder, work with your doctor or nurse to gain weight safely and treat the eating disorder. If the eating disorder is not treated, it may come back or continue and cause health problems. Gaining weight too suddenly, with an eating disorder, can cause serious heart problems and other health concerns.

Because many Americans are overweight, there are many resources geared toward losing weight. But some of these resources can also provide guidance for you to gain weight in a healthy way.

Should I Stop Exercising If I'm Underweight or Losing Weight Too Quickly?

Maybe. People who are underweight due to an eating disorder should not exercise unless their doctor tells them to. Physical activity is important for your health, muscle strength, balance, and flexibility. Your doctor or nurse can help you develop an exercise plan that is healthy and safe for a person of your current weight.

If you normally do high-intensity aerobic workouts, your doctor or nurse may talk to you about more moderate or less vigorous aerobic, strength training, and flexibility exercises.

When Should I Talk to a Doctor or Nurse about My Weight?

If you are worried about your weight, talk to your doctor or nurse.

Your weight can affect your health. Your weight can also make it harder to get pregnant. Talk to your doctor or nurse if you are underweight and have period problems or symptoms of malnutrition, such as extreme tiredness, headaches, or hair loss.

Your doctor or nurse will ask you questions and may do tests to learn more about what is causing your symptoms or weight loss. Your doctor or nurse may suggest making changes in your eating and exercise habits, depending on the cause of your weight loss.

Section 44.4

How to Gain a Healthy Weight

This section includes text excerpted from "If You Need to Gain Weight," girlshealth.gov, Office on Women's Health (OWH), May 7, 2018.

If your doctor tells you that you are underweight, it's important you try to gain some weight. Sometimes being underweight can be just as hard to handle as being overweight. Here are some tips for gaining weight in a healthy way:

- **Use the ChooseMyPlate website (www.choosemyplate. gov) to guide your eating.** Whether you are underweight, overweight, or the right weight, you should eat a variety of healthy foods. The ChooseMyPlate website can help you do that. If you are underweight, you just need to eat more calories each day. The website can tell you how many calories you need to eat each day in order to reach a healthy weight. Use the MyPlate Checklist Calculator (www.choosemyplate.gov/MyPlatePlan) to find a personalized healthy eating plan.

- **Eat more healthy fats.** Choose unsaturated fats. You can find these in nuts, avocados, olives, and "fatty" fish. Add extra olive oil to your pasta dish. Add more salad dressing to your salad, and more mayonnaise to your tuna.

- **Eat more healthy carbohydrates.** Select sweets that also provide nutrients, such as bran muffins, yogurt with fruit, fruit pies or juice, and granola bars.

- **Think about your drink.** Try drinks with extra calories and nutrients, like a smoothie made with milk or juice. And don't fill up on a drink at mealtime.

Chapter 45

Maintaining Your Weight

Chapter Contents

Section 45.1

Weight Cycling: An Unhealthy Pattern

This section includes text excerpted from "Weight
Loss Maintenance," U.S. Department of Veterans
Affairs (VA), December 27, 2016.

It is often quite simple to make an initial health behavior change,
but very hard to maintain that change. Mark Twain captured this
succinctly: "It is easy to quit smoking. I have done it hundreds of
times." With weight, many patients have a history of brief weight loss,
followed by re-gain.

Virtually all health behavior change programs have fairly high
recidivism/relapse rates. This is well known for smoking cessation and
substance abuse/dependence and is also true for weight management.
Just a decade ago, the consensus was that 80 percent of patients who
had lost weight through a weight loss program would re-gain that
weight within a year. With advancements in behavioral interventions, it is now estimated that 20 percent of overweight individuals
are successful at long-term weight loss when it is defined as losing at
least 10 percent of initial body weight and maintaining the loss for at
least one year.

Relapse rates for weight loss programs are higher than for smoking
cessation and substance abuse/dependence. There are some clear reasons for this. First, successful long-term weight loss requires changing
two behaviors—eating and physical activity. Second, it may be easier
for people to "quit" something that is not a requirement. Research
has shown that it is difficult for those who are addicted to cut back
on smoking or drinking. Unfortunately, one cannot just stop eating,
and therein lies a significant barrier to weight loss. We know that
smoking and problematic drinking are complex problems involving
social, behavioral, thinking/belief, and biological factors. One's weight
is likely an even more complex interaction of these and additional
factors. To be successful in weight management, a patient needs to
simultaneously manage their eating, thinking, behavior, and physical
activity. These changes must occur in spite of an environment and a
culture that promotes obesity.

The good news is that there are strategies that are effective for
helping patients maintain new behaviors. Furthermore, there is a core
of patients who lose weight and maintain it, and these patients have
been studied carefully. It is also important to note that even those

successful at losing weight and maintaining weight loss may regain up to 50 percent of their initial weight loss; thus, some weight regain should not be seen as failure.

Causes of Weight Regain

People who have lost weight usually regain that weight because they stop doing those things they did to lose weight in the first place. Once the big concentrated effort is finished and their weight goal has been achieved, people often stop recording their food intake, slowly revert to former eating habits, and start skipping opportunities for physical activity. This may be a "lapse" (partial relapse) initially, but often leads to a full-blown "relapse" if not recognized and addressed. Clinical researchers have found it helpful to study relapses and provide tools for preventing them.

Importance of Active Relapse Prevention

Specific and ongoing attention to relapse prevention is almost always necessary to prevent weight regain. Patients rarely engage in active relapse prevention efforts without prompting. To be effective, relapse prevention efforts should be started and emphasized long before a patient's goal weight is reached. A basic rule of thumb with relapse prevention is "forewarned is forearmed." The clinician must assist patients in identifying future situations that place them at risk for relapse and developing skills to master these anticipated challenges.

Everyone attempting a healthy behavior change has slips or lapses. Unfortunately, the lapses themselves pose an ever greater risk of relapse due to the negative thinking that can go with a slip. This is so common that clinicians have named this the abstinence violation effect. Those who slip tend to feel like failures. They feel guilty, and they begin to question their confidence for making the change. This extra baggage makes a full relapse even more likely. Patients need to be aware of what slips are and what to do to limit their impact to avoid the abstinence violation effect (AVE).

In the event of a lapse or a slip, patients should be helped to put the relapse in a broad perspective ("it's just a temporary dip in the trend line"). One should not make too much of a slip. Avoid giving permission for lapses, but remember that successful weight managers also have temporary lapses. Help patients avoid self-recrimination and other negative thoughts and emotional reactions and advise them not to give up because they briefly lapsed. Help them engage in realistic positive thinking and encourage them to immediately resume appropriate weight control habits. Lastly, turn the slip into a positive—figure out why the slip occurred and plan to manage a similar situation in a different way in the future.

Weight-Loss Maintenance Strategies

There are many strategies that contribute to the success of those who are able to lose weight and keep it off. While a patient is actively working on weight loss, the importance of maintenance should be introduced. Once weight loss goals are met and the patient enters into a maintenance phase, the following strategies may be helpful.

Monitor Weight Daily

A research has shown that daily weight monitoring is associated with better weight loss and prevention of weight regain. Daily weighing allows for rapid detection of small gains. Thus, corrective actions (e.g., reduction of intake, increasing activity, or both) can be taken immediately. If a patient notices that his/her weight is up a pound, cutting back on high-calorie foods for a day or two may be all that is required to return to the goal weight. With less frequent weighing, a trend of small, daily weight gains may go unnoticed. This may require a more sustained and intensive effort to lose the gained weight. Thus, daily monitoring and immediate corrective action may be more effective than less frequent monitoring.

Establish Weight and Behavior "Alarms"

Having an "alarm" system will help patients stop an undesirable trend in their behavior or weight quickly. This alarm system will be most successful if it is coupled with frequent weighing (see Monitor Weight Daily above). A study, "STOP regain," showed that patients who were taught to weigh daily and develop a specific plan to return to weight-loss behaviors when they detected small gains were more likely to avoid larger re-gains than those not taught this system. Weight gain of three to four pounds was a "caution" and patients in this program were encouraged to use general dietary strategies to cut back on intake. Problem-solving determined the causes of changes in daily routines which contributed to weight gain (increased eating out, decreased activity, increased snacking, etc.). A five-pound gain signaled time to reinstate a weight-loss plan. The active weight loss involved a return to weight-loss calorie goals and increasing physical activity. In addition, participants were encouraged to use meal plans, pre-portioned meals, or use strategies that were previously helpful for limiting calories.

Engage in Physical Activity

Physical activity is important for weight loss maintenance. Evidence suggests that patients who lose weight using diet and physical activity maintain greater weight loss after one year than those who lose weight with diet alone. Repeatedly, studies of successful weight maintainers show those who are successful with long-term maintenance tend to exercise consistently. While both diet and physical activity contribute to energy balance, consistent physical activity during maintenance allows patients to consume a slightly higher level of calories compared to those not exercising and maintain their weight.

Get Support from Others

Ongoing support from family and friends is also very helpful because it provides additional accountability, encouragement, and reinforcement. Encourage patients to have their supporters ask them about their progress and offer encouragement on a regular basis.

Plan for High-Risk Situations

Being prepared to manage tempting situations can be very helpful. Patients should be encouraged to make a written list of their overly, or "high-risk" situations. Some high-risk, may be influenced by mood, so be alert to emotional states, which can be both positive and negative. Common high-risk situations related to mood include:

- Celebrations (positive mood)
- Boredom (neutral mood)
- Stress, sadness, or depressed mood (negative)

It may be helpful for patients to identify their typical responses for these different emotional states and develop plans to detect and manage eating in response to these feelings. High-risk situations can be very challenging, and it is important to have backup plans as first attempts may be unsuccessful.

315

Section 45.2

Maintaining a Healthy Weight: Balancing Calories

This section includes text excerpted from "Maintaining a Healthy Weight," National Institute on Aging (NIA), National Institutes of Health (NIH), June 11, 2017.

Maintaining a healthy weight is important for overall health and well-being. The secret to maintaining a healthy weight is to balance "energy in" and "energy out." Energy in means the calories you get from the food and beverages you consume. Energy out means the calories you burn for basic body functions and during physical activity. Check your weight once a week. Then you'll know whether you are balancing the calories in and calories out or whether you need to be more active.

As you grow older, if you continue to eat the same types and amounts of food but don't become more active, you'll probably gain weight. That's because metabolism (how you burn the calories you eat) can slow down with age.

How Active Should You Be to Keep a Healthy Weight

The answer is different for each person, but generally:

- To keep your weight the same, you need to burn the same number of calories as you eat and drink.

- To lose weight, burn more calories than you eat and drink.

- To gain weight, burn fewer calories than you eat and drink.

Other Ways to Maintain a Healthy Weight

- Limit portion size to control calorie intake.

- Add healthy snacks during the day if you want to gain weight.

- Be as physically active as you can be.

- Talk to your doctor about your weight if you think that you weigh too much or too little.

How Much Physical Activity

Although any amount of regular physical activity is good for you, aim for at least 150 minutes of physical activity each week. Unless you are already that active, you won't do that much all at once—10-minute sessions several times a day on most days are fine.

People over age 65 should be as physically active as their abilities and conditions will allow. Doing anything is better than doing nothing at all.

Most older people can be moderately active. But, you might want to talk to your doctor if you aren't used to energetic activity and you want to start a vigorous exercise program or significantly increase your physical activity. You should also check with your doctor if you have health concerns like the following:

- Dizziness

- Shortness of breath

- Chest pain or pressure

- An irregular heartbeat

- Blood clots

- Joint swelling

- A hernia

- Recent hip or back surgery

Your doctor might have some safety tips or suggest certain types of exercise for you.

You don't have to spend a lot of money joining a gym or hiring a personal trainer. Think about the kinds of physical activities that you enjoy—for example, walking, running, bicycling, gardening, house-cleaning, swimming, or dancing. Try to make time to do what you enjoy on most days of the week. And then increase how long you do it, or add another fun activity.

What Is Body Mass Index?

Your doctor might mention body mass index (BMI) when talking about your weight. Your BMI—body mass index—is a number based on your height and weight that can be compared to a chart to see if you are considered overweight or underweight. Obesity is a growing problem for all age groups in the United States. In older adults who are overweight, the decision whether to lose some or all of that extra weight is complicated, and BMI is just one factor. Body changes that come with age and health problems may mean that an older person's desired weight is higher than for someone younger. The National Heart, Lung, and Blood Institute (NHLBI), part of National Institutes of Health (NIH), has information on obesity and physical activity and on BMI.

Balancing Calories

Balancing the calories you eat and drink with the calories burned by being physically active helps to maintain a healthy weight. Check your weight once a week. Then you'll know whether you are balancing the calories in and calories out or whether you need to be more active.

Table 45.1. Balancing Calories (Energy) In and Calories Out

	Balancing Calories (Energy) in and Calories out
Energy In = Energy Out	**Maintaining Weight** Your weight will stay the same when the calories you eat and drink equal the calories you burn.
Energy In < Energy Out	**Losing Weight** You will lose weight when the calories you eat and drink are less than the calories you burn.
Energy In > Energy Out	**Gaining Weight** You will gain weight when the calories you eat and drink are greater than the calories you burn.

Section 45.3

Cutting Calories

This section includes text excerpted from "Eat More,
Weigh Less?" Centers for Disease Control and Prevention (CDC),
May 15, 2015. Reviewed December 2018.

How to Manage Your Weight without Being Hungry

Have you tried to lose weight by cutting down the amount of food you eat? Do you still feel hungry and not satisfied after eating? Or have you avoided trying to lose weight because you're afraid of feeling hungry all the time? If so, you are not alone. Many people throw in the towel on weight loss because they feel deprived and hungry when they eat less. But there is another way. Aim for a slow, steady weight loss by decreasing calorie intake while maintaining an adequate nutrient intake and increasing physical activity. You can cut calories without eating less nutritious food. The key is to eat foods that will fill you up without eating a large amount of calories.

If I Cut Calories, Won't I Be Hungry?

Research shows that people get full by the amount of food they eat, not the number of calories they take in. You can cut calories in your favorite foods by lowering the amount of fat and or increasing the amount of fiber-rich ingredients, such as vegetables or fruit.

Let's take macaroni and cheese as an example. The original recipe uses whole milk, butter, and full-fat cheese. This recipe has about 540 calories in one serving (1 cup).

Here's How to Remake This Recipe with Fewer Calories and Less Fat

- Use 2 cups nonfat milk instead of 2 cups whole milk

- Use 8 ounces light cream cheese instead of 2¼ cups full-fat cheddar cheese

- Use 1 tablespoon butter instead of 2 or use 2 tablespoons of soft transfat free margarine

- Add about 2 cups of fresh spinach and 1 cup diced tomatoes (or any other veggie you like)

Your redesigned mac and cheese now has 315 calories in one serving (1 cup). You can eat the same amount of mac and cheese with 225 fewer calories.

What Foods Will Fill Me Up?

To be able to cut calories without eating less and feeling hungry, you need to replace some higher calorie foods with foods that are lower in calories and fat and will fill you up. In general, this means foods with lots of water and fiber in them. The chart below will help you make smart food choices that are part of a healthy eating plan.

Table 45.2. Balancing Calories (Energy) In and Calories Out

These Foods Will Fill You up with Less Calories. Choose Them More Often . . .	These Foods Can Pack More Calories into Each Bite. Choose Them Less Often . . .
Fruits and vegetables (prepared without added fat)	**Fried foods**
Spinach, broccoli, tomato, carrots, watermelon, berries, apples	Eggs fried in butter, fried vegetables, French fries
Low-fat and fat-free milk products	**Full-fat milk products**
Low- or fat-free milk, low or fat-free yogurt, low- or fat-free cottage cheese	Full-fat cheese, full-fat ice cream, whole and 2% milk
Broth-based soup	**Dry snack foods**
Vegetable-based soups, soups with chicken or beef broth, tomato soups (without cream)	Crackers or pretzels, cookies, chips, dried fruits
Whole grains	**Higher-fat and higher-sugar foods**
Brown rice, whole wheat bread, whole wheat pastas, popcorn	Croissants, margarine, shortening, and butter, doughnuts, candy bars, cakes, and pastries
Lean meat, poultry and fish	**Fatty cuts of meat**
Grilled salmon, chicken breast without skin, ground beef (lean or extra lean)	Bacon, brisket, ground beef (regular)
Legumes (beans and peas)	
Black, red kidney and pinto beans (without added fat), green peas, black-eyed peas	

A healthy eating plan is one that:

- Emphasizes fruits, vegetables, whole grains, and fat-free or low-fat milk and milk products

- Includes lean meats, poultry, fish, beans, eggs, and nuts

- Is low in saturated fats, trans fats, cholesterol, salt (sodium), and added sugars

- Stays within your calorie needs

The number of calories in a particular amount or weight of food is called "calorie density" or "energy density." Low-calorie dense foods are ones that don't pack a lot of calories into each bite.

Foods that have a lot of water or fiber and little fat are usually low in calorie density. They will help you feel full without an unnecessary amount of calories.

Here Are Some More Ideas for Cutting Back on Calories without Eating Less and Being Hungry

Table 45.3. Ideas for Cutting Back on Calories

Instead Of . . .	Try . . .
Fried chicken sandwich with 1 tbsp. mayonnaise = 599 calories	Grilled chicken salad with low-fat dressing 2 cups lettuce, 2 oz. grilled chicken breast, 2 tbsp. light balsamic vinaigrette dressing = 178 calories
Cream-based soup 1 cup mushroom bisque = 400 calories	Broth-based soup 1 cup minestrone = 112 calories
Chips or pretzels 1.5 oz. pretzels = 162 calories	Baby carrots with hummus 16 baby carrots with 1 tbsp. hummus = 75 calories

Good Things Can Come in Big Packages!

People eat more than they realize when faced with large portion sizes. This usually means eating too many calories. But, not all large portions are created equal. Larger portions of water and fiber-rich foods, like fruits, vegetables, and broth-based soups, can fill you up with less calories. Start with an appetizer. Research shows that if you eat a low-calorie appetizer before a meal, you will eat fewer total calories during the meal. Start your meals with a broth-based soup or a green salad without a large amount of cheese or croutons.

Fruits and Veggies: Keep It Simple!

Most fruits and veggies are low-calorie and will fill you up, but the way you prepare them can change that. Breading and frying, and using high-fat creams or butter with vegetables and fruit will add extra calories. Try steaming vegetables and using spices and low-fat sauces for flavor. And enjoy the natural sweetness of raw fruit.

What about Beverages?

While drinking beverages is important to good health, they don't help you feel full and satisfied the way food does. Choose drinks without calories, like water, sparkling water, or unsweetened iced tea. Drink fat-free or low-fat milk instead of two percent or whole milk.

Section 45.4

Maintain a Healthy Weight: Tips for Healthy Weight Management

This section includes text excerpted from "Keeping It Off,"
Centers for Disease Control and Prevention (CDC),
May 15, 2015. Reviewed December 2018.

If you've recently lost excess weight, congratulations! It's an accomplishment that will likely benefit your health now and in the future. Now that you've lost weight, let's talk about some ways to maintain that success.

The following tips are some of the common characteristics among people who have successfully lost weight and maintained that loss over time.

Watch Your Diet

- **Follow a healthy and realistic eating pattern.** You have embarked on a healthier lifestyle, now the challenge is maintaining the positive eating habits you've developed along the way. In studies of people who have lost weight and kept it off for at least a year, most continued to eat a diet lower in calories as compared to their preweight loss diet.

- **Keep your eating patterns consistent.** Follow a healthy eating pattern regardless of changes in your routine. Plan ahead for weekends, vacations, and special occasions. By making a plan, it is more likely you'll have healthy foods on hand for when your routine changes.

- **Eat breakfast every day.** Eating breakfast is a common trait among people who have lost weight and kept it off. Eating a healthful breakfast may help you avoid getting "over hungry" and then overeating later in the day.

Be Active

Get daily physical activity. People who have lost weight and kept it off typically engage in 60 to 90 minutes of moderate intensity physical activity most days of the week while not exceeding calorie needs. This doesn't necessarily mean 60 to 90 minutes at one time. It might mean 20 to 30 minutes of physical activity three times a day. For example, a brisk walk in the morning, at lunchtime, and in the evening. Some people may need to talk to their healthcare provider before participating in this level of physical activity.

Stay on Course

- **Monitor your diet and activity.** Keeping a food and physical activity journal can help you track your progress and spot trends. For example, you might notice that your weight creeps up during periods when you have a lot of business travel or when you have to work overtime. Recognizing this tendency can be a signal to try different behaviors, such as packing your own healthful food for the plane and making time to use your hotel's exercise facility when you are traveling. Or, if working overtime, maybe you can use your breaks for quick walks around the building.

- **Monitor your weight.** Check your weight regularly. When managing your weight loss, it's a good idea to keep track of your weight so you can plan accordingly and adjust your diet and exercise plan as necessary. If you have gained a few pounds, get back on track quickly.

- **Get support from family, friends, and others.** People who have successfully lost weight and kept it off often rely on support from others to help them stay on course and get over any "bumps." Sometimes having a friend or partner who is also losing weight or maintaining a weight loss can help you stay motivated.

Chapter 46

Healthy Weight-Loss Guidelines

Chapter Contents

Section 46.1

Losing Weight: Getting Started

This section includes text excerpted from "Losing Weight: Getting Started," Centers for Disease Control and Prevention (CDC), December 10, 2015. Reviewed December 2018.

Losing weight takes more than desire. It takes commitment and a well-thought-out plan. Here's a step-by-step guide to getting started.

Step One: Make a Commitment

Making the decision to lose weight, change your lifestyle, and become healthier is a big step to take. Start simply by making a commitment to yourself. Many people find it helpful to sign a written contract committing to the process. This contract may include things like the amount of weight you want to lose, the date you'd like to lose the weight by, the dietary changes you'll make to establish healthy eating habits, and a plan for getting regular physical activity.

Writing down the reasons why you want to lose weight can also help. It might be because you have a family history of heart disease, or because you want to see your kids get married, or simply because you want to feel better in your clothes. Post these reasons where they serve as a daily reminder of why you want to make this change.

Step Two: Take Stock of Where You Are

Consider talking to your healthcare provider. She or he can evaluate your height, weight, and explore other weight-related risk factors you may have. Ask for a follow-up appointment to monitor changes in your weight or any related health conditions.

Keep a "food diary" for a few days, in which you write down everything you eat. By doing this, you become more aware of what you are eating and when you are eating. This awareness can help you avoid mindless eating.

Next, examine your current lifestyle. Identify things that might pose challenges to your weight loss efforts. For example, does your work or travel schedule make it difficult to get enough physical activity? Do you find yourself eating sugary foods because that's what you buy for your kids? Do your coworkers frequently bring high-calorie items, such as doughnuts, to the workplace to share with everyone? Think through things you can do to help overcome these challenges.

Finally, think about aspects of your lifestyle that can help you lose weight. For example, is there an area near your workplace where you and some coworkers can take a walk at lunchtime? Is there a place in your community, such as a Young Men's Christian Association (YMCA), with exercise facilities for you and child care for your kids?

Step Three: Set Realistic Goals

Set some short-term goals and reward your efforts along the way. If your long-term goal is to lose 40 pounds and to control your high blood pressure, some short-term eating and physical activity goals might be to start eating breakfast, taking a 15-minute walk in the evenings, or having a salad or vegetable with supper.

Focus on two or three goals at a time. Great, effective goals are:

- Specific

- Realistic

- Forgiving (less than perfect)

For example, "Exercise More" is not a specific goal. But if you say, "I will walk 15 minutes, 3 days a week for the first week," you are setting a specific and realistic goal for the first week.

Remember, small changes every day can lead to big results in the long run. Also, remember that realistic goals are achievable goals. By achieving your short-term goals day-by-day, you'll feel good about your progress and be motivated to continue. Setting unrealistic goals, such as losing 20 pounds in 2 weeks, can leave you feeling defeated and frustrated.

Being realistic also means expecting occasional setbacks. Setbacks happen when you get away from your plan for whatever reason—maybe the holidays, longer work hours, or another life change. When setbacks happen, get back on track as quickly as possible. Also take some time to think about what you would do differently if a similar situation happens, to prevent setbacks.

Keep in mind everyone is different—what works for someone else might not be right for you. Just because your neighbor lost weight by taking up running, doesn't mean running is the best option for you. Try a variety of activities—walking, swimming, tennis, or group exercise classes to see what you enjoy most and can fit into your life. These activities will be easier to stick with over the long term.

Step Four: Identify Resources for Information and Support

Find family members or friends who will support your weight loss efforts. Making lifestyle changes can feel easier when you have others you can talk to and rely on for support. You might have coworkers or neighbors with similar goals, and together you can share healthful recipes and plan group exercise.

Joining a weight loss group or visiting a healthcare professional such as a registered dietitian, can help.

Step Five: Continually "Check-In" with Yourself to Monitor Your Progress

Revisit the goals you set for yourself (in Step 3) and evaluate your progress regularly. If you set a goal to walk each morning but are having trouble fitting it in before work, see if you can shift your work hours or if you can get your walk in at lunchtime or after work. Evaluate which parts of your plan are working well and which ones need tweaking. Then rewrite your goals and plan accordingly.

If you are consistently achieving a particular goal, add a new goal to help you continue on your pathway to success.

Reward yourself for your successes! Recognize when you're meeting your goals and be proud of your progress. Use nonfood rewards, such as a bouquet of freshly picked flowers, a sports outing with friends, or a relaxing bath. Rewards help keep you motivated on the path to better health.

Section 46.2

Choosing a Safe and Successful Weight-Loss Program

This section includes text excerpted from "Choosing a Safe and Successful Weight-Loss Program," National Institute of Diabetes and Digestive and Kidney Diseases (NIDDK), July 2017.

Do you think you need to lose weight? Have you been thinking about trying a weight-loss program?

You are not alone. More than 70 percent of U.S. adults are overweight or have obesity—and many of them try to lose the extra pounds through different kinds of weight-loss programs. A number of these programs are advertised in magazines and newspapers, as well as on the radio, TV, and Internet. But are they safe? And will they work for you?

Here you'll find tips on how to choose a program that may help you lose weight safely and keep it off over time. You'll also learn how to talk with a healthcare professional about your weight.

Your healthcare professional may be able to help you make lifestyle changes to reach and maintain a healthy weight. However, if you're having trouble making these lifestyle changes—or if these changes aren't enough to help you reach and stay at a healthy weight—you may want to consider a weight-loss program or other types of treatment.

Where Do I Start?

Talking with a healthcare professional about your weight is an important first step. Sometimes, healthcare professionals may not address issues such as healthy eating, physical activity, and weight during general office visits. You may need to raise these issues yourself. If you feel uneasy talking about your weight, bring your questions with you and practice talking about your concerns before your office visit. Aim to work with your healthcare professional to improve your health.

Prepare for Your Visit

Before your visit with a healthcare professional, think about the following questions:

- How can I change my eating habits so I can be healthier and reach a healthy weight?

- How much and what type of physical activity do I think I need to be healthier and reach a healthy weight?

- Could I benefit from seeing a nutrition professional or weight-loss specialist, or joining a weight-loss program?

You can be better prepared for a visit with a healthcare professional if you:

- Write down all of your questions ahead of time

- Record all of the medicines and dietary supplements you take, or bring them with you

- Write down the types of diets or programs you have tried in the past to lose weight

- Bring a pen and paper, smartphone, or other mobile devices to read your questions and take notes

During your visit, a healthcare professional may:

- Review any medical problems you have and medicines you take to see whether they may be affecting your weight or your ability to lose weight

- Ask you about your eating, drinking, and physical activity habits

- Determine your body mass index (BMI) to see whether you're overweight or have obesity

People who are overweight have a BMI between 25.0 and 29.9. People with obesity have a BMI of 30.0 or higher, and those with extreme obesity have a BMI of 40.0 or higher. You can use this online tool or chart to see what your BMI is.

If a healthcare professional says you should lose weight, you may want to ask for a referral to a weight-loss program, dietitian, or weight-loss specialist. If you decide to choose a weight-loss program on your own, consider talking with the healthcare professional about the program before you sign up, especially if you have any health problems.

Ask questions if you don't understand something your healthcare professional has said, or if you need more information.

Questions to Ask a Healthcare Professional

You may want to ask a healthcare professional the following questions:

- What is a healthy weight or BMI for me?

- Will losing weight improve my general health, as well as specific health problems I have?

- Could any of my medical conditions or medications be causing weight gain or making it harder for me to lose weight?

- Are there any types or amounts of physical activity I should not do because of my health?

- What dietary approaches do you recommend I try or avoid?

What Should I Look for in a Weight-Loss Program?

To reach and stay at a healthy weight over the long term, you must focus on your overall health and lifestyle habits, not just on what you eat. Successful weight-loss programs should promote healthy behaviors that help you lose weight safely, that you can stick with every day, and that help you keep the weight off.

Safe and successful weight-loss programs should include:

- Behavioral treatment, also called lifestyle counseling, that can teach you how to develop and stick with healthier eating and physical activity habits—for example, keeping food and activity records or journals

- Information about getting enough sleep, managing stress, and the benefits and drawbacks of weight-loss medicines

- Ongoing feedback, monitoring, and support throughout the program, either in person, by phone, online, or through a combination of these approaches

- Slow and steady weight-loss goals—usually 1 to 2 pounds per week (though weight loss may be faster at the start of a program)

- A plan for keeping the weight off, including goal setting, self-checks such as keeping a food journal, and counseling support

The most successful weight-loss programs provide 14 sessions or more of behavioral treatment over at least 6 months—and are led by trained staff.

Some commercial weight-loss programs have all of these components for a safe and successful weight-loss program. Check for these features in any program you are thinking about trying.

Although these diets may help some people lose a lot of weight quickly—for example, 15 pounds in a month—they may not help people keep the weight off long term. These diets also may have related health risks, the most common being gallstones.

For people who are overweight or have obesity, experts recommend a beginning weight-loss goal of 5 to 10 percent of your starting weight within 6 months.2 If you weigh 200 pounds, that would amount to a loss of 10 pounds, which is 5 percent of starting weight, to 20 pounds, which is 10 percent of starting weight, in 6 months.

Changing your lifestyle isn't easy, but adopting healthy habits that you don't give up after a few weeks or months may help you maintain your weight loss.

What If the Program Is Offered Online

Many weight-loss programs are now being offered partly or completely online and through apps for mobile devices. Researchers are studying how well these programs work on their own or together with in-person programs, especially long term. However, experts suggest that these weight-loss programs should provide the following:

- Organized, weekly lessons, offered online or by podcast, and tailored to your personal goals

- Support from a qualified staff person to meet your goals

- A plan to track your progress on changing your lifestyle habits, such as healthy eating and physical activity, using tools such as cell phones, activity counters, and online journals

- Regular feedback on your goals, progress, and results provided by a counselor through email, phone, or text messages

- The option of social support from a group through bulletin boards, chat rooms, or online meetings

Whether a program is online or in person, you should get as much background as you can before you decide to join.

Weight-Loss Programs to Avoid

Avoid weight-loss programs that make any of the following promises:

- Lose weight without diet or exercise!

- Lose weight while eating as much as you want of all your favorite foods!

- Lose 30 pounds in 30 days!

- Lose weight in specific problem areas of your body!

Other warning signs to look out for include:

- Very small print, asterisks, and footnotes, which may make it easy to miss important information

- Before-and-after photos that seem too good to be true

- Personal endorsements that may be made up

What Questions Should I Ask about a Weight-Loss Program?

Weight-loss program staff should be able to answer questions about the program's features, safety, costs, and results. Find out if the program you're interested in is based on current research about what works for reaching and maintaining a healthy weight.

A first and very important question to ask of commercial weight-loss programs is, "Has your company published any reports in peer-reviewed, scientific journals about the safety and effectiveness of your program?"

If the response is "yes," ask for a copy of the report or how you could get it. If the answer is "no," the program is harder to evaluate and may not be as favorable a choice as programs that have published such information. If you have questions about the findings, discuss the report with your healthcare professional.

Here are some other questions you may want to ask:

What Does the Program Include?
Eating

- Am I expected to follow a specific meal plan?

- Am I encouraged to write down what I eat each day?

- Do I have to buy special meals or supplements? If so, what are the daily or weekly costs?

- Does the program offer healthy meal-plan suggestions that I could stick with?

- If the program requires special foods, can I make changes based on my likes, dislikes, and any food allergies I may have?

Physical Activity

- Does the program include a physical activity plan?

- Does the program offer ways to help me be more physically active and stay motivated?

Counseling

- Does the program offer one-on-one or group counseling to help me develop and stick with my healthier habits?

- Does the program include a trained coach or counselor to help me overcome roadblocks and stay on track?

Weight Maintenance

- Does the program include a plan to help me keep off the weight I've lost?

- What does that program include? Will there be ongoing counseling support?

Other Features

- How long is the actual weight-loss program?

- How long is the weight-loss maintenance program?

- Does the program require that I take any kind of medicine?

- Can I speak with a doctor or certified health professional if I need to?

- Can I change the program to meet my lifestyle, work schedule, and cultural needs?

- Will the program help me cope with such issues as stress or social eating, getting enough sleep, changes in work schedules, lack of motivation, and injury or illness?

- Is the program in person? Is there an online part to the program?

What Kind of Education or Training Do Staff Members Have?

These questions are especially important if you are considering a medically supervised program that encourages quick weight loss (three or more pounds a week for several weeks):

- Does a doctor or other certified health professional run or oversee the program?

- Does the program include specialists in nutrition, physical activity, behavior change, and weight loss?

- What type of certifications, education, experience, and training do staff members have?

- How long, on average, have most of the staff been working with the program?

Does the Program or Product Carry Any Risks?

- Could the program cause health problems or be harmful to me in any way?

- Is there ongoing input and follow-up to ensure my safety while I'm in the program?

- Will the program's doctor or staff work with my healthcare professional if needed—for example, to address how the program may affect an ongoing medical issue?

How Much Does the Program Cost?

- What is the total cost of the program, from beginning to end?

- Are there costs that are not included in that total, such as membership fees or fees for:

  - Weekly visits

  - Food, meal replacements, supplements, or other products

  - Medical tests

  - Counseling sessions

  - Follow-up to maintain the weight I've lost

What Results Do People in the Program Typically Achieve?

- How much weight does the average person lose?

- How long does the average person keep the weight off?

- Do you have written information on these and other program results?

- Are the results of the program published in a peer-reviewed scientific journal?

What If I Need More Help Losing Weight?

If a weight-loss program is not enough to help you reach a healthy weight, ask your healthcare professional about other types of weight-loss treatments. Prescription medicines to treat overweight and obesity, combined with healthy lifestyle changes, may help some people reach a healthy weight. For some people who have extreme obesity, bariatric surgery may be an option.

Section 46.3

Weight-Loss and Nutrition Myths

This section includes text excerpted from "Weight-Loss and Nutrition Myths," National Institute of Diabetes and Digestive and Kidney Diseases (NIDDK), July 6, 2017.

"Lose 30 pounds in 30 days!"

"Eat as much as you want and still lose weight!"

"Try the thigh buster and lose inches fast!"

Have you heard these claims before? A large number of diets and tools are available, but their quality may vary. It can be hard to know what to believe.

This section discusses myths and provide facts and tips about weight loss, nutrition, and physical activity. This information may help you make healthy changes in your daily habits. You can also talk to your healthcare provider. She or he can help you if you have other questions or you want to lose weight. A registered dietitian may also give you advice on a healthy eating plan and safe ways to lose weight and keep it off.

Weight-Loss and Diet Myths
Myth

Fad diets will help me lose weight and keep it off.

Fact

Fad diets are not the best way to lose weight and keep it off. These diets often promise quick weight loss if you strictly reduce what you eat or avoid some types of foods. Some of these diets may help you lose weight at first. But these diets are hard to follow. Most people quickly get tired of them and regain any lost weight. Fad diets may be unhealthy. They may not provide all of the nutrients your body needs. Also, losing more than 3 pounds a week after the first few weeks may increase your chances of developing gallstones (solid matter in the gallbladder that can cause pain). Being on a diet of fewer than 800 calories a day for a long time may lead to serious heart problems.

Myth

Grain products such as bread, pasta, and rice are fattening. I should avoid them when trying to lose weight.

Fact

A grain product is any food made from wheat, rice, oats, cornmeal, barley, or another cereal grain. Grains are divided into two subgroups, whole grains and refined grains. Whole grains contain the entire grain kernel—the bran, germ, and endosperm. Examples include brown rice and whole-wheat bread, cereal, and pasta. Refined grains have been milled, a process that removes the bran and germ. This is done to give grains a finer texture and improve their shelf life, but it also removes dietary fiber, iron, and many B vitamins.

People who eat whole grains as part of a healthy diet may lower their chances of developing some chronic diseases. Government dietary guidelines advise making half your grains whole grains. For example, choose 100 percent whole-wheat bread instead of white bread, and brown rice instead of white rice. The Resources section at the end of this fact sheet offers helpful links to these guidelines and the ChooseMyPlate (www.choosemyplate.gov) website, which provides information, tips, and tools on healthy eating.

Meal Myths

Myth

Some people can eat whatever they want and still lose weight.

Fact

To lose weight, you need to burn more calories than you eat and drink. Some people may seem to get away with eating any kind of food they want and still lose weight. But those people, like everyone, must use more energy than they take in through food and drink to lose weight.

A number of factors such as your age, genes, medicines, and lifestyle habits may affect your weight. If you would like to lose weight, speak with your healthcare provider about factors that may affect your weight. Together, you may be able to create a plan to help you reach your weight and health goals.

Myth

"Low-fat" or "fat-free" means no calories.

Fact

A serving of low-fat or fat-free food may be lower in calories than a serving of the full-fat product. But many processed low-fat or fat-free foods have just as many calories as the full-fat versions of the same foods—or even more calories. These foods may contain added flour, salt, starch, or sugar to improve flavor and texture after fat is removed. These items add calories.

Myth

Fast foods are always an unhealthy choice. You should not eat them when dieting.

Fact

Many fast foods are unhealthy and may affect weight gain. However, if you do eat fast food, choose menu options with care. Both at home and away, choose healthy foods that are nutrient rich, low in calories, and small in portion size.

Myth

If I skip meals, I can lose weight.

Fact

Skipping meals may make you feel hungrier and lead you to eat more than you normally would at your next meal. In particular, studies show a link between skipping breakfast and obesity. People who skip breakfast tend to be heavier than people who eat a healthy breakfast.

Myth

Eating healthy food costs too much.

Fact

Eating better does not have to cost a lot of money. Many people think that fresh foods are healthier than canned or frozen ones. For example, some people think that spinach is better for you raw than frozen or canned. However, canned or frozen fruits and veggies provide as many nutrients as fresh ones, at a lower cost. Healthy options include low-salt canned veggies and fruit canned in its own juice or water-packed. Remember to rinse canned veggies to remove excess salt. Also, some canned seafood, like tuna, is easy to keep on the shelf, healthy, and low cost. And canned, dried, or frozen beans, lentils, and peas are also healthy sources of protein that are easy on the wallet.

Food Myths
Myth

Eating meat is bad for my health and makes it harder to lose weight.

Fact

Eating lean meat in small amounts can be part of a healthy plan to lose weight. Chicken, fish, pork, and red meat contain some cholesterol and saturated fat. But they also contain healthy nutrients like iron, protein, and zinc.

Myth

Dairy products are fattening and unhealthy.

Fact

Fat-free and low-fat cheese, milk, and yogurt are just as healthy as whole-milk dairy products, and they are lower in fat and calories. Dairy products offer protein to build muscles and help organs work well, and calcium to strengthen bones. Most milk and some yogurts have extra vitamin D added to help your body use calcium. Most Americans don't get enough calcium and vitamin D. Dairy is an easy way to get more of these nutrients.

Myth

"Going vegetarian" will help me lose weight and be healthier.

Fact

Research shows that people who follow a vegetarian eating plan, on average, eat fewer calories and less fat than nonvegetarians. Some research has found that vegetarian-style eating patterns are associated with lower levels of obesity, lower blood pressure, and a reduced risk of heart disease. Vegetarians also tend to have lower body mass index (BMI) scores than people with other eating plans. (The BMI measures body fat based on a person's height in relation to weight). But vegetarians—like others—can make food choices that impact weight gain, like eating large amounts of foods that are high in fat or calories or low in nutrients.

The types of vegetarian diets eaten in the United States can vary widely. Vegans do not consume any animal products, while lacto-ovo vegetarians eat milk and eggs along with plant foods. Some people have eating patterns that are mainly vegetarian but may include small amounts of meat, poultry, or seafood.

Section 46.4

Popular Fad Diets

The many popular diets and diet plans on the market today can be confusing and overwhelming for consumers to navigate. People who want to lose weight are bombarded with advertisements for various diets all claiming to provide the secret to rapid weight loss with little or no effort. Some of these diets eliminate or restrict various foods, while others focus on including only certain foods. A diet can be considered a fad if it promises to deliver drastic weight loss in a short amount of time, without exercise, and if it is based on an unbalanced approach to nutrition. Many popular fad diets can be organized by type: high protein, low carbohydrate, fasting, food-specific, liquid only, and so on.

High-Protein Diets

High protein diets promote an eating plan based largely on foods containing protein, usually meat, eggs, cheese, and other dairy products. The theory behind high-protein diets is that the body must work harder to digest protein, and in doing so, more calories are burned. Studies have found that diets high in protein can cause certain health problems, as the body works to process excess protein. High-protein diets can cause rapid initial weight loss as the body eliminates water while processing extra protein. Typically, any weight lost on a high-protein diet will be regained.

Low-Carbohydrate Diets

The main premise of low-carbohydrate diets is the severe restriction of calories from carbohydrates (sugar). Most low-carbohydrate diets suggest replacing foods high in carbohydrates with foods high in protein. In this way, low-carbohydrate diets are similar to high-protein diets. A low-carbohydrate diet is often high in fat. A high-fat diet causes a condition known as ketosis, which can act as an appetite suppressant. The theory of low-carbohydrate diets is that the suppressed appetite will result in the dieter consuming fewer calories overall. Studies of low-carbohydrate diets have shown that dieters are at risk for health problems including kidney malfunction and heart disease.

341

Many people who follow a low-carbohydrate diet report feeling sluggish and tired, and typically any weight that is lost will be regained.

Detoxifying Diets

Detoxifying diets are often high-fiber diets, and sometimes include increased consumption of fats and oils. The theory of this type of detoxification is that the fiber helps the dieter to feel full, therefore, consuming fewer calories throughout the day. It is also believed that a high-fiber diet will cleanse the digestive system through the elimination of more solid waste. Side effects of a high-fiber detoxifying diet often include gastrointestinal distress, bloating, cramps, and dehydration. Studies have shown no permanent weight loss from this type of detoxifying diet.

Fasting Diets

Fasting diets require dieters to consume nothing but clear liquids for a short period of time, typically one to five days. This is believed to help rid the body of toxins. Fasting can result in temporary weight loss due to consuming far fewer calories than normal, though the weight generally returns once the fast is ended. Fasting produces a host of side effects, including dizziness, lethargy, and feeling weak or tired.

Food-Specific Diets

Food-specific diets recommend consumption of a single type of food, such as grapefruit, cabbage or protein shakes. These diets are based on the theory that certain foods have special properties that promote weight-loss. Food-specific diets do not provide the range of vitamins, minerals, and other nutrients needed to support bodily functions. If maintained over an extended period of time, the side effects of food-specific diets can be serious.

Popular Diet Plans
The Atkins Diet

The Atkins Diet is a low-carbohydrate, high-protein diet created by Dr. Robert Atkins, an American cardiologist. The main premise of the Atkins Diet is that eating too many carbohydrates causes obesity and other health problems. A diet that is low in carbohydrates produces metabolic activity that results in less hunger and also in weight loss. The Atkins Diet is structured in four phases: induction; weight loss; premaintenance; lifetime maintenance. Dieters move through the four phases at their own pace. Early phases of the Atkins Diet allow consumption of seafood, poultry, meat, eggs, cheese, salad vegetables, oils, butter, and cream. Later phases allow consumption of foods such as nuts, fruits, wine, beans, whole grains, and other vegetables. The Atkins Diet recommends avoidance of certain foods such as fruit, bread, most grains, starchy vegetables, and dairy products other than cheese, cream, and butter. The Atkins Diet may help people feel full longer, and may result in weight loss as long as the diet is continued. Side effects may result from consuming low amounts of fiber and certain vitamins and minerals, while consuming larger amounts of saturated fat, cholesterol, and red meat.

The Zone Diet

The Zone Diet was created by Dr. Barry Spears and is based on the genetic evolution of humans. The main premise of the Zone Diet is that humans should maintain a diet similar to that of our ancient hunter-gatherer ancestors. The Zone Diet focuses on lean protein, natural carbohydrates (fruit) and natural fiber (vegetables) while avoiding or eliminating processed carbohydrates such as grains and products made from grains. The Zone Diet recommends a food plan that is made up of 40 percent natural carbohydrates. 30 percent fat, and 30 percent protein. The emphasis is on food choices, not amount of calories. This percentage should apply to every meal and snack that is eaten. Close evaluation of the Zone Diet has revealed that at its core, the Zone Diet is a very low-calorie eating plan that is lacking in certain nutrients, vitamins, and minerals.

Weight Watchers

Weight Watchers was founded by Jean Nidetch in 1963. The Weight Watchers program focuses on weight loss through diet, exercise, and the use of support networks. Members are given the option of joining a group or following the program online. In either case, educational materials and support are available to assist members. The Weight Watchers support network is considered a critical aspect of the program, as it is believed that dieters need constant positive reinforcement in order to achieve and maintain long-term weight loss. The Weight Watchers program is structured in two phases: weight loss and maintenance. During weight loss, dieters work to lose weight slowly, with the goal of one to two pounds per week. Once the goal weight has been attained, dieters move into the maintenance phase, during which they gradually adjust their food intake until they are neither losing nor gaining weight. In general, Weight Watchers is viewed as providing a healthy approach to dieting.

Ornish Lifestyle Medicine

The Ornish Lifestyle Medicine program was created by Dr. Dean Ornish. The main premise of the program is that foods are neither good nor bad, but some are healthier than others. The Ornish diet focuses on fruits, vegetables, whole grains, legumes, soy products, nonfat dairy, natural egg whites, and fats that contain omega three fatty acids. The Ornish diet is plant-based; meat, poultry, and fish are excluded. Portion control is recommended, but caloric intake is not restricted unless a person is trying to lose weight. The program recommends small, frequent meals spread out throughout the day to support constant energy and avoid hunger. The consumption of caffeine is discouraged though allowed in small amounts. The Ornish program recommends exercise and low-dose multivitamin supplements. In general, the Ornish program is viewed as a healthy diet.

Diet Safety

Fad diets may produce initial weight loss results, but the potential for undesirable side effects should not be ignored. The human body needs simple carbohydrates (glucose) for energy and brain function. Low-carbohydrate and high-protein diets are not nutritionally balanced enough to meet the needs of children and some adults, particularly women who are pregnant, plan to become pregnant, or are nursing a baby. If maintained for an extended period of time, high-protein, low-carbohydrate diets can result in health problems such as heart disease, kidney problems, and certain cancers.

Weight loss is achieved by eating fewer calories than are consumed by physical activity. Because most fad diets require people to consume very few calories, these diets can result in weight loss. However, because most fad diets are not nutritionally balanced and cannot be maintained for long periods of time, people usually find that any weight lost is regained once they stop following the diet and return to their old eating habits. The most effective weight-loss strategies are those that include a healthy, balanced diet combined with exercise.

References

1. "Diet Fads versus Diet Truths," January 2004.

2. Nordqvist, Christian. "The Eight Most Popular Diets Today," Medical News Today, October 1, 2015.

3. "Nutrition Fact Sheet," Alaska Department of State Health Services, Nutrition Services Section, 2005.

Section 46.5

Why Fad Diets Don't Work

This section contains text excerpted from the following sources:
Text in this section begins with excerpts from "Healthy Weight,"
Centers for Disease Control and Prevention (CDC), October 2, 2018;
Text under the heading "Benefits of Long Term Healthy Eating
(Versus Short-Term Dieting)" is excerpted from "Diets Don't Work,"
National Oceanic and Atmospheric Administration (NOAA), U.S.
Department of Commerce (DOC), April 27, 2017; Text under the
heading "A "Stick-to-It" Diet Is More Important Than a Popular One"
is excerpted from "Diets Don't Work," Agricultural Research
Service (ARS), U.S. Department of Agriculture (USDA),
March 2006. Reviewed December 2018.

When it comes to weight loss, there's no lack of fad diets promising fast results. But such diets limit your nutritional intake, can be unhealthy, and tend to fail in the long run. The key to achieving and maintaining a healthy weight isn't about short-term dietary changes. It's about a lifestyle that includes healthy eating, regular physical activity, and balancing the number of calories you consume with the number of calories your body uses. For many reasons, diets are not an effective long-term strategy for maintaining a healthy weight:

- Diets may work in the short-term but the majority of dieters regain the weight over the long-term

- Deprivation and dietary restrictions (not to mention hunger) lead to binge eating or "cheating" on the diet

- Many diets are based on outdated nutritional science and do not take into account the impact of hormones such as ghrelin and leptin on hunger and weight management or the effect of sugar and refined carbohydrates on fat storage

Benefits of Long-Term Healthy Eating

- More energy

- Better sleep

- Reduced illness and resistance to disease

- Decreased aches and pains (headaches, joint pain, etc.)

- Reduced digestive discomfort

- Better brain function and clearer thinking

- Improved hormonal balance, including menstrual cycles, menopause, adrenal response, and stress management

A "Stick-to-It" Diet Is More Important than a Popular One

With over 1,000 diet books available on bookstore shelves, popular diets clearly have become increasingly prevalent. At the same time, they have also become increasingly controversial, because some depart substantially from mainstream medical advice or have been criticized by various medical authorities.

A comparison of several popular diets by Agricultural Research Service (ARS)-funded researchers showed that at the end of the day, or in this case at the end of the year, sticking with a diet—more than the type of a diet—is the key to losing weight.

The study was conducted by Michael L. Dansinger, Ernst J. Schaefer, and Joi A. Gleason of the Lipid Metabolism Laboratory at the Jean Mayer U.S. Department of Agriculture (USDA) Human Nutrition Research Center on Aging (HNRCA) at Tufts University and Tufts-New England Medical Center in Boston.

Published in the *Journal of the American Medical Association (JAMA)*, the study compared the relative merits of four of the most popular weight-loss diets. These included the Atkins (carbohydrate restriction), Ornish (fat restriction), Weight Watchers (calorie and portion size restriction), and Zone (high-glycemic-load carbohydrate restriction and increased protein) diets.

The researchers randomly assigned 160 overweight or obese volunteers to use 1 of the 4 diets. All participants were provided with the diet book and four 1-hour instructional classes to help them assimilate the rules of their assigned diets. The 40 participants in each of the 4 diet groups were representative—in terms of age, race, sex, body mass index, and metabolic characteristics—of the overweight population in the United States.

The results in terms of both weight loss and reduction in heart disease risk factors were compared among "completers," or those who stayed with the study for an entire year.

Only about half the volunteers completed the program while on what the authors considered to be more extreme diet plans: Atkins and Ornish diets. In contrast, 65 percent were able to complete the more moderate diet plans: Weight Watchers and Zone. Still, those that stayed in the program tended to loosen their resolve by about six months, as determined by their self-reported food records.

"The bottom line was that it wasn't so much the type of diet followed that led to successful weight loss, but the ability of participants to stick with the program for the entire year's time," says Schaefer.

"The study showed that whether volunteers restricted carbohydrate calories or fat calories—whether they lowered intake overall, or balanced intake overall—everybody lost weight," says Schaefer. "Ultimately, it comes down to calorie restriction. The strongest predictor of weight loss was not the type of diet, but compliance with the diet plan that subjects were given."

The finding lends credence to the importance of adopting a caloric-restriction diet that doesn't conflict with one's natural affinities for specific allowable foods.

"Implementing a dietary regimen that can transition an individual into a healthful eating pattern after the diet ends is also very important," says USDA Human Nutrition National Program Leader Molly Kretsch. "Lifestyle practices that help people maintain a healthy body weight, incorporate the right balance of foods and appropriate portion sizes, and increase their physical activity are the keys to long-term weight management."

Among those who stayed in the program for the entire 12-month period, all four diet plans promoted a 10 percent improvement in the balance of "good" (high-density lipoproteins) and "bad" (low-density lipoproteins) cholesterol levels. "The particular diet plan the long-term dieter followed did not seem to matter that much," says Dansinger. "The long-term dieters reduced their ratio of good to bad cholesterol according to how much weight they lost."

Those who improved their cholesterol ratios by 10 percent improved their heart disease risk factors by 20 percent. "For every 1 percent of weight loss a dieter achieves, there will be a 2 percent, or twice as much, reduction in heart disease risk factors," says Dansinger.

In addition, all four diet plans promoted lower blood insulin levels as well as lower levels of C reactive protein (CRP). High levels of CRP in the blood have been linked to heart disease.

Future studies will focus on identifying practical techniques to increase dietary adherence—including ways to match individuals with the diets best suited to their food preferences and lifestyles. "We also plan to test different versions of the new USDA diet and look specifically at the results from a diet with higher and lower glycemic index values," says Schaefer.

Section 46.6

Detox Diets—the Lowdown

This section contains text excerpted from the following sources: Text in this section begins with excerpts from "Health and Environmental Research Online (HERO)," U.S. Environmental Protection Agency (EPA), December 31, 2018; Text beginning with the heading "Miami VA Healthcare System" is excerpted from "Miami VA Healthcare System," U.S. Department of Veterans Affairs (VA), January 24, 2018; Text under the heading "Juicing 101: Nutrition Tips for Consumers" is excerpted from "Juicing 101: Nutrition Tips for Consumers," Nutrition.gov, U.S. Department of Agriculture (USDA), December 21, 2018.

Detox diets are popular dieting strategies that claim to facilitate toxin elimination and weight loss, thereby promoting health and well-being. The present review examines whether detox diets are necessary, what they involve, whether they are effective and whether they present any dangers. Although the detox industry is booming, there is very little clinical evidence to support the use of these diets. A handful of clinical studies have shown that commercial detox diets enhance liver detoxification and eliminate persistent organic pollutants from the body, although these studies are hampered by flawed methodologies and small sample sizes. There is preliminary evidence to suggest that certain foods such as coriander, nori, and olestra have detoxification properties, although the majority of these studies have been performed in animals. To the best of our knowledge, no randomized controlled trials have been conducted to assess the effectiveness of commercial detox diets in humans. This is an area that deserves attention so that consumers can be informed of the potential benefits and risks of detox programmes.

Miami VA Healthcare System

"Detox" diets are all the craze during the new year promising a "quick-fix" to getting rid of all the extra weight that accumulated during the holidays. These types of diets can get you on a cycle of yo-yo dieting with short-term results. In order to get life-long results, you need to make lifestyle changes. Quick fixes are just patches. Eventually, the patch is going to break and you're going to get a quick rebound back to where you were in the first place. To make lifestyle changes, you have to become an explorer of new foods and recipes and break the monotony of eating the same things every day. Did you know your taste buds can change every few years? You might like the taste of something today that you used to dislike in the past. But you'll never know unless you try. So, in light of the "New Year" and the "New You," let's take that first leap together with this awesome recipe. This recipe is full of anti-inflammatory (omega 6 and 3 fatty acids) agents, antioxidants, immune boosting agents, vitamins and so much more.

Health Benefits
Brussels Sprouts

These cruciferous veggies are rich in nutrients! They are excellent sources of vitamins C and K. To add to this already great couple, Brussels sprouts contain folate, manganese, vitamins B6 and B1, potassium, phosphorus, and omega-3 fatty acids. And if it couldn't get any better, dietary fiber.

Carrots

These bright veggies help keep the world bright for you. They are a weight-loss friendly food that is a great source of beta-carotene, which is involved in improving eye health. Carotene antioxidants have also been linked to a reduced risk of cancer.

Edamame

A sweet, delicious fruit best used to help with your digestive system, dates are full of dietary fiber, iron, calcium, sulfur, manganese, potassium, phosphorus, and magnesium. Dates help to regulate your digestive system, strengthen your bones, treat anemia and intestinal disorders, and boost energy.

Flaxseed

Flaxseed has been used as a superfood for over 6,000 years and is full of omega-3 alpha linoleic acid, fiber, protein, vitamin B1, manganese, magnesium, phosphorus, and selenium. It helps lower cholesterol, improve digestion, promote weight loss and heart health.

Lemon Juice

Lemons are full of vitamin C, citric acid, calcium, B vitamins, magnesium, phosphorus, and potassium.

This is the perfect recipe for the New Year. The taste is so sweet and savory that you'll want to include it in your meals throughout the year. The rich supply of vitamins and minerals along with the added health benefits of each individual ingredient will help you start the new year feeling like your best self.

This recipe is meant for anyone following a regular healthy, vegetarian, diabetic, paleo, or gluten-free diet. Unfortunately, this recipe is not suited for renal diet due to high levels of potassium and phosphorus in most of the ingredients.

If you have any additional dietary restriction that may be of nutritional concern when making this recipe, consult your registered dietitian.

Juicing 101: Nutrition Tips for Consumers

Juicing in the home has gained popularity in recent years, but is it good for you? You may have read or heard things like "juice cleanse," "detox," or that juicing is a good way to lose weight. Juicing is a term that refers to combining fruits and/or vegetables in a juicer or juicing machine, which breaks these foods down into a liquid form.

The *Dietary Guidelines for Americans 2010* (DGA) reports that most Americans over the age of four years are not eating enough fruits and vegetables, and do not get enough dietary fiber, important minerals such as folate, potassium, magnesium, or vitamins A, C, and K in their diet. Fruits and vegetables are also a good source of folate which is especially important for women who may become pregnant. Juicing can be one way to add more fruits and/or veggies into your day. With so much information available in the media, it can sometimes be difficult to know what's true and what's false.

Are There Benefits to Adding Juicing into My Eating Plan?

This depends on many factors including your lifestyle, dietary preferences, health conditions, etc. The DGA recommends that the majority of fruit intake come from whole fruits, including canned, frozen, and dried forms. Juicing can be one way to increase your nutrient intake, and incorporate a variety of fruits and vegetables that you may not normally eat, such as kale or spinach, however, you should not rely on juice as your sole source of fruit or vegetable intake. To improve taste, some juicing recipes may include added sugars, such as sugar, honey, turbinado, raw sugar, maple syrup, or molasses. Most Americans need to reduce their intake of added sugars. Choose juicing recipes that don't include these ingredients or use noncaloric sweeteners instead.

Will Juicing Provide All the Nutrients I Need in My Diet?

No. Juicing can be a good way to introduce new fruits and vegetables, but a diet containing only these ingredients is missing some major nutrients. For example, protein and fat will only be present in very small amounts, so they will need to be obtained from other foods. Important vitamins and minerals like vitamin D, calcium, and iron may also be lacking. In addition, the amount of fiber may be reduced if the skin and pulp are removed in the juicing process. If you choose to juice, incorporate it into a healthy eating plan that includes foods from a variety of sources such as whole grains, fat-free or low-fat milk and milk products, and protein foods.

351

Is There a Difference between a Juice and a Smoothie?

Yes. A smoothie typically contains fruits and/or vegetables, but other ingredients, such as milk, yogurt or protein powder, may be added as well. Smoothies can contain lots of ingredients: flaxseed, green tea, kefir, herbs and more. This is another option to increase consumption of fruits and vegetables, which may also increase your intake of calories and nutrients, like protein, vitamins and minerals. Juicing typically includes just the fruit and/or vegetable that has been liquefied. Some juicers remove fiber from the whole fruit or vegetable. Fiber is an important nutrient and many Americans need more fiber in their diets.

Will You Always Lose the Fiber?

No. It can depend on the types of fruits and vegetables you use, as well as the equipment, and your personal preference. There are some products that do not extract, or remove the pulp, such as a blender. If you would like to keep the pulp in your juice, be sure to research the properties and functions of the equipment you are considering.

Will Juicing Help Me Lose Weight?

Not necessarily. A juice may contain a considerable amount of calories which should be taken into consideration when managing your weight. In order to maintain your body weight, you must expend, or "burn" the same amount of calories that you consume, and therefore, taking in more calories than you use will lead to weight gain. For example, if your daily calorie needs are about 1600, and you consume 2100, you will experience weight gain, which may not be desirable depending on your current weight status. Try these tools to help you understand your daily caloric needs, and to get a better idea of how many calories are in your juice:

- USDA National Nutrient Database for Standard Reference
- SuperTracker's Food Tracker
- My Recipe

Should I Talk to My Doctor before Juicing?

Yes. Juicing is not appropriate for everyone. For example, if you have diabetes or kidney disease, you may need to limit, or monitor your intake of certain nutrients such as carbohydrates, potassium or phosphorus, and adding certain fruits or vegetables may not be recommended. For example, fruits such as melon and banana are high in potassium, and someone with kidney disease may be instructed to avoid these foods. Also, a juice made of mostly fruits can be high in carbohydrates, and could cause a rise in blood sugar, which could be problematic, especially in diabetics. In addition, juicing may also be a source of considerable calories, depending on the size, and content of the juice you make. Consuming excess calories can lead to weight gain, which can increase risk of developing chronic diseases such as heart disease and type 2 diabetes. Talk to your doctor, registered dietitian, or other healthcare professional to help you determine if juicing is a healthy option for you.

Will Juicing Reduce My Risk for Certain Diseases?

The Dietary Guidelines state that that intake of at least 2 ½ cups of vegetables and fruits per day is associated with a reduced risk of cardiovascular disease, including heart attack and stroke. In addition, fruits and vegetables contain more fiber when eaten whole, which may reduce your risk of obesity, type 2 diabetes, and cardiovascular disease. Fiber can also play a role in providing a feeling of fullness, and promoting healthy laxation. Most Americans don't consume enough dietary fiber, and should increase their consumption of whole fruits and vegetables to help meet the recommendation for fiber. Since juicing fruits and vegetables can sometimes remove some of the fiber, it is not clear what the relationship is between juicing and health. If you choose to juice, try adding the leftover pulp from your juice to soups or muffins to help add the fiber into your diet.

Will Juicing Help to Detoxify My Body?

There is no evidence showing the benefits of a juicing detox, juice cleanse or juice fast, which is when one drinks only juice and does not eat any solid foods for a set period of time. Doing this doesn't detoxify your body. Your body naturally filters and removes most toxins.

How Much Should I Expect to Spend?

Juicing machines can be costly, and could range from $50 to $500 or more. In addition, depending on the quantity or type of fruits and vegetables you use, you may see an increase in your grocery bill. You can try using frozen or canned foods to help manage your budget, and look for options that are low in sodium and added sugars, such as fruit canned in water or lite syrup. Fruits and vegetables from your home garden are also a good option. Learn how to plan, shop, and budget your trip to the grocery store using resources available to you by visiting Shopping, Cooking and Meal Planning from www.Nutrition.gov.

What Are Some Other Things to Consider?

Wash your fruits and vegetables thoroughly under running water just before eating, cutting, or putting them in the juicer. Do not use soap, detergent, or commercial produce washes. If you are cutting your produce, use a clean knife and cutting board, as well as a clean juicer. Make only what you are able to drink or refrigerate in clean, covered containers. Wrap any leftover portions of fruits and vegetables tightly and refrigerate. They will keep for a day or two in the refrigerator; after that, they may spoil. Be careful when washing your juicer, as many contain sharp blades or other surfaces that might be harmful if mishandled, and clean it thoroughly after every use. If you buy fresh squeezed juice from a store or juicing stand, be aware that these may contain harmful bacteria if they have not been pasteurized, or treated to kill harmful bacteria. Unpasteurized (raw) juices are not recommended for those at risk for foodborne illness, such as children, the elderly, and people with weakened immune systems. Those at risk should look for a warning label before purchasing. Juicing should not be used as a quick way to lose weight. Consuming only fruits and vegetables, even though they are nutritious, is not considered a balanced diet. A healthy weight loss goal is ½ to 2 pounds per week, and can be achieved with healthy eating and activity habits. Talk with your doctor about safe and effective ways to control your weight.

Section 46.7

Dietary Supplements for Weight Loss

This section includes text excerpted from "Dietary
Supplements for Weight Loss Fact Sheet for Consumers,"
Office of Dietary Supplements (ODS), National Institutes of
Health (NIH), November 1, 2017.

What Are Weight-Loss Dietary Supplements and What Do They Do?

The proven ways to lose weight are eating healthful foods, cutting calories, and being physically active. But making these lifestyle changes isn't easy, so you might wonder if taking a dietary supplement that's promoted for weight loss might help.

This section describes what's known about the safety and effectiveness of many ingredients that are commonly used in weight-loss dietary supplements. Sellers of these supplements might claim that their products help you lose weight by blocking the absorption of fat or carbohydrates, curbing your appetite, or speeding up your metabolism. But there's little scientific evidence that weight-loss supplements work. Many are expensive, some can interact or interfere with medications, and a few might be harmful.

If you're thinking about taking a dietary supplement to lose weight, talk with your healthcare provider. This is especially important if you have high blood pressure, diabetes, heart disease, liver disease, or other medical conditions.

What Are the Ingredients in Weight-Loss Dietary Supplements?
African Mango

African mango seed extract is claimed to curb the formation of fat tissue.

Does It Work?

African mango might help you lose a very small amount of weight.

Is It Safe?

African mango seems to be safe, but its safety hasn't been well studied. It can cause headache, sleeping problems, flatulence, and gas.

355

Beta-Glucans

Beta-glucans are soluble dietary fibers in bacteria, yeasts, fungi, oats, and barley. They might slow down the time it takes for food to travel through your digestive system, making you feel fuller.

Does It Work?

Beta-glucans don't seem to have any effect on body weight.

Is It Safe?

Beta-glucans seem to be safe (at up to 10 grams [g] a day for 12 weeks). They can cause flatulence.

Bitter Orange

Bitter orange contains synephrine (a stimulant). It's claimed to burn calories, increase fat breakdown, and decrease appetite. Products with bitter orange usually also contain caffeine and other ingredients. Bitter orange is in some weight loss dietary supplements that used to contain ephedra, another stimulant containing herb that was banned from the U.S. market in 2004 (see the section on Ephedra).

Does It Work?

Bitter orange might slightly increase the number of calories you burn. It might also reduce your appetite a little, but whether it can help you lose weight is unknown.

Is It Safe?

Bitter orange might not be safe. Supplements with bitter orange can cause chest pain, anxiety, headache, muscle and bone pain, a faster heart rate, and higher blood pressure.

Caffeine

Caffeine is a stimulant that can make you more alert, give you a boost of energy, burn calories, and increase fat breakdown. Often added to weight-loss dietary supplements, caffeine is found naturally in tea, guarana, kola (cola) nut, yerba mate, and other herbs. The labels of supplements that contain caffeine don't always list it, so you might not know if a supplement has caffeine.

Does It Work?

Weight-loss dietary supplements with caffeine might help you lose a little weight or gain less weight over time. But when you use caffeine regularly, you become tolerant of it. This tolerance might lessen any effect of caffeine on body weight over time.

Is It Safe?

Caffeine is safe for most adults at doses up to 400 to 500 milligrams (mg) a day. But it can make you feel nervous, jittery, and shaky. It can also affect your sleep. At higher doses, it can cause nausea, vomiting, rapid heartbeat, and seizures. Combining caffeine with other stimulant ingredients can increase caffeine's effects.

Calcium

Calcium is a mineral you need for healthy bones, muscles, nerves, blood vessels, and many of your body's functions. It's claimed to burn fat and decrease fat absorption.

Does It Work?

Calcium—either from food or in weight-loss dietary supplements—probably doesn't help you lose weight or prevent weight gain.

Is It Safe?

Calcium is safe at the recommended amounts of 1,000 to 1,200 mg a day for adults. Too much calcium (more than 2,000 to 2,500 mg a day) can cause constipation and decrease your body's absorption of iron and zinc. Also, too much calcium from supplements (but not foods) might increase your risk of kidney stones.

Capsaicin

Capsaicin comes from chili peppers and makes them taste hot. It's claimed to help burn fat and calories and to help you feel full and eat less.

Does It Work?

Capsaicin hasn't been studied enough to know if it will help you lose weight.

Is It Safe?

Capsaicin is safe (at up to 33 mg a day for 4 weeks or 4 mg a day for 12 weeks), but it can cause stomach pain, burning sensations, nausea, and bloating.

Carnitine

Your body makes carnitine, and it's also found in meat, fish, poultry, milk, and dairy products. In your cells, it helps break down fats.

Does It Work?

Carnitine supplements might help you lose a small amount of weight.

Is It Safe?

Carnitine supplements seem to be safe (at up to 2 g a day for 1 year or 4 g a day for 56 days). They can cause nausea, vomiting, diarrhea, abdominal cramps, and a fishy body odor.

Chitosan

Chitosan comes from the shells of crabs, shrimp, and lobsters. It's claimed to bind fat in the digestive tract so that your body can't absorb it.

Does It Work?

Chitosan binds only a tiny amount of fat, not enough to help you lose much weight.

Is It Safe?

Chitosan seems to be safe (at up to 15 g a day for 6 months). But it can cause flatulence, bloating, mild nausea, constipation, indigestion, and heartburn. If you're allergic to shellfish, you could have an allergic reaction to chitosan.

Chromium

Chromium is a mineral that you need to regulate your blood sugar levels. It's claimed to increase muscle mass and fat loss and decrease appetite and food intake.

Does It Work?

Chromium might help you lose a very small amount of weight and body fat.

Is It Safe?

Chromium in food and supplements is safe at recommended amounts, which range from 20 to 45 micrograms a day for adults. In larger amounts, chromium can cause watery stools, headache, weakness, nausea, vomiting, constipation, dizziness, and hives.

Coleus Forskohlii

Coleus forskohlii is a plant that grows in India, Thailand, and other subtropical areas. Forskolin, made from the plant's roots, is claimed to help you lose weight by decreasing your appetite and increasing the breakdown of fat in your body.

Does It Work?

Forskolin hasn't been studied much. But so far, it doesn't seem to have any effect on body weight or appetite.

Is It Safe?

Forskolin seems to be safe (at 500 mg a day for 12 weeks), but it hasn't been well studied. It can cause frequent bowel movements and loose stools.

Conjugated Linoleic Acid (CLA)

CLA is a fat found mainly in dairy products and beef. It's claimed to reduce your body fat.

Does It Work?

CLA may help you lose a very small amount of weight and body fat.

Is It Safe?

CLA seems to be safe (at up to 6 g a day for 1 year). It can cause an upset stomach, constipation, diarrhea, loose stools, and indigestion.

Fucoxanthin

Fucoxanthin comes from brown seaweed and other algae. It's claimed to help with weight loss by burning calories and decreasing fat.

Does It Work?

Fucoxanthin hasn't been studied enough to know if it will help you lose weight. Only one study in people included fucoxanthin (the other studies were in animals).

Is It Safe?

Fucoxanthin seems to be safe (at 2.4 mg a day for 16 weeks), but it hasn't been studied enough to know for sure.

Garcinia Cambogia

Garcinia cambogia is a tree that grows throughout Asia, Africa, and the Polynesian islands. Hydroxycitric acid in the fruit is claimed to decrease the number of new fat cells your body makes, suppress your appetite and thus reduce the amount of food you eat, and limit the amount of weight you gain.

Does It Work?

Garcinia cambogia has little to no effect on weight loss.

Is It Safe?

Garcinia cambogia seems to be fairly safe. But it can cause headache, nausea, and symptoms in the upper respiratory tract, stomach, and intestines.

Glucomannan

Glucomannan is a soluble dietary fiber from the root of the konjac plant. It's claimed to absorb water in the gut to help you feel full.

Does It Work?

Glucomannan has little to no effect on weight loss. But it might help lower total cholesterol, LDL ("bad") cholesterol, triglycerides, and blood sugar levels.

Is It Safe?

Most forms of glucomannan seem to be safe (at up to 15.1 g a day for several weeks in a powder or capsule form). It can cause loose stools, flatulence, diarrhea, constipation, and abdominal discomfort.

Green Coffee Bean Extract

Green coffee beans are unroasted coffee beans. Green coffee bean extract is claimed to decrease fat accumulation and help convert blood sugar into energy that your cells can use.

Does It Work?

Green coffee bean extract might help you lose a small amount of weight.

Is It Safe?

Green coffee bean extract seems to be safe (at up to 200 mg a day for 12 weeks). It might cause headache and urinary tract infections. Green coffee beans contain the stimulant caffeine, which can cause problems at high doses or when it's combined with other stimulants (see the section on Caffeine).

Green Tea and Green Tea Extract

Green tea (also called Camellia sinensis) is a common beverage all over the world. Green tea and green tea extract in some weight-loss supplements are claimed to reduce body weight by increasing the calories your body burns, breaking down fat cells, and decreasing fat absorption and the amount of new fat your body makes.

Does It Work?

Green tea might help you lose a small amount of weight.

Is It Safe?

Drinking green tea is safe, but taking green tea extract might not be. Green tea extract can cause constipation, abdominal discomfort, nausea, and increased blood pressure. In some people, it has been linked to liver damage.

Guar Gum

Guar gum is a soluble dietary fiber in some dietary supplements and food products. It's claimed to make you feel full, lower your appetite, and decrease the amount of food you eat.

Does It Work?

Guar gum probably doesn't help you lose weight.

Is It Safe?

Guar gum seems to be safe (at up to 30 g a day for 6 months) when it is taken with enough fluid. But it can cause abdominal pain, flatulence, diarrhea, nausea, and cramps.

Guarana

(See the section on Caffeine)

Hoodia

Hoodia is a plant from southern Africa, where it's used as an appetite suppressant.

Does It Work?

There hasn't been much research on hoodia, but it probably won't help you eat less or lose weight. Analyses showed that some "hoodia" supplements sold in the past contained very little hoodia or none at all. It's not known whether this is true of hoodia supplements sold today.

Is It Safe?

Hoodia might not be safe. It can cause rapid heart rate, increased blood pressure, headache, dizziness, nausea, and vomiting.

Kola (Or Cola) Nut

(See the section on Caffeine)

Mate

(See the section on Caffeine)

Probiotics

Probiotics are microorganisms in foods, such as yogurt, that help maintain or restore beneficial bacteria in your digestive tract.

Does It Work?

Probiotic supplements seem to have little to no effect on weight loss, but they haven't been well studied.

Is It Safe?

Probiotics are safe but may cause gas or other gastrointestinal problems.

Pyruvate

Pyruvate is naturally present in your body. Pyruvate in weight loss supplements is claimed to increase fat breakdown, reduce body weight and body fat, and improve exercise performance.

Does It Work?

Pyruvate in supplements might help you lose a small amount of weight.

Is It Safe?

Pyruvate seems to be safe (at up to 30 g a day for 6 weeks). It can cause diarrhea, gas, bloating, and rumbling noises in the intestines due to gas.

Raspberry Ketone

Raspberry ketone, found in red raspberries, is claimed to be a "fat burner."

Does It Work?

Raspberry ketone has only been studied as a weight-loss aid in combination with other ingredients and not alone. Its effects on body weight are unknown.

Is It Safe?

Raspberry ketone hasn't been studied enough to tell if it's safe.

Vitamin D

Your body needs vitamin D for good health and strong bones. People who are obese tend to have lower levels of vitamin D, but there is no known reason why taking vitamin D would help people lose weight.

Does It Work?

Vitamin D doesn't help you lose weight.

Is It Safe?

Vitamin D from foods and dietary supplements is safe at the recommended amounts of 600 to 800 IU a day for adults. Too much vitamin D (more than 4,000 IU a day) can be toxic and cause nausea, vomiting, poor appetite, constipation, weakness, and irregular heartbeat.

White Kidney Bean / Bean Pod

White kidney bean or bean pod (also called Phaseolus vulgaris) is a legume grown around the world. An extract of this bean is claimed to block the absorption of carbohydrates and suppress your appetite.

Does It Work?

Phaseolus vulgaris extract might help you lose a small amount of weight and body fat.

Is It Safe?

Phaseolus vulgaris seems to be safe (at up to 3,000 mg a day for 12 weeks). But it might cause headaches, soft stools, flatulence, and constipation.

Yerba Mate

(See the section on Caffeine)

Yohimbe

Yohimbe is a West African tree. Yohimbe extract is an ingredient in supplements used to improve libido, increase muscle mass, and treat male sexual dysfunction. Yohimbe is also found in some weight-loss supplements and is claimed to increase weight loss.

Does It Work?

Yohimbe doesn't help you lose weight.

Is It Safe?

Yohimbe might not be safe (especially at doses of 20 mg or higher). Use it only with guidance from your healthcare provider because the side effects can be severe. Yohimbe can cause headaches, high blood pressure, anxiety, agitation, rapid heartbeat, heart attack, heart failure, and death.

Ephedra, an Ingredient-Banned Dietary Supplements?

Ephedra (also called má huáng) is a plant containing substances that can stimulate your nervous system, increase the amount of energy you burn, increase weight loss, and suppress your appetite. In the 1990s, ephedra was a popular ingredient in dietary supplements sold for weight loss and to enhance athletic performance. In 2004, the U.S. Food and Drug Administration (FDA) banned ephedra in dietary supplements, concluding that it isn't safe. Ephedra can cause nausea, vomiting, anxiety, mood changes, high blood pressure, abnormal heartbeat, stroke, seizures, heart attack, and death.

How Are Weight-Loss Dietary Supplements Regulated?

The FDA is the federal agency that oversees dietary supplements in the United States. Unlike over-the-counter (OTC) and prescription drugs—which must be approved by the FDA before they can be sold—dietary supplements don't require review or approval by the FDA before they are put on the market. Also, manufacturers don't have to provide evidence to the FDA that their products are safe or effective before selling these products. When the FDA finds an unsafe dietary supplement, it can remove the supplement from the market or ask the supplement maker to recall it. The FDA and the Federal Trade Commission can also take enforcement action against companies that make false weight-loss claims about their supplements; add pharmaceutical drugs to their supplements; or claim that their supplements can diagnose, treat, cure, or prevent a disease.

Can Weight-Loss Dietary Supplements Be Harmful?

Weight-loss supplements, like all dietary supplements, can have harmful side effects and might interact with prescription and OTC medications. Many weight-loss supplements have ingredients that haven't been tested in combination with one another, and their combined effects are unknown.

Fraudulent and Adulterated Products

Be very cautious when you see weight-loss supplements with tempting claims, such as "magic diet pill," "melt away fat," and "lose weight without diet or exercise." If the claim sounds too good to be true, it probably is. These products might not help you lose weight—and they could be dangerous. Weight-loss products marketed as dietary supplements are sometimes adulterated with prescription drugs or controlled substances. These ingredients won't be listed on the product label, and they could harm you. The FDA puts out public notifications about tainted weight-loss products.

Interactions with Medications

Like most dietary supplements, some weight-loss supplements can interact or interfere with other medicines or supplements you take. If you take dietary supplements and medications on a regular basis, be sure to talk about this with your healthcare provider.

Choosing a Sensible Approach to Weight Loss

Weight-loss supplements can be expensive, and they might not work. The best way to lose weight and keep it off is to follow a healthy eating plan, reduce calories, and exercise regularly under the guidance of your healthcare provider. As a bonus, lifestyle changes that help you lose weight might also improve your mood and energy level and lower your risk of heart disease, diabetes, and some types of cancer.

Section 46.8

Beware of Miracle Weight-Loss Products

This section contains text excerpted from the following sources: Text beginning with the heading "Tainted Products" is excerpted from "Beware of Products Promising Miracle Weight Loss," U.S. Food and Drug Administration (FDA), September 10, 2018; Text beginning with the heading "Weighing the Claims in Diet Ads" is excerpted from "Weighing the Claims in Diet Ads," Federal Trade Commission (FTC), July 2012. Reviewed December 2018.

Tainted Products

The U.S. Food and Drug Administration (FDA) has found weight-loss products tainted with the prescription drug ingredient sibutramine. This ingredient was in an FDA-approved drug called Meridia, which was removed from the market in October 2010 because it caused heart problems and strokes.

"We've also found weight-loss products marketed as supplements that contain dangerous concoctions of hidden ingredients including active ingredients contained in approved seizure medications, blood pressure medications, and antidepressants," says Jason Humbert, a senior regulatory manager at FDA. Most recently, FDA has found a number of products marketed as dietary supplements containing fluoxetine, the active ingredient found in Prozac, a prescription drug marketed for the treatment of depression and other conditions. Another product contained triamterene, a powerful diuretic (sometimes known as "water pills") that can have serious side-effects and should only be used under the supervision of a healthcare professional.

Many of these tainted products are imported, sold online, and heavily promoted on social media sites. Some can also be found on store shelves.

And if you're about to take what you think of as "natural" dietary supplements, such as bee pollen or Garcinia cambogia, you should be aware that FDA has found some of these products also contain hidden active ingredients contained in prescription drugs.

"The only natural way to lose weight is to burn more calories than you take in," says James P. Smith, M.D. That means a combination of healthful eating and physical activity.

Dietary Supplements Are Not FDA-Approved

Under the Federal Food, Drug and Cosmetics Act (FFDCA) (as amended by the Dietary Supplement Health and Education Act

(DSHEA) of 1994), dietary supplement firms do not need FDA approval prior to marketing their products. It is the company's responsibility to make sure its products are safe and that any claims made about such products are true.

But just because you see a supplement product on a store shelf does not mean it is safe, Humbert says. FDA has received numerous reports of harm associated with the use of weight loss products, including increased blood pressure, heart palpitations (a pounding or racing heart), stroke, seizure and death. When safety issues are suspected, FDA must investigate and, when warranted, take steps to have these products removed from the market.

FDA has issued over 30 public notifications and recalled 7 tainted weight loss products in 2014. The agency also has issued warning letters, seized products, and criminally prosecuted people responsible for marketing these illegal diet products. In addition, FDA maintains an online list of tainted weight-loss products.

To help people with long-term weight management, FDA has approved prescription drugs such as Belviq, Qysmia, and Contrave, but these products are intended for people at least 18 years of age who:

- Have a body mass index (BMI, a standard measure of body fat) of 30 or greater (considered obese); or

- Have a BMI of 27 or greater (considered overweight) and have at least one other weight-related health condition.

Moreover, if you are going to embark on any type of weight control campaign, you should talk to your healthcare professional about it first, Smith says.

Know the Warning Signs

Look for potential warning signs of tainted products, such as:

- Promises of a quick fix, for example, "lose 10 pounds in one week"

- Use of the words "guaranteed" or "scientific breakthrough"

- Products marketed in a foreign language

- Products marketed through mass e-mails

- Products marketed as herbal alternatives to an FDA-approved drug or as having effects similar to prescription drugs

Advice for Consumers

Generally, if you are using or considering using any product marketed as a dietary supplement, FDA suggests that you:

- Check with your healthcare professional or a registered dietitian about any nutrients you may need in addition to your regular diet

- Ask yourself if it sounds too good to be true

- Be cautious if the claims for the product seem exaggerated or unrealistic

- Watch out for extreme claims such as "quick and effective" or "totally safe"

- Be skeptical about anecdotal information from personal "testimonials" about incredible benefits or results from using a product

Weighing the Claims in Diet Ads

Whether it's a pill, patch, or cream, there's no shortage of ads promising quick and easy weight loss without diet or exercise. But the claims just aren't true, and some of these products could even hurt your health. The best way to lose weight is to eat fewer calories and get more exercise. Don't be hooked by promises, testimonials, or supposed endorsements from reporters; all you'll lose is money.

Will I Really Lose Weight?

Wouldn't it be nice if you could lose weight simply by taking a pill, wearing a patch, or rubbing in a cream? Unfortunately, claims that you can lose weight without changing your habits just aren't true.

Doctors, dieticians, and other experts agree that the best way to lose weight is to eat fewer calories and be more active. That's true even for people taking FDA-approved pills to help them lose weight. For most people, a reasonable goal is to lose about a pound a week, which means:

- Cutting about 500 calories a day from your diet

- Eating a variety of nutritious foods

- Exercising regularly

The Truth behind Weight-Loss Ads

Claims to watch out for include:

Lose Weight without Diet or Exercise!

Getting to a healthy weight takes work. Take a pass on any product that promises miraculous results without the effort. The only thing you'll lose is money.

Lose Weight No Matter How Much You Eat of Your Favorite Foods!

Beware of any product that claims that you can eat all the high-calorie food you want and still lose weight. Losing weight requires sensible food choices. Filling up on healthy vegetables and fruits can make it easier to say no to fattening sweets and snacks.

Lose Weight Permanently! Never Diet Again!

Even if you're successful in taking weight off, permanent weight loss requires permanent lifestyle changes. Don't trust any product that promises once-and-for-all results without ongoing maintenance.

Just Take a Pill!

Doctors, dieticians, and other experts agree that there's simply no magic way to lose weight without diet or exercise. Even pills approved by FDA to block the absorption of fat or help you eat less and feel full are to be taken with a low-calorie, low-fat diet and regular exercise.

Lose 30 Pounds in 30 Days!

Losing weight at the rate of a pound or two a week is the most effective way to take it off and keep it off. At best, products promising lightning-fast weight loss are a scam. At worst, they can ruin your health.

Everybody Will Lose Weight!

Your habits and health concerns are unique. There is no one-size-fits-all product guaranteed to work for everyone. Team up with your healthcare provider to design a nutrition and exercise program suited to your lifestyle and metabolism.

Lose Weight with Our Miracle Diet Patch or Cream!

You've seen the ads for diet patches or creams that claim to melt away the pounds. Don't believe them. There's nothing you can wear or apply to your skin that will cause you to lose weight.

Acai Berry Supplements in the "News"

More and more, scam artists are exploiting people's trust in well-known news organizations by setting up fake news sites with the logos of legitimate news organizations to peddle their wares. In particular, sites claiming to be objective news sources may describe a so-called "investigation" of the effectiveness of acai berry dietary supplements for weight loss. These sites are a marketing ploy created to sell acai berry supplements.

Tainted Weight Loss Products

In the last few years, FDA has discovered hundreds of dietary supplements containing drugs or other chemicals, often in products for weight loss and bodybuilding. These extras generally aren't listed on the label—and might even be sold with false and misleading claims like "100 percent natural" and "safe." They could cause serious side effects or interact in dangerous ways with medicines or other supplements you're taking.

The Skinny on Electronic Muscle Stimulators

You might have seen ads for electronic muscle stimulators claiming they will tone, firm, and strengthen abdominal muscles, help you lose weight, or get rock hard abs. But according to FDA, while these devices may temporarily strengthen, tone, or firm a muscle, no electronic muscle stimulator device alone will give you "six-pack" abs.

Chapter 47

Guidelines for Healthy Eating

Chapter Contents

Section 47.1

Healthy Eating for a Healthy Weight

This section contains text excerpted from the following sources: Text beginning with the heading "Healthy Eating for a Healthy Weight" is excerpted from "Healthy Eating for a Healthy Weight," Centers for Disease Control and Prevention (CDC), September 8, 2016; Text beginning with the heading "What Is Myplate?" is excerpted from "What Is Myplate?" ChooseMyPlate.gov, U.S. Department of Agriculture (USDA), December 4, 2018.

Healthy Eating for a Healthy Weight

A healthy lifestyle involves many choices. Among them, choosing a balanced diet or healthy eating plan. So how do you choose a healthy eating plan? Let's begin by defining what a healthy eating plan is.

According to the *Dietary Guidelines for Americans* (DGA) *2015–2020*, a healthy eating plan:

- Emphasizes fruits, vegetables, whole grains, and fat-free or low-fat milk and milk products

- Includes lean meats, poultry, fish, beans, eggs, and nuts

- Is low in saturated fats, trans fats, cholesterol, salt (sodium), and added sugars

- Stays within your daily calorie needs

Eat Healthfully and Enjoy It!

A healthy eating plan that helps you manage your weight includes a variety of foods you may not have considered. If "healthy eating" makes you think about the foods you can't have, try refocusing on all the new foods you can eat:

- **Fresh, frozen, or canned fruits**? Don't think just apples or bananas. All fresh, frozen, or canned fruits are great choices. Be sure to try some "exotic" fruits, too. How about a mango? Or a juicy pineapple or kiwi fruit! When your favorite fresh fruits aren't in season, try a frozen, canned, or dried variety of a fresh fruit you enjoy. One caution about canned fruits is that they may contain added sugars or syrups. Be sure and choose canned varieties of fruit packed in water or in their own juice.

374

- **Fresh, frozen, or canned vegetables**? Try something new. You may find that you love grilled vegetables or steamed vegetables with an herb you haven't tried like rosemary. You can sauté (panfry) vegetables in a nonstick pan with a small amount of cooking spray. Or try frozen or canned vegetables for a quick side dish—just microwave and serve. When trying canned vegetables, look for vegetables without added salt, butter, or cream sauces. Commit to going to the produce department and trying a new vegetable each week.

- **Calcium-rich foods**? You may automatically think of a glass of low-fat or fat-free milk when someone says "eat more dairy products." But what about low-fat and fat-free yogurts without added sugars? These come in a wide variety of flavors and can be a great dessert substitute for those with a sweet tooth.

- **A new twist on an old favorite**? If your favorite recipe calls for frying fish or breaded chicken, try healthier variations using baking or grilling. Maybe even try a recipe that uses dry beans in place of higher-fat meats. Ask around or search the Internet and magazines for recipes with fewer calories—you might be surprised to find you have a new favorite dish!

Do I Have to Give Up My Favorite Comfort Food?

No! Healthy eating is all about balance. You can enjoy your favorite foods even if they are high in calories, fat or added sugars. The key is eating them only once in a while, and balancing them out with healthier foods and more physical activity.

Some general tips for comfort foods:

- Eat them less often. If you normally eat these foods every day, cut back to once a week or once a month. You'll be cutting your calories because you're not having the food as often.

- Eat smaller amounts. If your favorite higher-calorie food is a chocolate bar, have a smaller size or only half a bar.

- Try a lower-calorie version. Use lower-calorie ingredients or prepare food differently. For example, if your macaroni and cheese recipe uses whole milk, butter, and full-fat cheese, try remaking it with nonfat milk, less butter, light cream cheese, fresh spinach, and tomatoes. Just remember to not increase your portion size.

- The point is, you can figure out how to include almost any food in your healthy eating plan in a way that still helps you lose weight or maintain a healthy weight.

What Is MyPlate?

MyPlate is a reminder to find your healthy eating style and build it throughout your lifetime. Everything you eat and drink matters. The right mix can help you be healthier now and in the future. This means:

- Focus on variety, amount, and nutrition

- Choose foods and beverages with less saturated fat, sodium, and added sugars

- Start with small changes to build healthier eating styles

- Support healthy eating for everyone

Eating healthy is a journey shaped by many factors, including our stage of life, situations, preferences, access to food, culture, traditions, and personal decisions we make over time. All your food and beverage choices count. MyPlate offers ideas and tips to help you create a healthier eating style that meets your individual needs and improves your health.

Fruits
What Foods Are in the Fruit Group?

Any fruit or 100 percent fruit juice counts as part of the fruit group. Fruits may be fresh, canned, frozen, or dried, and may be whole, cut-up, or pureed.

How Much Fruit Is Needed Daily?

The amount of fruit you need to eat depends on age, sex, and level of physical activity. Recommended daily amounts are shown in the table 47.1 below.

Table 47.1. Daily Fruit Table

Daily Recommendation*		
Children	2 to 3 years old	1 cup
	4 to 8 years old	1 to 1½ cups

Table 47.1. Continued

Daily Recommendation*		
Girls	9 to 13 years old	1½ cups
	14 to 18 years old	1½ cups
Boys	9 to 13 years old	1½ cups
	14 to 18 years old	2 cups
Women	19 to 30 years old	2 cups
	31 to 50 years old	1½ cups
	51+ years old	1½ cups
Men	19 to 30 years old	2 cups
	31 to 50 years old	2 cups
	51+ years old	2 cups

* These amounts are appropriate for individuals who get less than 30 minutes per day of moderate physical activity, beyond normal daily activities. Those who are more physically active may be able to consume more while staying within calorie needs.

What Counts as a Cup of Fruit?

In general, 1 cup of fruit or 100 percent fruit juice, or ½ cup of dried fruit can be considered as 1 cup from the fruit group. Table 47.2 below shows specific amounts that count as 1 cup of fruit (in some cases equivalents for ½ cup are also shown) towards your daily recommended intake.

Table 47.2. Cup of Fruit Table

	Amount That Counts as 1 Cup of Fruit	Other Amounts (Count as 1/2 Cup of Fruit Unless Noted)
Apple	½ large (3¼" diameter) 1 small (2¼" diameter) 1 cup, sliced or chopped, raw or cooked	½ cup, sliced or chopped, raw or cooked
Applesauce	1 cup	1 snack container (4oz.)
Banana	1 cup, sliced 1 large (8" to 9" long)	1 small (less than 6" long)
Cantaloupe	1 cup, diced or melon balls	1 medium wedge (⅛ of a med. melon)

Table 47.2. Continued

	Amount That Counts as 1 Cup of Fruit	Other Amounts (Count as 1/2 Cup of Fruit Unless Noted)
Grapes	1 cup, whole or cut-up 32 seedless grapes	16 seedless grapes
Grapefruit	1 medium (4" diameter) 1 cup, sections	½ medium (4" diameter)
Mixed fruit (fruit cocktail)	1 cup, diced or sliced, raw or canned, drained	1 snack container (4 oz.) drained = $^3/_8$ cup
Orange	1 large (3$^1/_{16}$" diameter) 1 cup, sections	1 small (2$^3/_8$" diameter)
Orange, Mandarin	1 cup, canned, drained	
Peach	1 large (2¾" diameter) 1 cup, sliced or diced, raw, cooked, or canned, drained 2 halves, canned	1 small (2" diameter) 1 snack container (4 oz.) drained = $^3/_8$ cup
Pear	1 medium pear (2½ per lb) 1 cup, sliced or diced, raw cooked, or canned, drained	1 snack container (4 oz.) drained = $^3/_8$ cup
Pineapple	1 cup, chunks, sliced or crushed, raw, cooked or canned, drained	1 snack container (4 oz.) drained = $^3/_8$ cup
Plum	1 cup, sliced raw or cooked 3 medium or 2 large plums	1 large plum
Strawberries	About 8 large berries 1 cup, whole, halved, or sliced, fresh or frozen	½ cup whole, halved, or sliced
Watermelon	1 small (1" thick) 1 cup, diced or balls	6 melon balls
Dried fruit (raisins, prunes, apricots, etc.)	½ cup dried fruit	¼ cup dried fruit or 1 small box raisins (1½ oz.)
100% fruit juice (orange, apple, grape, grapefruit, etc.)	1 cup	½ cup

Vegetables
What Foods Are in the Vegetable Group?

Any vegetable or 100 percent vegetable juice counts as a member of the vegetable group. Vegetables may be raw or cooked; fresh, frozen, canned, or dried/dehydrated; and may be whole, cut-up, or mashed.

Based on their nutrient content, vegetables are organized into five subgroups: dark-green vegetables, starchy vegetables, red and orange vegetables, beans and peas, and other vegetables.

How Many Vegetables Are Needed?

The amount of vegetables you need to eat depends on your age, sex, and level of physical activity. Recommended total daily amounts and recommended weekly amounts from each vegetable subgroup are shown in the two tables below.

Table 47.3. Daily Vegetable Table

Daily Recommendation*		
Children	2 to 3 years old	1 cup
	4 to 8 years old	1 ½ cups
Girls	9 to 13 years old	2 cups
	14 to 18 years old	2 ½ cups
Boys	9 to 13 years old	2 ½ cups
	14 to 18 years old	3 cups
Women	19 to 30 years old	2 ½ cups
	31 to 50 years old	2 ½ cups
	51+ years old	2 cups
Men	19 to 30 years old	3 cups
	31 to 50 years old	3 cups
	51+ years old	2 ½ cups

These amounts are appropriate for individuals who get less than 30 minutes per day of moderate physical activity, beyond normal daily activities. Those who are more physically active may be able to consume more while staying within calorie needs.

Vegetable subgroup recommendations are given as amounts to eat WEEKLY. It is not necessary to eat vegetables from each subgroup daily. However, over a week, try to consume the amounts listed from each subgroup as a way to reach your daily intake recommendation.

Table 47.4. Weekly Vegetable Subgroup Table

Amount per Week		Dark Green Vegetables	Red and Orange Vegetables	Beans and Peas	Starchy Vegetables	Other Vegetables
Children	2 to 3 yrs old	½ cup	2½ cups	½ cup	2 cups	1½ cups
	4 to 8 yrs old	1 cup	3 cups	½ cup	3½ cups	2½ cups
Girls	9 to 13 yrs old	1½ cups	4 cups	1 cup	4 cups	3½ cups
	14 to 18 yrs old	1½ cups	5½ cups	1½ cups	5 cups	4 cups
Boys	9 to 13 yrs old	1½ cups	5½ cups	1½ cups	5 cups	4 cups
	14 to 18 yrs old	2 cups	6 cups	2 cups	6 cups	5 cups
Women	19 to 30 yrs old	1½ cups	5½ cups	1½ cups	5 cups	4 cups
	31 to 50 yrs old	1½ cups	5½ cups	1 ½ cups	5 cups	4 cups
	51+ yrs old	1½ cups	4 cups	1 cup	4 cups	3½ cups
Men	19 to 30 yrs old	2 cups	6 cups	2 cups	6 cups	5 cups
	31 to 50 yrs old	2 cups	6 cups	2 cups	6 cups	5 cups
	51+ yrs old	1½ cups	5½ cups	1½ cups	5 cups	4 cups

What Counts as a Cup of Vegetables?

In general, one cup of raw or cooked vegetables or vegetable juice, or two cups of raw leafy greens can be considered as one cup from the vegetable group. The table below lists specific amounts that count as one cup of vegetables (in some cases equivalents for ½ cup are also shown) towards your recommended intake.

Table 47.5. Cup of Vegetable Table

		Amount That Counts as 1 Cup of Vegetable	Amount That Counts as 1/2 Cup of Vegetables
Dark green vegetables	Broccoli	1 cup, chopped or florets 3 spears 5" long raw or cooked	
	Greens (collards, mustard greens, turnip greens, kale)	1 cup, cooked	
	Spinach	1 cup, cooked 2 cups, raw	1 cup, raw
	Raw leafy greens: Spinach, romaine, watercress, dark green leafy lettuce, endive, escarole	2 cups, raw	1 cup, raw
Red and orange vegetables	Carrots	1 cup, strips, slices, or chopped, raw or cooked 2 medium 1 cup baby carrots (about 12)	1 medium carrot About 6 baby carrots
	Pumpkin	1 cup, mashed, cooked	
	Red peppers	1 cup, chopped, raw, or cooked 1 large pepper (3" diameter, 3¾" long)	1 small pepper
	Tomatoes	1 large raw whole (3") 1 cup, chopped or sliced, raw, canned, or cooked	1 small raw whole (2¼" diameter) 1 medium canned
	Tomato juice	1 cup	½ cup
	Sweet potato	1 large baked (2¼" or more diameter) 1 cup, sliced or mashed, cooked	
	Winter squash (acorn, butternut, hubbard)	1 cup, cubed, cooked	½ acorn squash, baked = ¾ cup

Table 47.5. Continued

		Amount That Counts as 1 Cup of Vegetable	Amount That Counts as 1/2 Cup of Vegetables
Beans and peas	Dry beans and peas (such as black, garbanzo, kidney, pinto, or soybeans, or black-eyed peas or split peas)	1 cup, whole or mashed, cooked	
Starchy vegetables	1Corn, yellow or white	1 cup 1 large ear (8" to 9" long)	1 small ear (about 6" long)
	Green peas	1 cup	
	White potatoes	1 cup, diced, mashed 1 medium boiled or baked potato (2½" to 3" diameter)	
Other vegetables	Bean sprouts	1 cup, cooked	
	Cabbage, green	1 cup, chopped or shredded raw or cooked	
	Cauliflower	1 cup, pieces or florets raw or cooked	
	Celery	1 cup, diced or sliced, raw or cooked 2 large stalks (11" to 12" long)	1 large stalk (11" to 12" long)
	Cucumbers	1 cup, raw, sliced or chopped	
	Green or wax beans	1 cup, cooked	
	Green peppers	1 cup, chopped, raw or cooked 1 large pepper (3" diameter, 3 ¾" long)	1 small pepper
	Lettuce, iceberg or head	2 cups, raw, shredded or chopped	1 cup, raw, shredded or chopped
	Mushrooms	1 cup, raw or cooked	
	Onions	1 cup, chopped, raw or cooked	
	Summer squash or zucchini	1 cup, cooked, sliced or diced	

Grains

What Foods Are in the Grains Group?

Any food made from wheat, rice, oats, cornmeal, barley, or another cereal grain is a grain product. Bread, pasta, oatmeal, breakfast cereals, tortillas, and grits are examples of grain products.

Grains are divided into two subgroups, whole grains, and refined grains. Whole grains contain the entire grain kernel—the bran, germ, and endosperm. Examples of whole grains include whole-wheat flour, bulgur (cracked wheat), oatmeal, whole cornmeal, and brown rice. Refined grains have been milled, a process that removes the bran and germ. This is done to give grains a finer texture and improve their shelf life, but it also removes dietary fiber, iron, and many B vitamins. Some examples of refined grain products are white flour, de-germed cornmeal, white bread, and white rice.

Most refined grains are enriched. This means certain B vitamins (thiamin, riboflavin, niacin, folic acid) and iron are added back after processing. Fiber is not added back to enriched grains. Check the ingredient list on refined grain products to make sure that the word "enriched" is included in the grain name. Some food products are made from mixtures of whole grains and refined grains.

How Many Grain Foods Are Needed Daily?

The amount of grains you need to eat depends on your age, sex, and level of physical activity. Recommended daily amounts are listed in this table below. Most Americans consume enough grains, but few are whole grains. At least half of all the grains eaten should be whole grains.

Table 47.6. Daily Grain Table

		Daily Recommendation*	Daily Minimum Amount of Whole Grains
Children	2 to 3 years old 4 to 8 years old	3 ounce equivalents 5 ounce equivalents	1½ ounce equivalents 2½ ounce equivalents
Girls	9 to 13 years old 14 to 18 years old	5 ounce equivalents 6 ounce equivalents	3 ounce equivalents 3 ounce equivalents

Table 47.6. Continued

		Daily Recommendation*	Daily Minimum Amount of Whole Grains
Boys	9 to 13 years old	6 ounce equivalents	3 ounce equivalents
	14 to 18 years old	8 ounce equivalents	4 ounce equivalents
Women	19 to 30 years old	6 ounce equivalents	3 ounce equivalents
	31 to 50 years old	6 ounce equivalents	3 ounce equivalents
	51+ years old	5 ounce equivalents	3 ounce equivalents
Men	19 to 30 years old	8 ounce equivalents	4 ounce equivalents
	31 to 50 years old	7 ounce equivalents	3½ ounce equivalents
	51+ years old	6 ounce equivalents	3 ounce equivalents

* These amounts are appropriate for individuals who get less than 30 minutes per day of moderate physical activity, beyond normal daily activities. Those who are more physically active may be able to consume more while staying within calorie needs.

What Counts as an Ounce-Equivalent of Grains?

In general, 1 slice of bread, 1 cup of ready-to-eat cereal, or ½ cup of cooked rice, cooked pasta, or cooked cereal can be considered as 1 ounce-equivalent from the grains group. The table below lists specific amounts that count as 1 ounce-equivalent of grains towards your daily recommended intake. In some cases, the number of ounce-equivalents for common portions are also shown.

Table 47.7. Ounce-Equivalent of Grains Table

		Amount That Counts as 1 Ounce-Equivalent of Grains	Common Portions and Ounce-Equivalents
Bagels	WG**: Whole wheat RG**: Plain, egg	1" mini bagel	1 large bagel = 4 ounce-equivalents

Table 47.7. Continued

		Amount That Counts as 1 Ounce-Equivalent of Grains	Common Portions and Ounce-Equivalents
Biscuits	(baking powder/buttermilk-G*)	1 small (2" diameter)	1 large (3" diameter) = 2 ounce-equivalents
Breads	WG**: 100% Whole Wheat RG**: White, wheat, French, sourdough	1 regular slice 1 small slice, French 4 snack-size slices rye bread	2 regular slices = 2 ounce-equivalents
Bulgur	Cracked wheat (WG**)	½ cup, cooked	
Cornbread	(RG**)	1 small piece (2½" x 1¼" x 1¼")	1 medium piece (2½" x 2½" x 1¼") = 2 ounce-equivalents
Crackers	WG**: 100% whole wheat, rye RG**: Saltines, snack crackers	5 whole wheat crackers 2 rye crisp breads 7 square or round crackers	
English muffins	WG**: Whole wheat RG**: Plain, raisin	½ muffin	1 muffin = 2 ounce-equivalents
Muffins	WG**: Whole wheat RG**: Bran, corn, plain	1 small (2½" diameter)	1 large (3½" diameter) = 3 ounce equivalents
Oatmeal	(WG**)	½ cup, cooked 1 packet instant 1 ounce (1/3 cup), dry (regular or quick)	
Pancakes	WG**: Whole wheat, buckwheat RG**: Buttermilk, plain	1 pancake (4½" diameter) 2 small pancakes (3" diameter)	3 pancakes (4½" diameter) = 3 ounce-equivalents
Popcorn	(WG**)	3 cups, popped	1 mini microwave bag or 100-calorie bag, popped = 2 ounce-equivalents
Ready-to-eat breakfast cereal	WG**: Toasted oat, whole wheat flakes RG**: Corn flakes, puffed rice	1 cup, flakes or rounds 1¼ cup, puffed	

Table 47.7. Continued

		Amount That Counts as 1 Ounce-Equivalent of Grains	Common Portions and Ounce-Equivalents
Rice	WG*: Brown, wild RG*: Enriched, white, polished	½ cup cooked 1 ounce, dry	1 cup, cooked = 2 ounce-equivalents
Pasta— spaghetti, macaroni, noodles	WG**: Whole wheat RG**: Enriched, durum	½ cup, cooked 1 ounce, dry	1 cup, cooked = 2 ounce-equivalents
Tortillas	WG**: Whole wheat, whole grain corn RG**: Flour, corn	1 small flour tortilla (6" diameter) 1 corn tortilla (6" diameter)	1 large tortilla (12" diameter) = 4 ounce-equivalents

* WG = whole grains, RG = refined grains. This is shown when products are available both in whole grain and refined grain forms.

Proteins
What Foods Are in the Protein Foods Group?

All foods made from meat, poultry, seafood, beans and peas, eggs, processed soy products, nuts, and seeds are considered part of the protein foods group. Beans and peas are also part of the vegetable group.

Select a variety of protein foods to improve nutrient intake and health benefits, including at least 8 ounces of cooked seafood per week. Young children need less, depending on their age and calorie needs. The advice to consume seafood does not apply to vegetarians. Vegetarian options in the Protein Foods Group include beans and peas, processed soy products, and nuts and seeds. Meat and poultry choices should be lean or low-fat.

How Much Food from the Protein Foods Group Is Needed Daily?

The amount of food from the protein foods group you need to eat depends on age, sex, and level of physical activity. Most Americans eat enough food from this group, but need to make leaner and more varied selections of these foods. Recommended daily amounts are shown in the table below.

Table 47.8. Daily Protein Foods Table

Daily Recommendation*		
Children	2 to 3 years old 4 to 8 years old	2 ounce equivalents 4 ounce equivalents
Girls	9 to 13 years old 14 to 18 years old	5 ounce equivalents 5 ounce equivalents
Boys	9 to 13 years old 14 to 18 years old	5 ounce equivalents 6 ½ ounce equivalents
Women	19 to 30 years old 31 to 50 years old 51+ years old	5 ½ ounce equivalents 5 ounce equivalents 5 ounce equivalents
Men	19 to 30 years old 31 to 50 years old 51+ years old	6 ½ ounce equivalents 6 ounce equivalents 5 ½ ounce equivalents

These amounts are appropriate for individuals who get less than 30 minutes per day of moderate physical activity, beyond normal daily activities. Those who are more physically active may be able to consume more while staying within calorie needs.

What Counts as an Ounce-Equivalent in the Protein Foods Group?

In general, 1 ounce of meat, poultry or fish, ¼ cup cooked beans, 1 egg, 1 tablespoon of peanut butter, or ½ ounce of nuts or seeds can be considered as 1 ounce-equivalent from the protein foods group.

This table below lists specific amounts that count as 1 ounce-equivalent in the protein foods group towards your daily recommended intake.

Table 47.9. Ounce-Equivalent of Protein Foods Table

	Amount That Counts as 1 Ounce-Equivalent in the Protein Foods Group	**Common Portions and Ounce-Equivalents**
Meats	1 ounce cooked lean beef 1 ounce cooked lean pork or ham	1 small steak (eye of round, filet) = 3½ to 4 ounce-equivalents 1 small lean hamburger = 2 to 3 ounce-equivalents
Poultry	1 ounce cooked chicken or turkey, without skin 1 sandwich slice of turkey (4½" x 2½" x 1/8")	1 small chicken breast half = 3 ounce-equivalents ½ Cornish game hen = 4 ounce-equivalents

Table 47.9. Continued

	Amount That Counts as 1 Ounce-Equivalent in the Protein Foods Group	Common Portions and Ounce-Equivalents
Seafood	1 ounce cooked fish or shellfish	1 can of tuna, drained = 3 to 4 ounce-equivalents 1 salmon steak = 4 to 6 ounce-equivalents 1 small trout = 3 ounce-equivalents
Eggs	1 egg	3 egg whites = 2 ounce-equivalents 3 egg yolks = 1 ounce-equivalent
Nuts and seeds	½ ounce of nuts (12 almonds, 24 pistachios, 7 walnut halves) ½ ounce of seeds (pumpkin, sunflower, or squash seeds, hulled, roasted) 1 Tablespoon of peanut butter or almond butter	1 ounce of nuts or seeds = 2 ounce-equivalents
Beans and peas	¼ cup of cooked beans (such as black, kidney, pinto, or white beans) ¼ cup of cooked peas (such as chickpeas, cowpeas, lentils, or split peas) ¼ cup of baked beans, refried beans ¼ cup (about 2 ounces) of tofu 1 oz. tempeh, cooked ¼ cup roasted soybeans 1 falafel patty (2¼", 4 oz.) 2 Tablespoons hummus	1 cup split pea soup = 2 ounce-equivalents 1 cup lentil soup = 2 ounce-equivalents 1 cup bean soup = 2 ounce-equivalents 1 soy or bean burger patty = 2 ounce-equivalents

Dairy
What Foods Are Included in the Dairy Group?

All fluid milk products and many foods made from milk are considered part of this food group. Foods made from milk that retain their calcium content are part of the group. Foods made from milk that have little to no calcium, such as cream cheese, cream, and butter, are not. Calcium-fortified soymilk (soy beverage) is also part of the dairy group.

How Much Food from the Dairy Group Is Needed Daily?

The amount of food from the dairy group you need to eat depends on age. Recommended daily amounts are shown in the table below.

Table 47.10. Daily Dairy Table

Daily Recommendation		
Children	2 to 3 years old	2 cups
	4 to 8 years old	2½ cups
Girls	9 to 13 years old	3 cups
	14 to 18 years old	3 cups
Boys	9 to 13 years old	3 cups
	14 to 18 years old	3 cups
Women	19 to 30 years old	3 cups
	31 to 50 years old	3 cups
	51+ years old	3 cups
Men	19 to 30 years old	3 cups
	31 to 50 years old	3 cups
	51+ years old	3 cups

What Counts as a Cup in the Dairy Group?

In general, 1 cup of milk, yogurt, or soymilk (soy beverage), 1½ ounces of natural cheese, or 2 ounces of processed cheese can be considered as 1 cup from the dairy group. When choosing dairy, fat-free, and low-fat dairy are good options. The table below lists specific amounts that count as 1 cup in the dairy group towards your daily recommended intake.

Table 47.11. Cup of Dairy Table

	Amount That Counts as a Cup in the Dairy Group	Common Portions and Cup Equivalents
Milk	1 cup milk	
	1 half-pint container milk	
	½ cup evaporated milk	

Table 47.11. Continued

	Amount That Counts as a Cup in the Dairy Group	Common Portions and Cup Equivalents
Yogurt	1 regular container (8 fluid ounces)	1 small container (6 ounces) = ¾ cup
	1 cup yogurt	1 snack size container (4 ounces) = ½ cup
Cheese	1½ ounces hard cheese (cheddar, mozzarella, Swiss, Parmesan)	1 slice of hard cheese is equivalent to ½ cup milk
	1/3 cup shredded cheese	
	2 ounces processed cheese (American)	1 slice of processed cheese is equivalent to 1/3 cup milk
	½ cup ricotta cheese	
	2 cups cottage cheese	½ cup cottage cheese is equivalent to ¼ cup milk
Milk-based desserts	1 cup pudding made with milk	
	1 cup frozen yogurt	
	1½ cups ice cream	1 scoop ice cream is equivalent to 1.3 cup milk
Soymilk (soy beverage)	1 cup calcium-fortified soymilk	
	1 half-pint container calcium-fortified soymilk	

Oils
What Are "Oils"?

Oils are fats that are liquid at room temperature, like the vegetable oils used in cooking. Oils come from many different plants and from fish. Oils are NOT a food group, but they provide essential nutrients. Therefore, oils are included in U.S. Department of Agriculture (USDA) food patterns.

Some commonly eaten oils include: canola oil, corn oil, cottonseed oil, olive oil, safflower oil, soybean oil, and sunflower oil. Some oils are used mainly as flavorings, such as walnut oil and sesame oil. A number of foods are naturally high in oils, like nuts, olives, some fish, and avocados.

Foods that are mainly oil include mayonnaise, certain salad dressings, and soft (tub or squeeze) margarine with no trans fats. Check the Nutrition Facts label to find margarines with 0 grams of trans fat. Amounts of trans fat are required to be listed on labels.

Most oils are high in monounsaturated or polyunsaturated fats, and low in saturated fats. Oils from plant sources (vegetable and nut oils) do not contain any cholesterol. In fact, no plant foods contain cholesterol. A few plant oils, however, including coconut oil, palm oil, and palm kernel oil, are high in saturated fats and for nutritional purposes should be considered to be solid fats.

Solid fats are fats that are solid at room temperature, like butter and shortening. Solid fats come from many animal foods and can be made from vegetable oils through a process called hydrogenation. Some common fats are butter, milk fat, beef fat (tallow, suet), chicken fat, pork fat (lard), stick margarine, shortening, and partially hydrogenated oil.

How Much Is My Allowance for Oils?

Some Americans consume enough oil in the foods they eat, such as:

- Nuts

- Fish

- Cooking oil

- Salad dressings

Others could easily consume the recommended allowance by substituting oils for some solid fats they eat. A person's allowance for oils depends on age, sex, and level of physical activity. Daily allowances for oils are shown in the table below.

Table 47.12. Daily Allowance for Specific Age Group

Daily Allowance		
Children	2 to 3 years old 4 to 8 years old	3 teaspoons 4 teaspoons
Girls	9 to 13 years old 14 to 18 years old	5 teaspoons 5 teaspoons
Boys	9 to 13 years old 14 to 18 years old	5 teaspoons 6 teaspoons

Table 47.12. Continued

Daily Allowance		
Women	19 to 30 years old 31 to 50 years old 51+ years old	6 teaspoons 5 teaspoons 5 teaspoons
Men	19 to 30 years old 31 to 50 years old 51+ years old	7 teaspoons 6 teaspoons 6 teaspoons

How Do I Count the Oils I Eat?

The table below gives a quick guide to the amount of oils in some common foods.

Table 47.13. Oil Table

	Amount of Food	Amount of Oil	Calories from Oil	Total Calories
		Teaspoons/ grams	Approximate calories	Approximate calories
Oils:				
Vegetable oils (such as canola, corn, cottonseed, olive, peanut, safflower, soybean, and sunflower)	1 Tbsp	3 tsp/14 g	120	120
Foods rich in oils:				
Margarine, soft (trans fat-free)	1 Tbsp	2½ tsp/11 g	100	100
Mayonnaise	1 Tbsp	2½ tsp/11 g	100	100
Mayonnaise-type salad dressing	1 Tbsp	1 tsp/5 g	45	55
Italian dressing	2 Tbsp	2 tsp/8 g	75	85

Table 47.13. Continued

	Amount of Food	Amount of Oil	Calories from Oil	Total Calories
		Teaspoons/grams	Approximate calories	Approximate calories
Olives*, ripe, canned	4 large	½ tsp/2 g	15	20
Avocado*	½ med	3 tsp/15 g	130	160
Peanut butter*	2 T	4 tsp/16 g	140	190
Peanuts, dry roasted*	1 oz.	3 tsp/14 g	120	165
Mixed nuts, dry roasted*	1 oz.	3 tsp/15 g	130	170
Cashews, dry roasted*	1 oz.	3 tsp/13 g	115	165
Almonds, dry roasted*	1 oz.	3 tsp/15 g	130	170
Hazelnuts*	1 oz.	4 tsp/18 g	160	185
Sunflower seeds*	1 oz.	3 tsp/14 g	120	165

* Avocados and olives are part of the Vegetable Group; nuts and seeds are part of the Protein Foods Group. These foods are also high in oils. Soft margarine, mayonnaise, and salad dressings are mainly oil and are not considered to be part of any food group.

Section 47.2

A Guide to Portion Size

This section includes text excerpted from "Just Enough for You: About Food Portions," National Institute of Diabetes and Digestive and Kidney Diseases (NIDDK), December 2016.

To reach or stay at a healthy weight, how much you eat is just as important as what you eat. Do you know how much food is enough for you? Do you understand the difference between a portion and a serving? The information below explains portions and servings, and provides tips to help you eat just enough for you.

What Is the Difference between a Portion and a Serving?

A portion is how much food you choose to eat at one time, whether in a restaurant, from a package, or at home. A serving, or serving size, is the amount of food listed on a product's Nutrition Facts, or food label (see Figure 47.1 below).

Different products have different serving sizes, which could be measured in cups, ounces, grams, pieces, slices, or numbers—such as three crackers. A serving size on a food label may be more or less than the amount you should eat, depending on your age, weight, whether you are male or female, and how active you are. Depending on how much you choose to eat, your portion size may or may not match the serving size.

Figure 47.1. *Updated Nutrition Facts Label* (Source: U.S. Food and Drug Administration (FDA).)

As a result of updates to the Nutrition Facts label in May 2016, some serving sizes on food labels may be larger or smaller than they had been before (see Figure 47.2 below). For instance, a serving size of ice cream is now 2/3 cup, instead of 1/2 cup. A serving size of yogurt is six ounces rather than eight ounces. The U.S. Food and Drug Administration (FDA) changed some food and beverage serving sizes so that labels more closely match how much people actually eat and drink.

Figure 47.2. *FDA Serving Size Changes* (Source: U.S. Food and Drug Administration (FDA).)

Serving Size and Servings per Container

Go back to the updated food label in Figure 47.1. To see how many servings a container has, you would check "servings per container" listed at the top of the label above "Serving size." The serving size is 2/3 cup, but the container has eight servings. If you eat two servings, or 1⅓ cups, you need to double the number of calories and nutrients listed on the food label to know how much you are really getting. For example, if you eat two servings of this product, you are taking in 460 calories:

230 calories per serving x two servings eaten = 460 calories

How Much Should I Eat?

How many calories you need each day to lose weight or maintain your weight depends on your age, weight, metabolism, whether you are male or female, how active you are, and other factors. For example, a 150-pound woman who burns a lot of calories through intense physical activity, such as fast running, several times a week will need more calories than a woman about the same size who only goes for a short walk once a week.

The *Dietary Guidelines for Americans 2015–2020* can give you an idea of how many calories you may need each day based on your age, sex, and physical activity level. Use the Body Weight Planner tool (www.niddk.nih.gov/health-information/weight-management/body-weight-planner) to make your own calorie and physical activity plans to help you reach and maintain your goal weight.

How Can the Nutrition Facts Food Label Help Me?

The FDA food label is printed on most packaged foods. The food label is a quick way to find the amount of calories and nutrients in a certain amount of food. For example, reading food labels tells you how many calories and how much fat, protein, sodium, and other ingredients are in one food serving. Many packaged foods contain more than a single serving. The updated food label lists the number of calories in one serving size in larger print than before so it is easier to see.

Other Helpful Facts on the Food Label

The food label has other useful information about what is included in one food serving. For example, one serving on the food label in Figure 47.1 has one gram of saturated fat and 0 grams of trans fat, a type of fat that is unhealthy for your heart.

The updated food label also includes information about "added sugars." Added sugars include table sugar, or sucrose, including beet and cane sugars; corn syrup; honey; malt syrup; and other sweeteners, such as fructose or glucose, that have been added to food and beverages. Fruit and milk contain naturally-occurring sugars and are not included in the label as added sugars. *The Dietary Guidelines for*

Americans 2015 to 2020 calls for consuming less than ten percent of calories daily from added sugars.

Because Americans do not always get enough vitamin D and potassium, the updated food label includes serving information for both of these nutrients. Since a lack of vitamin A and vitamin C in the general population is rare, these nutrients are no longer included on the food label. However, food makers may include them if they choose. Most food makers will have to start using the new food label by July 26, 2018. Figure 47.3 below compares the updated food label with the original label.

Nutrition Facts

Serving Size 2/3 cup (55g)
Servings Per Container About 8

Amount Per Serving

Calories 230   Calories from Fat 72

	% Daily Value*
Total Fat 8g	12%
Saturated Fat 1g	5%
Trans Fat 0g	
Cholesterol 0mg	0%
Sodium 160mg	7%
Total Carbohydrate 37g	12%
Dietary Fiber 4g	16%
Sugars 1g	
Protein 3g	

Vitamin A	10%
Vitamin C	8%
Calcium	20%
Iron	45%

* Percent Daily Values are based on a 2,000 calorie diet. Your daily value may be higher or lower depending on your calorie needs.

		Calories:	2,000	2,500
Total Fat	Less than		65g	80g
Sat Fat	Less than		20g	25g
Cholesterol	Less than		300mg	300mg
Sodium	Less than		2,400mg	2,400mg
Total Carbohydrate			300g	375g
Dietary Fiber			25g	30g

Nutrition Facts

8 servings per container
Serving size   **2/3 cup (55g)**

Amount per serving

Calories   **230**

	% Daily Value*
Total Fat 8g	**10%**
Saturated Fat 1g	**5%**
Trans Fat 0g	
Cholesterol 0mg	**0%**
Sodium 160mg	**7%**
Total Carbohydrate 37g	**13%**
Dietary Fiber 4g	**14%**
Total Sugars 12g	
Includes 10g Added Sugars	**20%**
Protein 3g	

Vitamin D 2mcg	10%
Calcium 260mg	20%
Iron 8mg	45%
Potassium 235mg	6%

* The % Daily Value (DV) tells you how much a nutrient in a serving of food contributes to a daily diet. 2,000 calories a day is used for general nutrition advice.

Figure 47.3. *Side-by-Side Comparison of Original and New Nutrition Facts Label* (Source: U.S. Food and Drug Administration (FDA).)

Current label (left) and updated label (right)

How Can I Keep Track of How Much I Eat?

In addition to checking food labels for calories per serving, keeping track of what you eat—as well as when, where, why, and how much you eat—may help you manage your food portions. Create a food tracker on your cell phone, calendar, or computer to record the information.

You also could download apps that are available for mobile devices to help you track how much you eat—and how much physical activity you get—each day.

The Sample Food Tracker in Table 47.14 below shows what a 1-day page of a food tracker might look like. In the example, the person chose fairly healthy portions for breakfast and lunch, and ate to satisfy hunger. The person also ate five cookies in the afternoon out of boredom rather than hunger.

By 8 p.m., the person was very hungry and ate large portions of high-fat, high-calorie food at a social event. An early evening snack of a piece of fruit and 4 ounces of fat-free or low-fat yogurt might have prevented overeating less healthy food later. The number of calories for the day totaled 2,916, which is more than most people need. Taking in too many calories may lead to weight gain over time.

If, like the person in the food tracker example, you eat even when you're not hungry, try doing something else instead. For instance, call or visit a friend. Or, if you are at work, take a break and walk around the block, if work and schedule permit. If you can't distract yourself from food, try a healthy option, such as a piece of fruit or stick of low-fat string cheese.

Table 47.14. Sample Food Tracker

Time	Food	Amount	Place	Hunger/ Reason	Estimated Calories
8 a.m.	Coffee, Black	6 fl. oz.	Home	Slightly hungry	2
	Banana	1 medium			105
	Low-fat-yogurt	1 cup			250
1 p.m.	Grilled cheese sandwich		Work	Hungry	281
	Apple	1 medium			72
	Potato chips	Single-serving bag, 1 ounce			152
	Water	16 fl. oz.			—
3 p.m.	Chocolate-chip cookies	5 medium-sized	Work	Not hungry/ Bored	345

Table 47.14. Continued

Time	Food	Amount	Place	Hunger/ Reason	Estimated Calories
8 p.m.	Mini chicken drumsticks with hot pepper sauce	4	Restaurant/ Out with friends	Very hungry	312
	Taco salad	3 cups in fried flour tortilla with beans and cheese			586
	Chocolate cheesecake	1 piece, 1/12 of 9-inch cake			479
	Soft drink	12 fl. oz.			136
	Latte	Espresso coffee with whole milk, 16 ounces			196
Total Calories =					2,916

Through your tracker, you may become aware of when and why you consume less healthy foods and drinks. The tracker may help you make different choices in the future.

How Can I Manage Food Portions at Home?

You don't need to measure and count everything you eat or drink for the rest of your life. You may only want to do this long enough to learn typical serving and portion sizes. Try these ideas to help manage portions at home:

- Take one serving according to the food label and eat it off a plate instead of straight out of the box or bag

- Avoid eating in front of the TV, while driving or walking, or while you are busy with other activities

- Focus on what you are eating, chew your food well, and fully enjoy the smell and taste of your food

- Eat slowly so your brain can get the message that your stomach is full, which may take at least 15 minutes

- Use smaller dishes, bowls, and glasses so that you eat and drink less

- Eat fewer high-fat, high-calorie foods, such as desserts, chips, sauces, and prepackaged snacks

- Freeze food you won't serve or eat right away, if you make too much. That way, you won't be tempted to finish the whole batch. If you freeze leftovers in single- or family-sized servings, you'll have ready-made meals for another day.

- Eat meals at regular times. Leaving hours between meals or skipping meals altogether may cause you to overeat later in the day.

- Buy snacks, such as fruit or single-serving, prepackaged foods, that are lower in calories. If you buy bigger bags or boxes of snacks, divide the items into single-serve packages right away so you aren't tempted to overeat.

How Can I Manage Portions When Eating Out?

Although it may be easier to manage your portions when you cook and eat at home, most people eat out from time to time—and some people eat out often. Try these tips to keep your food portions in check when you are away from home:

- Share a meal with a friend, or take half of it home

- Avoid all-you-can-eat buffets

- Order one or two healthy appetizers or side dishes instead of a whole meal. Options include steamed or grilled—instead of fried—seafood or chicken, a salad with dressing on the side, or roasted vegetables.

- Ask to have the bread basket or chips removed from the table

- If you have a choice, pick the small-sized—rather than large-sized—drink, salad, or frozen yogurt

- Stop eating and drinking when you're full. Put down your fork and glass, and focus on enjoying the setting and your company for the rest of the meal.

Is Getting More Food for Your Money Always a Good Value?

Have you noticed that it costs only a few cents more to get the large fries or soft drinks instead of the regular or small size? Although getting the super-sized meal for a little extra money may seem like a good deal, you end up with more calories than you need for your body to stay healthy. Before you buy your next "value meal combo," be sure you are making the best choice for your wallet and your health.

How Can I Manage Portions and Eat Well When Money Is Tight?

Eating healthier doesn't have to cost a lot of money. For instance:

- Buy fresh fruit and vegetables when they are in season. Check out a local farmers market for fresh, local produce if there is one in your community. Be sure to compare prices, as produce at some farmers markets cost more than the grocery store. Buy only as much as you will use to avoid having to throw away spoiled food.

- Match portion sizes to serving sizes. To get the most from the money you spend on packaged foods, try eating no more than the serving sizes listed on food labels. Eating no more than a serving size may also help you better manage your fat, sugar, salt, and calories.

Section 47.3

How to Read Food Labels

This section includes text excerpted from "Using the
Nutrition Facts Label: A How-To Guide for Older Adults,"
U.S. Food and Drug Administration (FDA), July 31, 2018.

Why Nutrition Matters for You

Good nutrition is important throughout your life!

It can help you feel your best and stay strong. It can help reduce
the risk of some diseases that are common among older adults. And,
if you already have certain health issues, good nutrition can help you
manage the symptoms.

Nutrition can sometimes seem complicated. But the good news is
that the U.S. Food and Drug Administration (FDA) has a simple tool
to help you know exactly what you're eating.

It's called the Nutrition Facts Label. You will find it on all packaged
foods and beverages. It serves as your guide for making choices that
can affect your long-term health.

Good nutrition can help you avoid or manage these common
diseases:

- Certain cancers

- High blood pressure

- Type 2 diabetes

- Obesity

- Heart disease

- Osteoporosis

The Nutrition Facts Label at a Glance

Understanding what the Nutrition Facts Label includes can help
you make food choices that are best for your health.

1. Serving Size

This section shows how many servings are in the package,
and how big the serving is. Serving sizes are given in familiar
measurements, such as "cups" or "pieces."

Remember: All of the nutrition information on the label is based upon one serving of the food. A package of food often contains more than one serving!

2. Amount of Calories

The calories listed are for one serving of the food. "Calories from fat" shows how many fat calories there are in one serving.

Remember—a product that's fat-free isn't necessarily calorie-free. Read the label!

3. Percent (%) Daily Value

This section tells you how the nutrients in one serving of the food contribute to your total daily diet. Use it to choose foods that are high in the nutrients you should get more of, and low in the nutrients you should get less of.

Daily Values are based on a 2,000-calorie diet. However, your nutritional needs will likely depend on how physically active you are. Talk to your healthcare provider to see what calorie level is right for you.

Figure 47.4. *Nutritional Facts*

4. Limit These Nutrients

Eating too much total fat (especially saturated fat and trans fat), cholesterol, or sodium may increase your risk of certain chronic diseases, such as heart disease, some cancers, or high blood pressure.

Try to keep these nutrients as low as possible each day.

5. Get Enough of These Nutrients

Americans often don't get enough dietary fiber, vitamin A, vitamin C, calcium, and potassium in their diets. These nutrients are essential for keeping you feeling strong and healthy.

Eating enough of these nutrients may improve your health and help reduce the risk of some diseases.

Three Key Areas of Importance

As you use the Nutrition Facts Label, pay particular attention to serving size, percent daily value, and nutrients.

Serving Size

The top of the Nutrition Facts Label shows the serving size and the servings per container. Serving size is the key to the rest of the information on the Nutrition Facts Label.

- The nutrition information about the food—like the calories, sodium, and fiber—is based upon one serving.

- If you eat two servings of the food, you are eating double the calories and getting twice the amount of nutrients, both good and bad.

- If you eat three servings, that means three times the calories and nutrients—and so on.

That is why knowing the serving size is important. It's how you know for sure how many calories and nutrients you are getting.

Check Serving Size!

It is very common for a food package to contain more than one serving. One bottled soft drink or a small bag of chips can actually contain two or more serving.

Percent Daily Value (%DV)

The %DV is a general guide to help you link nutrients in one serving of food to their contribution to your total daily diet. It can help you determine if a food is high or low in a nutrient: five percent or less is low, 20 percent or more is high.

You can also use the %DV to make dietary trade-offs with other foods throughout the day.

%DV: Quick Tips

You can tell if a food is high or low in a particular nutrient by taking a quick look at the %DV.

- If it has five percent of the daily value or less, it is low in that nutrient.

This can be good or bad, depending on if it is a nutrient you want more of or less of.

- If it has 20 percent or more, it is high in that nutrient.

This can be good for nutrients like fiber (a nutrient to get more of) . . . but not so good for something like saturated fat (a nutrient to get less of).

Using %DV

- Once you are familiar with %DV, you can use it to compare foods and decide which is the better choice for you. Be sure to check for the particular nutrients you want more of or less of.

- Using %DV information can also help you "balance things out" for the day.

- For example: If you ate a favorite food at lunch that was high in sodium, a "nutrient to get less of," you would then try to choose foods for dinner that are lower in sodium.

Nutrients

A nutrient is an ingredient in a food that provides nourishment. Nutrients are essential for life and to keep your body functioning properly.

Nutrients to get more of:

There are some nutrients that are especially important for your health. You should try to get adequate amounts of these each day. They are:

- Calcium

- Dietary fiber

- Potassium*

- Vitamin A

- Vitamin C

* **Note:** The listing of potassium is optional on the Nutrition Facts Label.

Nutrients to get less of:

There are other nutrients that are important, but that you should eat in moderate amounts. They can increase your risk of certain diseases.

They are:

- Total fat (especially saturated fat)

- Cholesterol

- Sodium

Your Guide to a Healthy Diet

The Nutrition Facts Label can help you make choices for overall health. But some nutrients can also affect certain health conditions and diseases.

Use this section as a guide for those nutrients that could impact your own health. Each nutrient section discusses:

- What the nutrient is

- What it can mean for your health

- Label-reading tips

Watch for "nutrients to get less of" (the ones that you should try to limit), and "nutrients to get more of" (the ones that are very important to be sure to get enough of). You also might want to talk to your healthcare provider about which nutrients you should track closely for your continued health. And remember—the Nutrition Facts Label is a tool that is available to you on every packaged food and beverage!

Nutrients and Your Needs

On the following pages, you'll find specific information about certain nutrients.

Some are nutrients to get less of; others are nutrients to get more of. All of them can have an impact on your long-term health.

In addition, here is an example of how the Nutrition Facts Label can guide you in making good decisions for long-term health and nutrition.

Example

Heart disease is the number one cause of death in the United States. You can use the Nutrition Facts Label to compare foods and decide which ones fit with a diet that may help reduce the risk of heart disease. Choose foods that have fewer calories per serving and a lower percent DV of these "nutrients to get less of"

- Total fat

- Saturated fat

- Cholesterol

- Sodium

To lower your risk of heart disease, it is also recommended that you eat more fiber.

Dietary Salt/Sodium: Get Less Of
What It Is

Salt is a crystal-like compound that is used to flavor and preserve food. The words "salt" and "sodium" are often used interchangeably. Salt is listed as "sodium" on the Nutrition Facts Label.

What You Should Know

A small amount of sodium is needed to help certain organs and fluids work properly. But most people eat too much of it - and they may not even know it! That's because many packaged foods have a high amount of sodium, even when they don't taste "salty." Plus, when you add salt to food, you're adding more sodium.

Sodium has been linked to high blood pressure. In fact, eating less sodium can often help lower blood pressure . . . which in turn can help reduce the risk of heart disease.

And since blood pressure normally rises with age, limiting your sodium intake becomes even more important each year.

Label Reading Tips: Salt/Sodium

- Read the label to see how much sodium is in the food you are choosing.

- 5 percent DV or less is low in sodium

- 20 percent DV or more is high in sodium

- When you are deciding between two foods, compare the amount of sodium. Look for cereals, crackers, pasta sauces, canned vegetables, and other packaged foods that are lower in sodium.

Fiber: Get More Of
What It Is

Fiber, or "dietary fiber," is sometimes called "roughage." It's the part of food that can't be broken down during digestion. So because it moves through your digestive system "undigested," it plays an important role in keeping your system moving and "in working order."

What You Should Know

Fiber is a "nutrient to get more of." In addition to aiding in digestion, fiber has a number of other health-related benefits. These benefits are especially effective when you have a high fiber diet that is also low in saturated fat, cholesterol, trans fat, added sugars, salt, and alcohol.

- Eating a diet that is low in saturated fat and cholesterol and high in fruits, vegetables, and grain products that contain some types of dietary fiber, particularly soluble fiber, may help lower your cholesterol and reduce your chances of getting heart disease, a disease associated with many factors.

- Healthful diets that are low in fat and rich in fruits and vegetables that contain fiber may reduce the risk of some types of cancer, including colon cancer, a disease associated with many factors. In addition, such healthful diets are also associated with a reduced risk of type 2 diabetes.

- Fiber also aids in the regularity of bowel movements and preventing constipation. It may help reduce the risk of diverticulosis, a common condition in which small pouches form in the colon wall. This condition often has few or no symptoms; people who already have diverticulosis and do have symptoms often find that increased fiber consumption can reduce these symptoms. It's also important to note that if the pouches caused by diverticulosis rupture and become infected, it results in a more severe condition called diverticulitis.

Soluble versus Insoluble Fiber: Where to Get It, and What It Does

Fiber comes in two forms—insoluble and soluble. Most plant foods contain some of each kind.

- **Insoluble fiber** is mostly found in whole-grain products, such as wheat bran cereal, vegetables, and fruit. It provides "bulk" for stool formation and helps wastes move quickly through your colon.

- **Soluble fiber** is found in peas, beans, many vegetables and fruits, oat bran, whole grains, barley, cereals, seeds, rice, and some pasta, crackers, and other bakery products. It slows the digestion of carbohydrates, and can help stabilize blood sugar if you have diabetes. In addition, it helps lower "bad cholesterol." This, in turn, reduces the risk of heart disease.

Check the Nutrition Facts Label to see which foods have a higher %DV of fiber.

Label Reading Tips: Fiber

- **Read food labels.** The Nutrition Facts Label tells you the amount of dietary fiber in each serving, as well as the %DV of fiber that food contains.

When comparing the amount of fiber in food, remember:

- 5 percent DV or less is low in fiber
- 20 percent DV or more is high in fiber

The label won't indicate whether fiber is "insoluble" or "soluble," so it's best to try to get some of both. (See information on previous page)

- Compare foods and choose the ones with higher fiber.

Look for and compare labels on whole-grain products such as bulgur, brown rice, whole wheat couscous or kasha and whole-grain breads, cereals, and pasta. In addition, compare different styles/types of canned or frozen beans and fruit.

Total Fat: Get Less Of
What It Is

Fat, or "dietary fat," is a nutrient that is a major source of energy for the body. It also helps you absorb certain important vitamins.

As a food ingredient, fat provides taste, consistency, and helps you feel full.

What You Should Know

Eating too much fat can lead to a wide range of health challenges. The total amount and type of fat can contribute to and/or increase the risk of:

- Heart disease

- High cholesterol

- Increased risk of many cancers (including colon-rectum cancer)

- Obesity

- High blood pressure

- Type 2 diabetes

It is important to know that there are different types of dietary fat. Some have health benefits when eaten in small quantities, but others do not.

"Good" Fat: unsaturated fats (monounsaturated and polyunsaturated)

- These are healthful if eaten in moderation. In fact, small amounts can even help lower cholesterol levels!

- Best Sources: Plant-based oils (sunflower, corn, soybean, cottonseed, and safflower), olive, canola and peanut oils, nuts, and soft margarines (liquid, tub or spray).

"Undesirable" Fat: saturated and trans fats. These can raise cholesterol levels in the blood—which in turn can contribute to heart disease.

- Common Sources: Meat, poultry, fish, butter, ice cream, cheese, coconut and palm kernel oils, solid shortenings, and hard margarines.

- Meat (including chicken and turkey) and fish supply protein, B vitamins, and iron. When selecting and preparing meat, poultry, fish and milk or milk products, choose those that are lean, low-fat, or fat-free. Doing this, along with removing the skin from fish and poultry, are good strategies for limiting "undesirable" fat from your diet. In addition, dry beans, which can be used as a meat substitute, are a good source of protein and are nonfat.

Understanding Trans Fat

Trans fat is one of the newest additions to the Nutrition Facts Label, so you may be hearing more about it. Here's what you need to know:

Most trans fat is made when manufacturers "hydrogenize" liquid oils, turning them into solid fats, like shortening or some margarines. Trans fat is commonly found in crackers, cookies, snack foods, and other foods made with or fried in these solid oils.

Trans fat, like saturated fat and cholesterol, raises your LDL (bad) cholesterol and can increase your risk of coronary heart disease.

Trans Fat on the Label

There is no recommended total daily value for trans fat, so you won't find the %DV of trans fat on a food's Nutrition Facts Label. However, you can still use the label to see if a food contains trans fat and to compare two foods by checking to see if grams of trans fat are listed. If there is anything other than 0 grams listed, then the food contains trans fat. Because it is extremely difficult to eat a diet that is completely trans fat-free without decreasing other nutrient intakes, just aim to keep your intake of trans fat as low as possible.

Label Reading Tips: Total Fat

- When comparing foods, check the Nutrition Facts Label and choose the food with the lower %DV of total fat and saturated fat, and low or no grams of trans fat.
  - 5 percent DV or less of total fat is low
  - 20 percent DV or more of total fat is high
- When choosing foods that are labeled "fat-free" and "low-fat," be aware that fat-free doesn't mean calorie-free. Sometimes, to make a food tastier, extra sugars are added, which adds extra calories. Be sure to check the calories per serving.

Cholesterol: Get Less Of
What It Is

Cholesterol is a crystal-like substance carried through the bloodstream by lipoproteins—the "transporters" of fat. Cholesterol is required for certain important body functions, like digesting dietary fats, making hormones, and building cell walls.

Cholesterol is found in animal-based foods, like meats and dairy products.

411

What You Should Know

Too much cholesterol in the bloodstream can damage arteries, especially the ones that supply blood to the heart. It can build up in blood vessel linings. This is called atherosclerosis, and it can lead to heart attacks and stroke.

However, it's important to know that not all cholesterol is bad. There are two kinds of cholesterol found in the bloodstream. How much you have of each is what determines your risk of heart disease.

High-density lipoprotein (HDL): This "good" cholesterol is the form in which cholesterol travels back to the liver, where it can be eliminated.

- HDL helps prevent cholesterol buildup in blood vessels. A higher level of this cholesterol is better. Low HDL levels increase heart disease risk. Discuss your HDL level with your healthcare provider.

Low-density lipoprotein (LDL): This "bad" cholesterol is carried into the blood. It is the main cause of harmful fatty buildup in arteries.

- The higher the LDL cholesterol level in the blood, the greater the heart disease risk. So, a lower level of this cholesterol is better.

Label Reading Tips: Cholesterol

- Cholesterol is a "nutrient to get less of." When comparing foods, look at the Nutrition Facts Label, and choose the food with the lower %DV of cholesterol. Be sure not to go above 100 percent DV for the day.

  - 5 percent DV or less of cholesterol is low

  - 20 percent DV or more of cholesterol is high

- One of the primary ways LDL ("bad") cholesterol levels can become too high in the blood is by eating too much saturated fat and cholesterol. Saturated fat raises LDL levels more than anything else in the diet.

Calcium: Get More Of
What It Is

Calcium is a mineral that has a lot of uses in the body, but it is best known for its role in building healthy bones and teeth.

What You Should Know

Lack of calcium causes osteoporosis, which is the primary cause of hip fractures. In fact, the word "osteoporosis" means "porous bones." It causes progressive bone loss as you age, and makes bones fragile—so that they can break easily. It's extremely important (especially for women) to get enough calcium throughout your life, especially after menopause. Women are at much higher risk for osteoporosis, but men can get it too.

It's true that many dairy products, which contain high levels of calcium, are relatively high in fat and calories. But keep in mind that fat-free or low-fat types of milk products are excellent calcium sources. Nutritionists recommend that you try to get most of your calcium from calcium-rich foods, rather than from calcium supplements. The Nutrition Facts Label can help you make good high-calcium choices.

Other good sources of calcium are:

- Canned salmon (with bones, which are edible)

- Calcium-fortified soy beverages

- Tofu (soybean curd that is "calcium-processed")

- Certain vegetables (for example, dark leafy greens such as collards and turnip greens)

- Legumes (black-eyed peas and white beans)

- Calcium-fortified grain products

- Calcium-fortified juice

Label Reading: Tips Calcium

- Read the label to see how much calcium is in the food you are choosing.
  - 5 percent DV or less is low in calcium
  - 20 percent DV or more is high in calcium
- Select foods that are high in calcium as often as possible.

Section 47.4

The Importance of Family Meals

This section contains text excerpted from the following sources:
Text in this section begins with excerpts from "Scientific Report of
the 2015 Dietary Guidelines Advisory Committee," Office of Disease
Prevention and Health Promotion (ODPHP), U.S. Department
of Health and Human Services (HHS), February 2015. Reviewed
December 2018; Text under the heading "Trends in Family
Mealtimes" is excerpted from "The Health and Well-Being of
Children: A Portrait of States and the Nation 2011–2012," Health
Resources and Services Administration (HRSA), January 1, 2012.
Reviewed December 2018; Text beginning with the heading "Why
Family Meals Matter" is excerpted from "Family Style Meals,"
Early Childhood Learning and Knowledge Center (ECLKC), March
2015. Reviewed December 2018; Text under the heading "Helping
Children Determine Hunger and Fullness" is excerpted from "Eating
Environment," Food and Nutrition Service (FNS), U.S. Department
of Agriculture (USDA), December 24, 2016.

In the past, American families seldom consumed food prepared outside their homes and, for the most part, consumed their meals as a family unit. However, these behaviors have changed dramatically in recent years. Today, 33 percent of calories are consumed outside the home and it is becoming more common for individuals to eat alone and to bring meals prepared outside into their homes. Eating away from home is associated with increased caloric intake and poorer dietary quality compared to eating at home. As recognized by the Dietary Guidelines Advisory Committee these major changes in eating behaviors can be expected to have a negative impact on the quality of the diets consumed and the risk of obesity among the U.S. population.

Data from cross-sectional studies suggest that when families share meals, they achieve better diet quality and improved nutrient intake, and to some extent, are better able to maintain appropriate body weight. The definition of family shared meals in the literature varies, with some defining it as the number of a specific meal eaten together (e.g., dinner), or any meal, prepared at home or outside of home, that is shared among individuals living in the same household. Family mealtime may act as a protective factor for many nutritional health-related problems. For example, they provide an opportunity for parents to model good eating behaviors and create a positive atmosphere by providing time for social interaction and thus a sense of social support for all members. Shared meals may be important in every stage of the lifecycle to support healthy growth, development, and weight, though the evidence for adults is mixed.

Trends in Family Mealtimes

Eating together as a family can promote family bonding and good nutrition and eating habits. Overall, the parents of 46.7 percent of children reported that their families had eaten at least one meal together every day during the previous week. More than 31 percent of children were reported to eat meals with their families on 4 to 6 days per week, while 18.1 percent ate meals together on only 1 to 3 days per week and 3.5 percent of families did not eat at least one meal together during the previous week. On average, children and families ate meals together on 5.2 days during the previous week.

Sharing meals together is more common in lower-income households. Among children with household incomes below 100 percent of the federal poverty level (FPL), 57 percent ate at least one meal together with their families every day, while 51.3 percent of children whose household incomes were between 100 and 199 percent of FPL did so. Nearly 43 percent of children with household incomes between 200 and 399 percent of FPL and 38.3 percent of children in households with incomes of 400 percent or more of FPL ate a meal together with their families every day.

Eating meals together every day also varies by race and ethnicity. Hispanic children and non-Hispanic children of other races were most likely to eat at least one meal together as a family every day (52 and 51 percent, respectively), followed by non-Hispanic White children (44.3%) and non-Hispanic Black children.

Why Family Meals Matter

Family meals allow supervising adults to serve as role models for children, teach social skills and provide learning activities that are centered on foods. This approach allows children to identify and be introduced to new foods, new tastes and new menus. It encourages a positive attitude toward nutritious foods and helps children develop good eating habits. Developing healthy eating habits relies on a division of responsibility between children and adults. Adults have the responsibility of providing healthy and safe foods served at regularly scheduled meals and snacks. Children have the responsibility of deciding whether and how much to eat. Adults play an important role in helping children to recognize their internal cues of hunger and fullness so that they are able to self-regulate food intake (i.e., eat when they are hungry and stop when they are full). When adults force children to eat or encourage them to clean their plates, children are taught to disregard their internal hunger cues. This can lead to overeating and childhood obesity.

Tips to Involve Children in Meal Planning and Meal Prep

- **Let children help prepare food and do other things to get the meal ready.** Children can wash fruits or vegetables or mix or stir ingredients. Younger children can help set the table. Start with easy tasks and build up to more challenging ones. Be patient! It takes time for children to learn new skills.

- **Talk at the table.** Ask children question about things they are interested in and about the shape, color, smell, or taste of the foods they are eating. If there is more than one adult at the table, have adults talk to each other, too. Keep conversation topics positive. Praise children for the things they are doing well, and support the skills they are still developing.

- **Encourage children to try new foods by serving them along with familiar foods.** Offer a new food to children many times. It may take 10 to 15 times before a child will accept a new food.

- **Model eating healthy foods.** Children copy what other adults do. They are more likely to eat and try new foods if they see their parents or other caregivers enjoying the foods.

- **Allow children to pick new foods to try.** For example, look for new fruits or vegetables at the grocery store and let the child choose one to try.

Helping Children Determine Hunger and Fullness

- Encourage appropriate portion sizes. Children have small stomachs and need small portions. Like adults, they can overeat when their plate contains too much food.

- Start with small portions and ask children if they are hungry before serving or allowing second helpings.

- Help children learn to put the right amount of food on their plate.

- Create a positive eating environment. Listen when children say they are full.

- Observe younger children for fullness cues. For example, toddlers may not say they are full but they may be distracted from eating or start to play.

- Model healthy behaviors while sitting with the children. Let them see adults eating when they are hungry and pushing their plates away and stopping eating when they are full, even if there is still food on the plate.

Section 47.5

Eating Healthy When Eating Out

This section contains text excerpted from the following sources: Text in this section begins with excerpts from "Tipsheet: Eating Healthy When Dining Out," National Heart, Lung, and Blood Institute (NHLBI), July 31, 2014. Reviewed December 2018; Text beginning with the heading "Order Healthy" is excerpted from "Eating Healthy When Eating out," National Heart, Lung, and Blood Institute (NHLBI), February 13, 2013. Reviewed December 2018; Text under the heading "Tips for Eating Out" is excerpted from "Tips for Eating Out," National Heart, Lung, and Blood Institute (NHLBI), December 2013. Reviewed December 2018; Text under the heading "Ten Tips: Eating Foods Away from Home" is excerpted from "10 Tips: Eating Foods Away from Home," ChooseMyPlate.gov, U.S. Department of Agriculture (USDA), January 2016.

Regardless of whether you're trying to lose weight, you can eat healthy when dining out, if you know how. So, if you're treating yourself to a meal out, here are some tips to help make it a dining experience that is both tasty and good for you.

Ask!

Will the restaurant:

- Serve margarine rather than butter with the meal?

417

- Serve fat-free (skim) milk rather than whole milk or cream?
- Trim visible fat from poultry or meat?
- Leave all butter, gravy, or cream sauces off a dish?
- Serve salad dressing on the side?
- Accommodate special requests?
- Use less cooking oil when cooking?

Act!

Select foods that are:

- Steamed in their own juice (au jus)
- Broiled
- Baked
- Roasted
- Poached
- Lightly sauteed

Staying in energy balance can be tough when you and your family go out to eat. But you can still eat healthy and enjoy your meal. Don't be afraid to ask questions about the ingredients and how the food was cooked. You also can ask to leave some items out or replace them with healthier choices.

Order Healthy

When you are choosing foods, choose items that have less fat or added sugar. Or ask for a healthier substitution. When you order:

- Choose foods that are steamed, broiled, baked, roasted, poached, or lightly sautéed or stir-fried
- Ask for fat-free or low-fat milk instead of cream for coffee or tea
- Pick food without butter, gravy, or sauces—or ask to have the food without it
- Choose a lower-calorie salad dressing
- Ask for salad dressing on the side, and use only some of it

- Pick drinks without added sugar, like water, fat-free or low-fat milk, unsweetened tea, or diet iced-tea, lemonade, or soda

Eat Healthy

You can make healthy choices throughout your meal, just:

- Trim visible fat from poultry or meat
- Do not eat the skin on chicken or turkey
- Share your meal, or take half home for later
- Skip dessert or order fruit
- Split dessert with a friend

Tips for Eating Out

You do not have to give up eating fast foods to eat right. Here are some tips on how to make heart-healthy choices when eating out.

General Tips

- Let the restaurant know your dietary needs, so they can suggest ways to meet your needs, if possible.
- Instead of buffets, order healthy choices from the menu.
- On the day you are planning to eat out, eat foods with less sodium in your other meals and snacks. Many meals at restaurants are high in sodium.
- Ask that no salt be added to your meal.
- When eating Asian food, use light soy sauce to season the food.

Main Dishes

- Choose rotisserie-style chicken rather than fried chicken. Always remove the skin.
- Order pizza with vegetable toppings, such as peppers, mushrooms, or onions. Ask for half the usual amount of cheese.
- Choose grilled, steamed, or baked fish instead of deep-fried fish.
- Leave off all butter, gravy, and sauces.

419

- Make sure the restaurant does not use monosodium glutamate (MSG) in the dishes. MSG is high in sodium!

Sandwiches

- Order sandwiches without mayonnaise, tartar sauce, or special sauces. Try mustard or low-fat mayonnaise instead.
- Ask for vegetables to be added to your sandwich.
- Order plain, instead of deluxe hamburgers.
- Order sandwiches made with lean, low-sodium meat.
- Avoid chicken salad and tuna salad. They are usually made with regular mayonnaise and are high in fat.
- Choose grilled, instead of breaded, chicken sandwiches.

Side Dishes

- Choose a baked potato over french fries.
- Share a small order of french fries instead of eating a large order by yourself.
- Use low-calorie, low-fat salad dressing. Ask that it be served on the side, and use less.
- Order a green vegetable or salad instead of two or more starches.
- Ask for low-fat cheese and low-fat sour cream.

Beverages

- Choose water, 100 percent fruit juice, unsweetened iced tea, or fat-free or low-fat (1%) milk rather than a soft drink or a milkshake.
- If you really want to have a soft drink order a small or sugar-free one.

Desserts

- Order the smallest size of fat-free frozen yogurt, low-fat ice cream, or sherbet instead of cakes, cookies, pies, or other desserts.

Ten Tips: Eating Foods Away from Home

Restaurants, convenience and grocery stores, or fast-food places offer a variety of options when eating out. But larger portions can make it easy to eat or drink too many calories. Larger helpings can also increase your intake of saturated fat, sodium, and added sugars. Think about ways to make healthier choices when eating food away from home.

1. **Consider your drink**

   Choose water, fat-free or low-fat milk, unsweetened tea, and other drinks without added sugars to complement your meal.

2. **Savor a salad**

   Start your meal with a salad packed with vegetables to help you feel satisfied sooner. Ask for dressing on the side and use a small amount of it.

3. **Share a main dish**

   Divide a main entree between family and friends. Ask for small plates for everyone at the table.

4. **Select from the sides**

   Order a side dish or an appetizer-sized portion instead of a regular entree. They're usually served on smaller plates and in smaller amounts.

5. **Pack your snack**

   Pack fruit, sliced vegetables, low-fat string cheese, or unsalted nuts to eat during road trips or long commutes. No need to stop for other food when these snacks are ready-to-eat.

6. **Fill your plate with vegetables and fruit**

   Stir-fries, kabobs, or vegetarian menu items usually have more vegetables. Select fruits as a side dish or dessert.

7. **Compare the calories, fat, and sodium**

   Many menus now include nutrition information. Look for items that are lower in calories, saturated fat, and sodium. Check with your server if you don't see them on the menu.

8. **Pass on the buffet**

   Have an item from the menu and avoid the "all-you-can-eat"
   buffet. Steamed, grilled, or broiled dishes have fewer calories
   than foods that are fried in oil or cooked in butter.

9. **Get your whole grains**

   Request 100 percent whole-wheat breads, rolls, and pasta
   when choosing sandwiches, burgers, or main dishes.

10. **Quit the "clean your plate" club**

    Decide to save some for another meal. Take leftovers home in
    a container and chill in the refrigerator right away.

Chapter 48

Guidelines for Healthy Exercise

Chapter Contents

Section 48.1

Physical Activity for a Healthy Weight

This section includes text excerpted from "Physical Activity for a Healthy Weight," Centers for Disease Control and Prevention (CDC), May 15, 2015. Reviewed December 2018.

Why Is Physical Activity Important?

Regular physical activity is important for good health, and it's especially important if you're trying to lose weight or to maintain a healthy weight.

- When losing weight, more physical activity increases the number of calories your body uses for energy or "burns off." The burning of calories through physical activity, combined with reducing the number of calories you eat, creates a "calorie deficit" that results in weight loss.

- Most weight loss occurs because of decreased caloric intake. However, evidence shows the only way to maintain weight loss is to be engaged in regular physical activity.

- Most importantly, physical activity reduces risks of cardiovascular disease and diabetes beyond that produced by weight reduction alone.

Physical activity also helps to:

- Maintain weight
- Reduce high blood pressure
- Reduce risk for type two diabetes, heart attack, stroke, and several forms of cancer
- Reduce arthritis pain and associated disability
- Reduce risk for osteoporosis and falls
- Reduce symptoms of depression and anxiety

How Much Physical Activity Do I Need?

When it comes to weight management, people vary greatly in how much physical activity they need. Here are some guidelines to follow:

- **To maintain your weight:** Work your way up to 150 minutes of moderate-intensity aerobic activity, 75 minutes of vigorous-intensity aerobic activity, or an equivalent mix of the two each week. Strong scientific evidence shows that physical activity can help you maintain your weight over time. However, the exact amount of physical activity needed to do this is not clear since it varies greatly from person to person. It's possible that you may need to do more than the equivalent of 150 minutes of moderate-intensity activity a week to maintain your weight.

- **To lose weight and keep it off:** You will need a high amount of physical activity unless you also adjust your diet and reduce the amount of calories you're eating and drinking. Getting to and staying at a healthy weight requires both regular physical activity and a healthy eating plan.

What Do Moderate- and Vigorous-Intensity Mean?

Moderate: While performing the physical activity, if your breathing and heart rate is noticeably faster but you can still carry on a conversation—it's probably moderately intense. Examples include:

- Walking briskly (a 15-minute mile)

- Light yard work (raking/bagging leaves or using a lawnmower)

- Light snow shoveling

- Actively playing with children

- Biking at a casual pace

Vigorous: Your heart rate is increased substantially and you are breathing too hard and fast to have a conversation, it's probably vigorously intense. Examples include:

- Jogging/running

- Swimming laps

- Rollerblading/inline skating at a brisk pace

- Cross-country skiing

- Most competitive sports (football, basketball, or soccer)

- Jumping rope

How Many Calories Are Used in Typical Activities?

The following table 48.1 shows calories used in common physical activities at both moderate and vigorous levels.

Table 48.1. Calories Used per Hour in Common Physical Activities

Moderate Physical Activity	Approximate Calories/30 Minutes for a 154 lb Person[1]	Approximate Calories/ Hr for a 154 lb Person[1]
Hiking	185	370
Light gardening/yard work	165	330
Dancing	165	330
Golf (walking and carrying clubs)	165	330
Bicycling (<10 mph)	145	290
Walking (3.5 mph)	140	280
Weightlifting (general light workout)	110	220
Stretching	90	180
Vigorous Physical Activity	**Approximate Calories/30 Minutes for a 154 lb Person[1]**	**Approximate Calories/ Hr for a 154 lb Person[1]**
Running/jogging (5 mph)	295	590
Bicycling (>10 mph)	295	590
Swimming (slow freestyle laps)	255	510
Aerobics	240	480
Walking (4.5 mph)	230	460
Heavy yard work (chopping wood)	220	440
Weight lifting (vigorous effort)	220	440
Basketball (vigorous)	220	440

(*Source: Adapted from* Dietary Guidelines for Americans 2005.*)*
[1] *Calories burned per hour will be higher for persons who weigh more than 154 lbs (70 kg) and lower for persons who weigh less.*

Section 48.2

Benefits of Exercise

This section includes text excerpted from "Benefits of Exercise," MedlinePlus, National Institutes of Health (NIH), August 30, 2017.

We have all heard it many times before—regular exercise is good for you, and it can help you lose weight. But if you are like many Americans, you are busy, you have a sedentary job, and you haven't yet changed your exercise habits. The good news is that it's never too late to start. You can start slowly, and find ways to fit more physical activity into your life. To get the most benefit, you should try to get the recommended amount of exercise for your age. If you can do it, the payoff is that you will feel better, help prevent or control many diseases, and likely even live longer.

What Are the Health Benefits of Exercise?

Regular exercise and physical activity may:

- **Help you control your weight.** Along with diet, exercise plays an important role in controlling your weight and preventing obesity. To maintain your weight, the calories you eat and drink must equal the energy you burn. To lose weight, you must use more calories than you eat and drink.

- **Reduce your risk of heart diseases.** Exercise strengthens your heart and improves your circulation. The increased blood flow raises the oxygen levels in your body. This helps lower your risk of heart diseases such as high cholesterol, coronary artery disease, and heart attack. Regular exercise can also lower your blood pressure and triglyceride levels.

- **Help your body manage blood sugar and insulin levels.** Exercise can lower your blood sugar level and help your insulin work better. This can cut down your risk for metabolic syndrome and type two diabetes. And if you already have one of those diseases, exercise can help you to manage it.

- **Help you quit smoking.** Exercise may make it easier to quit smoking by reducing your cravings and withdrawal symptoms. It can also help limit the weight you might gain when you stop smoking.

- **Improve your mental health and mood.** During exercise, your body releases chemicals that can improve your mood and make you feel more relaxed. This can help you deal with stress and reduce your risk of depression.

- **Help keep your thinking, learning, and judgment skills sharp as you age.** Exercise stimulates your body to release proteins and other chemicals that improve the structure and function of your brain.

- **Strengthen your bones and muscles.** Regular exercise can help kids and teens build strong bones. Later in life, it can also slow the loss of bone density that comes with age. Doing muscle-strengthening activities can help you increase or maintain your muscle mass and strength.

- **Reduce your risk of some cancers,** including colon, breast, uterine, and lung cancer.

- **Reduce your risk of falls.** For older adults, research shows that doing balance and muscle-strengthening activities in addition to moderate-intensity aerobic activity can help reduce your risk of falling.

- **Improve your sleep.** Exercise can help you to fall asleep faster and stay asleep longer.

- **Improve your sexual health.** Regular exercise may lower the risk of erectile dysfunction (ED) in men. For those who already have ED, exercise may help improve their sexual function. In women, exercise may increase sexual arousal.

- **Increase your chances of living longer.** Studies show that physical activity can reduce your risk of dying early from the leading causes of death, like heart disease and some cancers.

How Can I Make Exercise a Part of My Regular Routine?

- **Make everyday activities more active.** Even small changes can help. You can take the stairs instead of the elevator. Walk down the hall to a coworker's office instead of sending an email. Wash the car yourself. Park further away from your destination.

- **Be active with friends and family.** Having a workout partner may make you more likely to enjoy exercise. You can also plan social activities that involve exercise. You might also consider joining an exercise group or class, such as a dance class, hiking club, or volleyball team.

- **Keep track of your progress.** Keeping a log of your activity or using a fitness tracker may help you set goals and stay motivated.

- **Make exercise more fun.** Try listening to music or watching television (TV) while you exercise. Also, mix things up a little bit—if you stick with just one type of exercise, you might get bored. Try doing a combination of activities.

- **Find activities that you can do even when the weather is bad.** You can walk in a mall, climb stairs, or work out in a gym even if the weather stops you from exercising outside.

Section 18.3

Exercise and Bone Health for Women

This section includes text excerpted from "Exercise and Bone Health for Women: The Skeletal Risk of Overtraining," NIH Osteoporosis and Related Bone Diseases ~ National Resource Center (NIH ORBD~NRC), May 2016.

Are you exercising too much? Eating too little? Have your menstrual periods stopped or become irregular? If so, you may be putting yourself at high risk for several serious problems that could affect your health, your ability to remain active, and your risk for injuries. You also may be putting yourself at risk for developing osteoporosis, a disease in which bone density is decreased, leaving your bones vulnerable to fracture (breaking).

Why Is Missing My Period Such a Big Deal?

Some athletes see amenorrhea (the absence of menstrual periods) as a sign of successful training. Others see it as a great answer to a monthly inconvenience. And some young women accept it blindly, not stopping to think of the consequences. But missing your periods is often a sign of decreased estrogen levels. And lower estrogen levels can lead to osteoporosis, a disease in which your bones become brittle and more likely to break.

Usually, bones don't become brittle and break until women are much older. But some young women, especially those who exercise so much that their periods stop, develop brittle bones, and may start to have fractures at a very early age. Some 20-year-old female athletes have been said to have the bones of an 80-year-old woman. Even if bones don't break when you're young, low estrogen levels during the peak years of bone-building, the preteen and teen years, can affect bone density for the rest of your life. And studies show that bone growth lost during these years may never be regained.

Broken bones don't just hurt—they can cause lasting physical malformations. Have you noticed that some older women and men have stooped postures? This is not a normal sign of aging. Fractures from osteoporosis have left their spines permanently altered.

Overtraining can cause other problems besides missed periods. If you don't take in enough calcium and vitamin D (among other nutrients), bone loss may result. This may lead to decreased athletic performance, decreased ability to exercise or train at desired levels of intensity or duration, and increased risk of injury.

Who Is at Risk for These Problems?

Girls and women who engage in rigorous exercise regimens or who try to lose weight by restricting their eating are at risk for these health problems. They may include serious athletes, "gym rats" (who spend considerable time and energy working out), and girls and women who believe "you can never be too thin."

How Can I Tell If Someone I Know, Train with, or Coach May Be at Risk for Bone Loss, Fracture, and Other Health Problems?

Here are some signs to look for:

- Missed or irregular menstrual periods

- Extreme or "unhealthy-looking" thinness

- Extreme or rapid weight loss

- Behaviors that reflect frequent dieting, such as eating very little, not eating in front of others, trips to the bathroom following meals, preoccupation with thinness or weight, focus on low-calorie and diet foods, possible increase in the consumption of water and other no- and low-calorie foods and beverages, possible increase in gum chewing, limiting diet to one food group, or eliminating a food group

- Frequent intense bouts of exercise (e.g., taking an aerobics class, then running five miles, then swimming for an hour, followed by weightlifting)

- An "I can't miss a day of exercise/practice" attitude

- An overly anxious preoccupation with an injury

- Exercising despite illness, inclement weather, injury, and other conditions that might lead someone else to take the day off

- An unusual amount of self-criticism or self-dissatisfaction

- Indications of significant psychological or physical stress, including depression, anxiety or nervousness, inability to concentrate, low levels of self-esteem, feeling cold all the time, problems sleeping, fatigue, injuries, and constantly talking about weight

How Can I Make Needed Changes to Improve My Bone Health?

If you recognize some of these signs in yourself, the best thing you can do is to make your diet more healthful. That includes consuming enough calories to support your activity level. If you've missed periods, it's best to check with a doctor to make sure it's not a sign of some other problem and to get his or her help as you work toward a more healthy balance of food and exercise. Also, a doctor can help you take steps to protect your bones from further damage.

What Can I Do If I Suspect a Friend May Have Some of These Signs?

First, be supportive. Approach your friend or teammate carefully, and be sensitive. She probably won't appreciate a lecture about how she should be taking better care of herself. But maybe you could share a copy of this fact sheet with her or suggest that she talk to a trainer, coach, or doctor about the symptoms she's experiencing.

My Friend Drinks a Lot of Diet Sodas. She Says This Helps Keep Her Trim.

Girls and women who may be dieting often drink diet sodas rather than milk. Yet, milk and other dairy products are a good source of calcium, an essential ingredient for healthy bones. Drinking sodas instead of milk can be a problem, especially during the teen years when rapid bone growth occurs. If you (or your friend) find yourself drinking a lot of sodas, try drinking half as many sodas each day, and gradually add more milk and dairy products to your diet. A frozen yogurt shake can be an occasional low-fat, tasty treat. Or try a fruit smoothie made with frozen yogurt, fruit, or calcium-enriched orange juice.

My Coach and I Think I Should Lose Just a Little More Weight. I Want to Be Able to Excel at My Sport!

Years ago, it was not unusual for coaches to encourage athletes to be as thin as possible for many sports (e.g., dancing, gymnastics, figure skating, swimming, diving, and running). However, many coaches now realize that being too thin is unhealthy and can negatively affect performance. It's important to exercise and watch what you eat. However, it's also important to develop and maintain healthy bones and bodies. Without these, it will not matter how fast you can run, how thin you are, or how long you exercise each day. Balance is the key!

I'm Still Not Convinced. If My Bones Become Brittle, so What? What's the Worst Thing That Could Happen to Me?

Brittle bones may not sound as scary as a fatal or rare disease. The fact is that osteoporosis can lead to fractures. It can cause disability.

Imagine having so many spine fractures that you've lost inches in height and walk bent over. Imagine looking down at the ground everywhere you go because you can't straighten your back. Imagine not being able to find clothes that fit you. Imagine having difficulty breathing and eating because your lungs and stomach are compressed into a smaller space. Imagine having difficulty walking, let alone exercising, because of pain and misshapen bones. Imagine constantly having to be aware of what you are doing and having to do things so slowly and carefully because of a very real fear and dread of a fracture—a fracture that could lead to a drastic change in your life, including pain, loss of independence, loss of mobility, loss of freedom, and more.

Osteoporosis isn't just an "older person's" disease. Young women also experience fractures. Imagine being sidelined because of a broken bone and not being able to get those good feelings you get from regular activity.

Eating for Healthy Bones

How Much Calcium Do I Need?

It's very important to your bone health that you receive adequate daily amounts of calcium, vitamin D, phosphorus, and magnesium. These vitamins and minerals are the most influential in building bones and teeth. This table 54.2 will help you decide how much calcium you need.

Table 48.2. Recommended Calcium Intakes (Mg/Day)

Age	Amount
9 to 13	1,300
14 to 18	1,300
19 to 30	1,000

(Source: Food and Nutrition Board (FNB), Institute of Medicine (IOM), National Academy of Sciences (NAS), 2010.)

Where Can I Get Calcium and Vitamin D?

Dairy products are the primary food sources of calcium. Choose low-fat milk, yogurt, cheeses, ice cream, or products made or served with these choices to fulfill your daily requirement. Three servings of dairy products per day should give you at least 900 mg (milligrams) of calcium. Green vegetables are another source. A cup of broccoli, for example, has about 136 mg of calcium.

Milk and Dairy Products

Many great snack and meal items contain calcium. With a little planning and "know-how," you can make meals and snacks calcium-rich!

- **Milk:** Wouldn't a tall, cold glass of this refreshing thirst quencher be great right now? If you're concerned about fat and calories, choose reduced-fat or fat-free milk. You can drink it plain or with a low- or no-fat syrup or flavoring, such as chocolate syrup, vanilla extract, hazelnut flavoring, or cinnamon.

- **Cheese:** Again, you can choose the low- or no-fat varieties. Use all different types of cheese for sandwiches, bagels, omelets, vegetable dishes, pasta creations, or as a snack by itself!

- **Pudding (prepared with milk):** You can now purchase (or make from a mix) pudding in a variety of flavors with little or no fat, such as chocolate fudge, lemon, butterscotch, vanilla, and pistachio. Try them all!

- **Yogurt:** Add fruit. Eat it plain. Add a low- or no-fat sauce or syrup. No matter how you choose to eat this calcium-rich food, yogurt remains a quick, easy, and convenient choice. It's also available in a variety of flavors. Try mocha-fudge-peppermint-swirl if you're more adventurous at heart and vanilla if you're a more traditional yogurt snacker!

- **Frozen yogurt (or fat-free ice cream):** Everybody loves ice cream. And now, without the unnecessary fat, you can enjoy it more often! Mix yogurt, milk, and fruit to create a breakfast shake. Have a cone at lunchtime or as a snack. A scoop or two after dinner can be cool and refreshing.

What Are Other Sources of Calcium?

Many foods you already buy and eat maybe "calcium-fortified." Try calcium-fortified orange juice or calcium-fortified cereal. Check food labels to see if some of your other favorite foods may be good sources of calcium. You also can take calcium supplements if you think you may not be getting enough from your diet.

Chapter 49

Coping with Holidays and Food-Related Challenges

The holiday season can be a very stressful time for individuals suffering or recovering from an eating disorder. Eating disorders are often about coping with stress and achieving a sense of control over oneself. The holiday season—Halloween through New Year's Day—can be extremely overwhelming with food taking center stage and putting undue pressure on individuals with disruptive patterns of eating behavior. Recovery from an eating disorder is not as straightforward as recovery from substance-abuse disorders. While a person can quit drugs or alcohol "cold turkey," the same is not true with "food." The implication is that relapses are an anticipated part of the recovery process and, needless to say, holidays can serve as triggers for disordered eating behaviors.

Holidays and Food Challenges

Holiday traditions, for the most part, are built around food and fellowship. The immoderate focus on food, coupled with plentiful opportunities to eat, can be emotionally challenging for those coping with eating disorders and can serve as a trigger for unhealthy eating behaviors. Thanksgiving conversations almost always tend

"Coping with Holidays and Food-Related Challenges," © 2019 Omnigraphics. Reviewed December 2018.

to center on food, physical appearance, and weight-loss regimens. This can be extremely trying for those dealing with a dysfunctional relationship to their body and food. It is also believed that in addition to the food on the table, people around it also may play a significant role in triggering abnormal eating behaviors during the holiday season. While people with an anorexia disorder may have a hard time responding to the well-meaning urges to "eat, eat, eat," people with bulimia and a binge-eating disorder must deal with the extreme temptation to overindulge. Some individuals with eating disorders may isolate themselves during the holiday season to continue their disruptive-eating behavior and avoid being judged or negatively evaluated by their extended family and peers. Others may have a difficult time trying to hide their eating rituals from their family and friends.

Tips to Help You Thrive through the Holiday Season

While there is no definitive cure for surviving the holiday season without relapsing into unhealthy eating behaviors, there are some measures a person with an eating disorder can take to minimize the risk of relapse and develop resilience in dealing with the challenges they face during the holiday season.

1. **Mindfulness:** It is important to understand and internalize the core beliefs and traditions around holidays and prepare yourself to deal with food-related challenges typical of the holiday season.

2. **Preparation:** Planning ahead on how to deal with triggers or cues can sometimes help to minimize distress. You can eat a small meal before going to parties so you don't have to berate yourself for indulging in your favorite foods a little more than you planned. Tomorrow is another day, and you need to live in the present for now.

3. **Self-care:** Seeking the true meaning of the holidays and steering the focus away from food can help one deal with the food challenges of the holiday season. Avoid stressors associated with the holidays. You don't have to find the "perfect gift" or attend every party. Take time off to just relax and do that things you enjoy rather than attempting to fulfill all your social obligations.

4. **Support:** Seeking support from a family member or friend may help you cope with addictive or obsessive eating behaviors. Be honest about your fears and anxiety around eating and have somebody you trust look out for you in times of crisis.

5. **Therapy:** You can always seek the assistance of your dietitian, or therapist, if you are still in therapy, and they can work with you to create a plan to help you during this time of the year. Others can contact 24-hour helplines to deal with their fears and anxieties.

Supporting Your Loved One with an Eating Disorder

Families are considered an integral part of the treatment team, and validation is an important way you can support your loved one with an eating disorder. Regarded as an essential element of therapy, validation is all about acknowledging that the patient's emotions and experiences are real. This is an effective way to convey empathy and win the patient's trust. Families need to understand that eating disorders are complex mental illnesses that stem from a multitude of factors, including internal mechanisms such as dysregulation in cognitive and emotional functioning. Families who step up during treatment should continue to offer support to their loved ones to prevent relapses. At the same time, they need to understand that there are no quick fixes for eating disorders and that it is important to respect a patient's recovery process without prevailing upon them to conform to societal expectations and traditions around the holiday season.

Family and friends should ensure that meal-time conversations are never about weight, size, or physical appearance. They should also be wary of engaging in "food policing" with casual remarks about the type of food eaten or portion sizes, since this may trigger anxiety and negatively impact those in recovery. It is also important to ask your loved one if they are comfortable sharing meals or celebrating the holiday season with family and friends. If they are not ready, it is important to let them know that you understand their concerns and that you will be there to support them in their recovery process. Finally, it is important to emphasize health and inner well-being while remaining calm and supportive during fraught times, as this helps your loved one navigate the holiday season with minimal distress.

References

1. McLaughlin, August. "Lessons in Self-Care: 5 Ways to Survive and Thrive through the Holidays When You Have an Eating Disorder," National Eating Disorders Association, n.d.

2. "Effect of the Holiday Season on Weight Gain: A Narrative Review," National Center for Biotechnology Information (NCBI), July 4, 2017.

3. "9 Ways to Manage Binge Eating Disorder during the Holidays," WebMD LLC, December 5, 2016.

Part Seven

Additional Help and Information

Chapter 50

Glossary of Terms Related to Eating Disorders

abuse: Misuse, wrong use, especially excessive use, of anything.

added sugars: These sugars, syrups, and other caloric sweeteners are added when foods are processed or prepared. Added sugars do not include sugars that occur naturally, like fructose in fruit or lactose in milk.

addiction: An illness in which you become dependent on, or can't do without, certain physical substances or an activity. When a person is addicted to something, they cannot control or stop their urges.

aerobic: Fat-fueled; aerobic exercise increases basal metabolic rate, reduces appetite, firms muscles, improves cardiac and respiratory function, and burns flab.

alcohol: A chemical substance found in drinks such as beer, wine, and liquor. It is also found in some medicines, mouthwashes, household products, and essential oils (scented liquid taken from certain plants). It is made by a chemical process called fermentation that uses sugars and yeast.

This glossary contains terms excerpted from documents produced by several sources deemed reliable.

441

allergies: A sensitivity to things that are usually not harmful, such as certain foods or animals. When a person is exposed to an allergen (something she or he is allergic to), the person's immune system gives off a much bigger response than it normally would.

amenorrhea: The loss of the menstrual cycle. In terms of eating disorders, this is usually the result of excessive weight loss and often accompanied by excessive exercise.

anorexia nervosa (AN): Self-induced starvation with at least 15 percent of original body weight lost. Victims also have amenorrhea, fatphobia, and a severe distortion of body image.

antidepressants: Drugs given by your doctor to treat depression.

anxiety disorder: Serious medical illness that fills people's lives with anxiety and fear. Some anxiety disorders include panic disorder, obsessive-compulsive disorder (OCD), posttraumatic stress disorder (PTSD), social phobia (or social anxiety disorder), specific phobias, and generalized anxiety disorder (GAD).

artery: Any of the thick-walled blood vessels that carry blood away from the heart to other parts of the body.

arthritis: A group of diseases affecting the joints. Common symptoms include pain, swelling, and reduced range of motion in the affected joints. Treatment options may include physical therapy or medications to alleviate symptoms.

autism: A disorder in the brain that affects both verbal and nonverbal communication.

bariatric surgery: Also known as gastrointestinal surgery or weight-loss surgery, this is surgery on the stomach and/or intestines to help patients with extreme obesity lose weight.

behavior therapy: An offshoot of psychotherapy involving the use of procedures and techniques associated with research in the fields of conditioning and learning for the treatment of a variety of psychologic conditions; distinguished from psychotherapy because specific symptoms (e.g., phobia, enuresis, high blood pressure) are selected as the target for change, planned interventions or remedial steps to extinguish or modify these symptoms are then employed, and the progress of changes is continuously and quantitatively monitored.

behavioral therapy: *See* **behavior therapy**

binge-eating disorder (BED): An eating disorder caused by a person being unable to control the need to overeat.

biological: Pertaining to biology or to life and living things. In medicine, refers to a substance made from a living organism or its products. Biologicals may be used to prevent, diagnose, treat or relieve of symptoms of a disease.

bipolar disorder: Medical illness that causes unusual shifts in mood, energy, and activity levels. It is also known as manic-depressive illness.

birth defect: A problem that happens while a baby is forming in the mother's body. Most birth defects happen during the first three months of pregnancy and may affect how the baby's body looks, works, or both.

blood pressure: The force of circulating blood on the walls of the arteries. Blood pressure is taken using two measurements: systolic (measured when the heart beats, when blood pressure is at its highest) and diastolic (measured between heart beats, when blood pressure is at its lowest).

body dysmorphic disorder (BDD): A psychosomatic (somatoform) disorder characterized by preoccupation with some imagined defect in appearance in a normal-appearing person.

body image: Personal conception of one's own body as distinct from one's actual anatomic body or the conception other persons have of it.

body mass index (BMI): An anthropometric measure of body mass, defined as weight in kilograms divided by height in meters squared; a method of determining caloric nutritional status.

bone mass: A measure of the amount of minerals (mostly calcium and phosphorous) contained in a certain volume of bone. Bone mass measurements are used to diagnose osteoporosis (a condition marked by decreased bone mass), to see how well osteoporosis treatments are working, and to predict how likely the bones are to break.

bone mineral density: A measure of the amount of minerals (mostly calcium and phosphorous) contained in a certain volume of bone. Bone mineral density measurements are used to diagnose osteoporosis (a condition marked by decreased bone mass), to see how well osteoporosis treatments are working, and to predict how likely the bones are to break.

bulimia nervosa (BN): Uncontrolled eating in the presence of a strong desire to lose weight.

calcium: A mineral that is an essential nutrient for bone health. It is also needed for the heart, muscles and nerves to function properly and for blood to clot.

calories: The energy provided by food/nutrients. On the label, calories shown are for one serving.

cancer: A term for diseases in which abnormal cells divide without control and can invade nearby tissues. Cancer cells can also spread to other parts of the body through the blood and lymph systems.

carbohydrates: A "carb" is a major source of energy for the body. The digestive system changes carbohydrates into blood glucose (sugar). The body uses this sugar to make energy for cells, tissues, and organs, and stores any extra sugar in the liver and muscles for when it is needed.

celiac disease: An inherited intestinal disorder in which the body cannot tolerate gluten, which is found in foods made with wheat, rye, and barley.

cholesterol: A necessary nutrient from animal-based foods that is carried in the bloodstream.

chronic disease: A sickness that lasts over a long period of time, perhaps your whole life.

cognitive behavioral therapy: Any of a variety of techniques in psychotherapy that utilizes guided self-discovery, imaging, self-inspection, symbolic modeling, and related forms of explicitly elicited cognitions as the principal mode of treatment.

daily Value: The amount of certain nutrients that most people need each day.

diabetes: A disease in which the body does not produce or properly use insulin. Insulin is a hormone that is needed to convert sugar, starches, and other food into energy.

diet: The things a person eats and drinks.

diuretic: A chemical that stimulates the production of urine. Also known as a water pill.

eating disorder not otherwise specified (EDNOS): A classification for eating disorders that do not meet the criteria of anorexia nervosa or bulimia nervosa; however, it involves a combination of multiple symptoms of eating disorders. It is the most common diagnosis of eating disorder among individuals seeking treatment.

eating disorders: A group of mental disorders including anorexia nervosa, bulimia nervosa, pica, and rumination disorder of infancy.

electroencephalogram: A test that measures the electrical activity of the brain, which indicates how well brain cells communicate with one another. Electrodes placed on the scalp monitor the electrical signals, which are recorded as patterns of waves.

enema: The injection of a liquid into the lower bowel through the rectum to compel elimination.

enzyme: A biological catalyst and is almost always a protein. It speeds up the rate of a specific chemical reaction in the cell.

estrogen: A type of chemical signal called a hormone that is produced by the ovaries. It allows women to develop female physical features, and contributes to the timing of the menstrual cycle.

fiber: In food, fiber is the part of fruits, vegetables, legumes, and whole grains that cannot be digested. The fiber in food may help prevent cancer.

flexibility: The range of motion of a muscle or group of muscles. Along with balance and strength, improving flexibility can significantly reduce the risk of falling.

fracture: Broken bone. People with osteoporosis, osteogenosis imperfecta, and Paget disease are at greater risk for bone fracture.

gallbladder: A sac that stores a fluid called bile, which is produced by the liver. After eating, bile is secreted into the small intestine, where it helps digest fats.

gallstone: Solid material that forms in the gallbladder or common bile duct. Gallstones are made of cholesterol or other substances found in the gallbladder.

gastroesophageal reflux: The backward flow of stomach acid contents into the esophagus (the tube that connects the mouth to the stomach).

genes: A gene is the basic physical unit of inheritance. Genes are passed from parents to offspring and contain the information needed to specify traits.

glands: Cell, group of cells, or organ that makes chemicals and releases them for use by other parts of the body or to be excreted.

glucose: A major source of energy for our bodies and a building block for many carbohydrates.

healthy weight: Healthy weight status is often based on having a body mass index (BMI) that falls in the normal (or healthy) range.

heart disease: A number of abnormal conditions affecting the heart and the blood vessels in the heart. Coronary artery disease is the most common type of heart disease. It involves a gradual buildup of plaque in the coronary artery, the blood vessel that brings blood to the heart.

hyperthyroidism: Too much thyroid hormone. Symptoms include weight loss, chest pain, cramps, diarrhea, and nervousness. Also called overactive thyroid.

hypoglycemia: It refers to having low blood sugar, or glucose. Glucose is used to provide energy to the body. When glucose levels are low, one may have hunger, dizziness, and feel weak.

hypogonadism: Abnormally low levels of sex hormone. Low levels of testosterone is sometimes a secondary cause of osteoporosis in men.

indigestion: A common problem that causes a vague feeling of abdominal discomfort after meals. Symptoms also can include an uncomfortable fullness, belching, bloating, and nausea. Also called dyspepsia.

insulin: A hormone made by the pancreas, insulin helps move glucose (sugar) from the blood to muscles and other tissues. Insulin controls blood sugar levels.

intervention: An action or ministration that produces an effect or that is intended to alter the course of a pathologic process.

kinase: A type of enzyme (a protein that speeds up chemical reactions in the body) that adds chemicals called phosphates to other molecules, such as sugars or proteins.

laxative: Mildly cathartic, having the action of loosening the bowels; a mild cathartic, a remedy that moves the bowels slightly without pain or violent action.

legume: A seed or pod of a certain kind of plant that is used as food. Legumes include beans, peas, lentils, and peanuts.

low birth weight: Having a weight at birth that is less than 2500 grams, or 5 pounds, 8 ounces.

lupus: A chronic inflammatory disease that occurs when the body's immune system attacks its own tissues and organs. Also called systemic lupus erythematosus (SLE).

malnutrition: Faulty nutrition resulting from malabsorption, poor diet, or overeating.

menopause: The cessation of menstruation in women. Bone health in women often deteriorates after menopause due to a decrease in the female hormone estrogen.

metabolism: It refers to all of the processes in the body that make and use energy, such as digesting food and nutrients and removing waste through urine and feces.

nutrient: An ingredient in a food that provides nourishment or nutritional benefit.

nutrition: A function of living plants and animals, consisting in the taking in and metabolism of food material whereby tissue is built up and energy liberated.

nutrition facts label: The black-and-white box found on food and beverage packages.

obesity: It refers to excess body fat. Because body fat is usually not measured directly, a ratio of body weight to height is often used instead. An adult who has a BMI of 30 or higher is considered obese.

obsessive-compulsive disorder (OCD): An anxiety disorder in which a person suffers from obsessive thoughts and compulsive actions, such as cleaning, checking, counting, or hoarding.

occupational therapist: A healthcare specialist who helps people with a disability, illness, injury, or other health issue learn or relearn how to do daily activities like eating, dressing, or bathing.

osteoporosis: Reduction in the quantity of bone or atrophy of skeletal tissue; an age-related disorder characterized by decreased bone mass and increased susceptibility to fractures.

overweight: It refers to an excessive amount of body weight that includes muscle, bone, fat, and water. A person who has a body mass index (BMI) of 25 to 29.9 is considered overweight.

percent daily value (%DV): The percentage of a nutrient found in one serving of food, based on the established standard of 2000 calories per day.

phobia: An unrealistic fear, often with obsessional characteristics.

pica: A perverse appetite for substances not fit as food or of no nutritional value.

portion size: The amount of a food served or eaten in one occasion. A portion is not a standard amount. The amount of food it includes may vary by person and occasion

postpartum: A depression that follows child birth in some mothers. Cases can be mild or severe enough to be labeled psychosis and require hospitalization.

posttraumatic stress disorder (PTSD): A psychological condition that can happen when a person sees or experiences something traumatic, such as rape, murder, torture, or wartime combat.

psychotherapy: Counseling or talk therapy with a qualified practitioner in which a person can explore difficult, and often painful, emotions and experiences, such as feelings of anxiety, depression, or trauma.

purging: A forced cleansing or release. In terms of eating disorders this is usually done by vomiting or laxative abuse.

recovery: A getting back or regaining; recuperation.

relapse: Return of the manifestations of a disease after an interval of improvement.

rumination: The apparently voluntary regurgitation, chewing, and reswallowing of food.

saturated fat: A type of fat that is solid at room temperature. It is usually animal-based. This type of fat is associated with certain health risks.

seizure: Uncontrollable contractions of muscles that can result in sudden movement or loss of control, also known as convulsions.

sodium: Dietary salt that is important in the diet. However, too much sodium can lead to high blood pressure and risk of heart disease.

solid fats: These types of fats are usually not liquid at room temperature. Solid fats are found in most animal foods but also can be made from vegetable oils through hydrogenation.

starvation: Lengthy and continuous deprivation of food.

stroke: A stroke occurs when blood flow to your brain stops. Within minutes, brain cells begin to die.

thyroid: A small gland in the neck that makes and stores hormones that help regulate heart rate, blood pressure, body temperature, and the rate at which food is converted into energy.

total fat: The combined fats that provide energy to the body. Some types of fat are healthier than others.

trans fat: A type of fat, usually made by food manufacturers so that foods last longer on shelves or in cans. Eating trans fats increases the risk of some illnesses, like heart disease.

triglycerides: A type of fat in your blood, triglycerides can contribute to the hardening and narrowing of your arteries if levels are too high. This puts you at risk of having a heart attack or stroke.

unsaturated fat: A type of fat that is liquid at room temperature; can be plant-based or animal-based. These are usually "good fats."

vitamin A: A family of fat-soluble compounds that play an important role in vision, bone growth, reproduction, cell division, and cell differentiation.

vitamin D: A nutrient that the body needs to absorb calcium.

weight control: This refers to achieving and maintaining a healthy weight with healthy eating and physical activity.

whole grains: Grains and grain products made from the entire grain seed, usually called the kernel, which consists of the bran, endosperm, and/or germ. If the kernel has been cracked, crushed, or flaked, it must retain nearly the same relative proportions of bran, endosperm, and germ as the original grain in order to be called whole grain. Many, but not all, whole grains are also a source of dietary fiber.

X-ray: A type of radiation used in the diagnosis and treatment of cancer and other diseases. In low doses, X-rays are used to diagnose diseases by making pictures of the inside of the body. In high doses, X-rays are used to treat cancer.

Chapter 51

Directory of Eating Disorder Resources

Government Organizations

Agency for Healthcare Research and Quality (AHRQ)
5600 Fishers Ln.
Rockville, MD 20857
Phone: 301-427-1364
Website: www.ahrq.gov
E-mail: info@ahrq.gov

Centers for Disease Control and Prevention (CDC)
1600 Clifton Rd.
Atlanta, GA 30333-4027
Toll-Free: 800-CDC-INFO
(800-232-4636)
Toll-Free TTY: 888-232-6348
Website: www.
allianceforeatingdisorders.com
E-mail: cdcinfo@cdc.gov

Resources in this chapter were compiled from several sources deemed reliable; all contact information was verified and updated in December 2018.

girlshealth.gov
Office on Women's Health
(OWH), U.S. Department of
Health and Human Services
(HHS)
200 Independence Ave. S.W.
Rm. 712E
Washington, DC 20201
Toll-Free: 800-994-9662
Website: www.girlshealth.gov

National Heart, Lung, and Blood Institute (NHLBI)
Bldg. 31
31 Center Dr.
Bethesda, MD 20892
Phone: 301-592-8573
TTY: 240-629-3255
Fax: 240-629-3246
Website: www.nhlbi.nih.gov
E-mail: nhlbiinfo@nhlbi.nih.gov

National Institute of Diabetes and Digestive and Kidney Diseases (NIDDK)
31 Center Dr., MSC 2560
Bldg. 31, Rm. 9A06
Bethesda, MD 20892-2560
Toll-Free: 800-860-8747
Phone: 301-496-3583
Toll-Free TTY: 866-569-1162
Fax: 301-594-9358
Website: www.niddk.nih.gov
E-mail: healthinfo@niddk.nih.gov

National Institute of Mental Health (NIMH)
6001 Executive Blvd.
Rm. 6200 MSC 9663
Bethesda, MD 20892-9663
Toll-Free: 866-615-8051
TTY: 301-443-8431, TTY Toll-Free: 866-415-8051
Fax: 301-443-4279
Website: www.nimh.nih.gov
E-mail: nimhinfo@nih.gov

National Institutes of Health (NIH)
9000 Rockville Pike
Bethesda, MD 20892
Toll-Free: 800-222-2225
Phone: 301-496-4000
TTY: 301-402-9612
Fax: 301-496-4000
Website: www.nih.gov
E-mail: NIHinfo@od.nih.gov

National Institutes of Health (NIH) Osteoporosis and Related Bone Diseases ~ National Resource Center (NIH ORBD~NRC)
2 AMS Cir.
Bethesda, MD 20892-3676
Toll-Free: 800-624-BONE
(800-624-2663)
Phone: 202-223-0344
TTY: 202-466-4315
Fax:202-293-2356
Website: www.bones.nih.gov
E-mail: NIHBoneInfo@mail.nih.gov

*National Women's Health
Information Center (NWHIC)*
9000 Rockville Pike
Bethesda, MD 20892
Website: www.womenshealth.
gov

*National Institute
of Arthritis and
Musculoskeletal and Skin
Diseases (NIAMS)*
1 AMS Cir.
Bethesda, MD 20892-3676
Toll-Free: 877-22-NIAMS
(877-226-4267)
Phone: 301-495-4484
TTY: 301-565-2966
Fax: 301-718-6366
Website: www.niams.nih.gov
E-mail: NIAMSinfo@mail.nih.
gov

*Office on Women's Health
(OWH)*
U.S. Department of Health and
Human Services (HHS)
200 Independence Ave. S.W.
Rm. 712E
Washington, DC,20201
Toll-Free: 800-994-9662
Phone: 202-690-7650
Toll-Free TDD: 888-220-5446
Fax: 202-205-2631
Website: www.womenshealth.
gov
E-mail: womenshealth@hhs.gov

*President's Council on
Fitness, Sports & Nutrition
(PCSFN)*
1101 Wootton Pkwy
Ste. 560
Rockville, MD 20852
Phone: 240-276-9567
Website: www.fitness.gov
E-mail: fitness@hhs.gov

*U.S. Department of Veterans
Affairs (VA)*
810 Vermont Ave. N.W.
Washington, DC 20420
Toll-Free: 800-273-8255
Phone: 202-720-2791
Website: www.va.gov
E-mail: vaoighotline@va.gov

*U.S. Food and Drug
Administration (FDA)*
10903 New Hampshire Ave.
Silver Spring, MD 20993-0002
Toll-Free: 888-INFO-FDA
(888-463-6332)
Phone: 301-796-3900
Website: www.fda.gov
E-mail: druginfo@fda.hhs.gov

*U.S. Department of
Agriculture (USDA)*
1400 Independence Ave. S.W.
Washington, DC 20250
Phone:202-720-2791
Website: www.usda.gov

Weight-control Information Network (WIN)
Bethesda, MD 20892–3665
Toll-Free: 877-946-4627
Phone: 202-828–1025
Fax: 202-828-1028
Website: www.win.niddk.nih.gov
E-mail: healthinfo@niddk.nih.
gov

Private Organizations

The Academy for Eating Disorders (AED)
12100 Sunset Hills Rd.
Ste. 130
Reston, VA 20190
Toll-Free: 888-236-2427
Phone: 703-234-4079
Fax: 703-435-4390
Website: www.aedweb.org
E-mail: info@aedweb.org

Academy of Nutrition and Dietetics
120 S. Riverside Plaza
Ste. 2190
Chicago, IL 60606-6995
Toll-Free: 800-877-1600
Phone: 312-899-0040
Website: www.eatright.org
E-mail: affiliate@eatright.org

The Alliance for Eating Disorders Awareness ("The Alliance")
1649 Forum Pl., Ste. 2
West Palm Beach, FL 33401
Toll-Free: 866-662-1235
Phone: 561-841-0900
Website: www.
allianceforeatingdisorders.com
E-mail: info@
allianceforeatingdisorders.com

Association For Size Diversity and Health (ASDAH)
P.O. Box 3093
Redwood City, CA 94064
Toll-Free: 877-576-1102
Website: www.
SizeDiversityandHealth.org
E-mail: contact@
sizediversityandhealth.org

The Binge Eating Disorder Association (BEDA)
637 Emerson Pl.
Severna Park, MD 21146
Toll-Free: 855-855-BEDA
(855-855-2332)
Fax: 410-741-3037
Website: bedaonline.com
E-mail: lizabeth@bedaonline.com.

Body Positive
P.O. Box 7801
Berkeley, CA 94707
Phone: 510-528-0101
Fax: 510-558-0979
Website: www.thebodypositive.org
E-mail: info@thebodypositive.org

Bulimia Anorexia Nervosa Association (BANA)
1500 Ouellette Ave.
Ste. 100
Windsor, ON N8X 1K7 Canada
Toll-Free: 855-969-5530
Phone: 519-969-2112
Fax: 519-969-0227
Website: www.bana.ca
E-mail: info@bana.ca

Bulimia Nervosa Resource Guide
5200 Butler Pike
Plymouth Meeting, PA 19462
Phone: 610-825-6000
Fax: 610-834-1275
Website: www.bulimiaguide.org
E-mail: dzenzel@ecri.org

Caring Online
Toll-Free: 888-884-4913
Website: www.caringonline.com
E-mail: AmAnBu@aol.com

Casa Palmera
14750 El Camino Real
Del Mar, CA 92014
Toll-Free: 866-504-2956
Website: www.casapalmera.com
E-mail: info@casapalmera.com

Center for Eating Disorders (CED)
111 N. First St.
Ste. 2
Ann Arbor, MI 48104
Phone: 734-668-8585
Fax: 734-668-2645
Website: www.center4ed.org
E-mail: info@center4ed.org

Diabulimia Helpline
Phone: 425-985-3635
Website: www.diabulimiahelpline.org
E-mail: info@diabulimiahelpline.org

Eating Disorders Coalition
P.O. Box 96503-98807
Washington, D.C. 20090
Phone: 202-543-9570
Website: www.eatingdisorderscoalition.org
E-mail: manager@eatingdisorderscoalition.org

The Eating Disorder Foundation
1901 E. 20th Ave.
Denver, CO 80205
Phone: 303-322-3373
Fax: 303-322-3364
Website:
eatingdisorderfoundation.org
E-mail: info@
eatingdisorderfoundation.org

Eating Disorders Foundation of Canada (EDF)
100 Collip Cir., Research Park,
Western University
Ste. 230A
London, ON N6G 4X8
Phone: 519-858-5111
Fax: 519-858-5086
Website: www.edfc.ca
E-mail: info@edfc.ca

Eating Disorder Hope
8520 Golden Pheasant Ct.
Redmond, OR 97756
Toll-Free: 888-206-1175
Website: www.
eatingdisorderhope.com
E-mail: info@eatingdisorderhope.com

Eating Disorder Referral and Information Center
Website: www.edreferral.com

Eating Disorder Support Network of Alberta (EDSNA)
Phone: 780-729-3376
Website: www.edsna.ca
E-mail: info@EDSNA.ca

Families Empowered and Supporting Treatment of Eating Disorders (FEAST)
P.O. Box 1281
Warrenton, VA 20188
Toll-Free: 855-503-3278
Website: www.feast-ed.org
E-mail: info@feast-ed.org

Female Athlete Triad Coalition
Website: www.
femaleathletetriad.org
E-mail: president@
femaleathletetriad.org

Harris Center for Education and Advocacy in Eating Disorders
55 Fruit St.
Ste. 200
Boston, MA 2114
Phone: 617-726-2000
Website: www.massgeneral.org/
harriscenter/index.asp

Hopewell
Heartwood House 404 McArthur
Ave Ottawa, ON K1K 1G8
Phone: 613-241-3428
Website: www.hopewell.ca
E-mail: info@hopewell.ca

The Krevoy Institute For Eating Disorders
9454 Wilshire Blvd.
Beverly Hills, CA 90212
Phone: 310-550-1776
Website: www.drkrevoy.com
E-mail: info@drkrevoy.com

The Kyla Fox Centre
174 Bedford Rd.
Toronto, ON M5R 2K9
Phone: 416-518-0440
Toll-Free Fax: 888-398-5952
Website: kylafoxcentre.com

The Joy Project
P.O. Box 16488
St Paul, MN 55116
Phone: 310-825-9822
Website: joyproject.org
E-mail: volunteercoordinator@
joyproject.org

KidsHealth®
The Nemours Foundation
1600 Rockland Rd.
Wilmington, DE 19803
Phone: 302-651-4046
Website: www.kidshealth.org
E-mail: info@kidshealth.org

Looking Glass Foundation
4116 Angus Dr.
Vancouver, BC V6J 4I9 Canada
Toll-Free: 888-980-5874
Phone: 604-314-0548
Fax: 604-829-2586
Website: www.lookingglassbc.
com
E-mail: info@lookingglassbc.com

Monte Nido & Affiliates
6100 S.W. 76th St.
Miami, FL 33143
Toll-Free: 888-228-1253
Phone: 310-457-9958
TTY: 310-457-8442
Fax: 310-457-8442
Website: www.montenido.com
E-mail: montenidoadmissions@
montenido.com

**Multi-Service Eating
Disorders Association, Inc.
(MEDA)**
288 Walnut St.
Ste. 130
Newton, MA 02460
Phone: 617-558-1881
Website: www.medainc.org
E-mail: info@medainc.org

**The National Association for
Males with Eating Disorders
(NAMED)**
2840 S.W. Third Ave.
Miami, FL 33129
Website: namedinc.org
E-mail: info@findacurepanel.com

**National Association of
Anorexia Nervosa and
Associated Disorders (ANAD)**
220 N. Green St.
Ste. 127
Chicago, IL 60607
Phone: 630-577-1330
Website: www.anad.org
E-mail: hello@anand.org

The National Eating Disorder Information Centre (NEDIC)
ES 7-421, 200 Elizabeth St.
Toronto, ON M5G 2C4 Canada
Toll-Free: 866-NEDIC-20
(866-633-4220)
Phone: 416-340-4156
Fax: 416-340-4736
Website: nedic.ca
E-mail: nedic@uhn.ca

National Eating Disorders Association (NEDA)
165 W. 46th St.
Ste. 402
New York, NY 10036
Toll-Free: 800-931-2237
Phone: 212-575-6200
Fax: 212-575-1650
Website: www.
nationaleatingdisorders.org
E-mail: info@
NationalEatingDisorders.org

National Initiative for Eating Disorders (NIED)
Phone: 647-347-2393
Website: nied.ca
E-mail: info@nied.ca

New Directions Eating Disorders Center
4419 Van Nuys Blvd.
Ste. 410
Sherman Oaks, CA 91403
Phone: 818-377-4442
Website:
newdirectionseatingdisorders.
com

Oklahoma Eating Disorders Association (OEDA)
6003 N. Robinson Ave.
Ste. 112
OKC, OK 73118
Phone: 405-896-0599
Website: okeatingdisorders.org

Ophelia's Place
407 Tulip St.
Liverpool, NY 13088
Phone: 315-451-5544
Website: www.opheliasplace.org
E-mail: director@opheliasplace.
org

Overeaters Anonymous
P.O. Box 44727
Rio Rancho, NM 87174-4727
Phone: 505-891-2664
Fax: 505-891-4320
Website: www.oa.org
E-mail: conventioninfo@oa.org

Project Heal
38-18 W. Dr.
Douglaston, NY 11363
Toll-Free: 833-365-4325.
Phone: 718 709 7787
Website: theprojectheal.org
Email: contact@theprojecttheal.
org

The Renfrew Center Foundation
475 Spring Ln.
Philadelphia, PA 19128
Toll-Free: 800-RENFREW
(800-736-3739)
Fax: 215-482-2695
Website: renfrewcenter.com

The Something Fishy
Website on Eating Disorders
P.O. Box 837
Holbrook, NY 11741
Toll-Free: 866-690-7239
Website: www.something-fishy.
org
E-mail: admin@something-fishy.
org

Sheena's Place
87 Spadina Rd.
Toronto, ON M5R 2T1
Phone: 416-927-8900
Fax: 416-927-8844
Website: sheenasplace.org
E-mail: info@sheenasplace.org

Upstate New York Eating
Disorder Service
1003 Walnut St.
Elmira, NY 14901
Toll-Free: 877-765-7866
Phone: 607-732-5646
Fax: 607-732-0373
Website: unyed.com
E-mail: enc1003@aol.com

Valenta Inc.
9479 Haven Ave.
Rancho Cucamonga, CA 91730
Phone: 909-771-8023
Website: www.valentaonline.com

We Are Diabetes (WAD)
P.O. Box 16263
Minneapolis, MN 55416
Website: www.wearediabetes.org
E-mail: contact@wearediabetes.
org

Index

Index

Page numbers followed by 'n' indicate a footnote. Page numbers in *italics* indicate a table or illustration.